Skate

100 YEARS OF FIGURE SKATING

Skate

100 YEARS OF FIGURE SKATING

STEVE MILTON

Principal Photography by Barbara McCutcheon

Trafalgar Square Publishing

In memory of
Sergei Grinkov, 1967–1995.
A Pairs Skater for the Ages.

First published in the United States of America in 1996 by Trafalgar Square Publishing,
North Pomfret, Vermont 05053

First published in Canada in 1996 by Key Porter Books, Toronto, Ontario M5E 1R2

Printed and bound in Canada

ISBN: 1-57076-056-X

Library of Congress Catalog Card Number: 96-60041

96 97 98 99 6 5 4 3 2 1

Dedication

To El, Jess, and Toby, without whose love, support, and sense of humor this book would never have been completed. To Michael Mouland, a superb editor, with patience and wit. To the men and women who have made figure skating among the most vibrant of vocations. And to Brian Orser and Doug Leigh, the two men who have spent 20 years guiding me through the most complicated, and rewarding, of sports.

JSM, October, 1995

Acknowledgments

Throughout the preparation of this book many people have helped me not only produce and find the photographs you see here, but also retain my "focus" on a life that doesn't always include a camera. A heartfelt thank you to:

My mother, Anne McCutcheon, who taught by example and love that a woman can take a non-traditional path and still live happily ever after.

Michael Mouland, a wonderful editor who always knows when to laugh and when not to.

The Stojko family for their friendship and support over the years, and especially to Elvis for the use of his medals in this book.

Brenda Gorman and Lynne Clifford-Ward of the Canadian Figure Skating Association for allowing me to play explorer in their archives and for their unfailing good humor.

Stephan Potopnyk, who in a competitive business willingly lent his time, expertise, and equipment to this project, but as a friend gave much more.

Ron Demers, skating memorabilia collector extraordinaire, for generously opening up his collection and allowing me to photograph it, and to Noreen Arnold for bringing us together.

Michael Rosenberg, Tom Collins, and the International Management Group for the skating shows. Every production was different and each was amazing.

To the following people whose mere presence in my life enriches it with respect, laughter, great conversations, and love: Tom Bailey, my Bell Sygma family, Yvette Brauch, Kate Carlson, Ed Futerman, Alan and Elizabeth Marsh, Marion Maye, Glendon McKinney, Enna Pearlston, Judith Pownall, Beverley Smith, Carole Swan, Patricia Thomson, and Pat Weir.

And to all the skaters you see in this book and the hundreds more that you don't.

BMcC, October, 1995

Contents

Skate

100 YEARS OF FIGURE SKATING

The Rock 'n' Roll Tradition

Early December, 1994. Thursday. Skating night in Memphis, Tennessee. Scott Hamilton slowly strokes his way under an archway of lights, keeping time to the music of Aerosmith, an aging rock 'n' roll group that, like Hamilton, has retained energy and youthful appeal and found huge success in the 1990s. As he nears his starting position at mid-ice, Hamilton anticipates the distinctive, generation-defining guitar riff that opens Aerosmith's "Walk This Way" and that will launch him into three-and-a-half demanding minutes of performance.

As soon as the audience see his distinctive profile, they break into cheers and screams. Figure skating may be as native to Tennessee as sunbathing is to Alaska, but these Southerners know Scott Hamilton. Just as they know every other skater in this new, professional event. They have seen them all on TV many times, and they will see them again when this competition is taped, packaged, and broadcast for Fox Television Network as the Rock 'n' Roll Championship.

Unlike fans at a more traditional championship, they also know the judges: not the dour, impenetrable panel of amateur competitions, but youth-culture stars like Downtown Julie Brown. They also know the music. If you want to skate in Fox's Rock 'n' Roll Championship, you've got to walk the walk and talk the talk; you've got to skate to rock 'n' roll.

Preparing backstage is three-time Canadian champion Josée Chouinard, a newcomer to professional skating. Later in the program she performs to "Devil in Disguise," a mixture of Elvis Presley and Tricia Yearwood interpretations of the rock classic. Chouinard does not skate her best – the women's event is won by Oksana Baiul, the 1994 Olympic champion from Ukraine with the delicate exterior and flinty, competitive spirit. But afterward Chouinard recalls that she felt so energized an idea took hold: to make the last-chance deadline for pros to file for reinstatement in the amateur ranks and then to try to reclaim her Canadian title and land the World Championship medal that had always eluded her.

THE NAME SAYS IT ALL: ELVIS STOJKO IS THE QUINTESSENTIAL ROCK 'N' ROLL PERFORMER.

Here were Chouinard and Hamilton, exercising two of the dozens of new options open to skaters heading into the twenty-first century. Chouinard, moving fluidly back and forth between the amateur and professional worlds; Hamilton, the confirmed pro, so carefully crafting his career that it is unthreatened by the countless

WHEN ALL ASPECTS OF A CAREER ARE CONSIDERED, SCOTT HAMILTON IS THE GREATEST MALE FIGURE SKATER OF ALL TIME. AMONG THE VAST ARRAY OF NUMBERS IN HIS REPERTOIRE IS THIS COMPETITIVE PROGRAM, "CUBAN PETE," FROM THE MOVIE *THE MASK*.

skaters graduating with momentum and fame from the amateur ranks.

"I just felt so good on the ice at Memphis," says Chouinard. "There you're being judged by celebrities – the jumps were not the main thing. You knew that if you did a double or a triple, half the judges wouldn't notice anyway. So you knew you had to be entertaining. It was a competition, but it was more of a show."

"They had no idea what skating is all about," explains Hamilton, who is probably – when professional and amateur accomplishments are considered – the greatest men's figure skater of all time. "But [the show] had an edge to it that kind of made it special. Everyone was trying to step out of themselves and do something different ... the whole idea was to grab the crowd. I think of it more as an event or happening than as a competition."

More than anything, the Rock 'n' Roll Championship was a symbol. Figure skating has become "the" sport of the 1990s, even in the South, even for crowds and judges who don't know a double Axel from a truck axle. Skating is a people sport, full of emotion, intrigue, and the vitality of youth. Fox is the network of the young, and rock is the music of the young at heart. It seems like a natural fit.

"Very definitely," says H. Kermit Jackson, managing editor of the influential magazine *American Skating World*. "You can program something like Fox Rock 'n' Roll right after *Beverly Hills 90210* without missing a beat."

Yet it has been only nine years since Canadian ice-dance stars Tracy Wilson and the late Rob McCall had one of their programs rejected by international judges – none of whom was under fifty years of age – who claimed that their music was not real rock 'n' roll. Wilson and McCall produced letters of authentication from rock stars, and the music stayed.

Strangely, Hamilton saw this skating-as-rock phenomenon coming more than a decade ago when he turned professional after winning four World Championships and an Olympic gold medal. He went immediately to MTV, the then-new American video network, and tried to sell them on the concept of skaters in rock videos. He was a backstage guest of Sting's manager when the former lead singer of The Police performed solo. But nothing came of Hamilton's idea because it was ten years ahead of its time.

"We could have had this even twenty years ago," said Hamilton. "But people weren't ready. Now skating is so hot they have to package it in different ways."

Figure skating is riding a crest of unprecedented popularity and has become the darling of the airwaves and the turnstiles. Televised competitions and exhibitions boast glittering ratings and demographics, and touring shows are expanding their schedules, playing to packed houses across the continent. As a live event, skating is a big sell; as a televised one, it's even bigger. Top skaters have always enjoyed a certain fame, but within a limited sphere. In the last half of the last decade of the century – 100 years after Gilbert Fuchs of Germany won the first World Championship with little fanfare on February 9, 1896, in St. Petersburg, Russia – figure skaters have become

THREE-TIME CANADIAN CHAMPION JOSÉE CHOUINARD WAS ALWAYS TICKETED AS A POSSIBLE MEDAL WINNER AT THE WORLD CHAMPIONSHIPS, BUT LET HER NERVES GET THE BETTER OF HER AT CRITICAL MOMENTS. TECHNICALLY PROFICIENT AND CHARISMATIC, CHOUINARD DECIDED WHILE PERFORMING NIGHT AFTER NIGHT BEFORE BIG CROWDS AS A PROFESSIONAL THAT SHE WOULD GIVE "AMATEUR" SKATING ANOTHER TRY DURING THE 1996 SEASON. BUT SHE HAD A DISAPPOINTING 1996 CANADIAN CHAMPIONSHIPS, FINISHING SECOND TO CHAMPION JENNIFER ROBINSON AND MISSING A BERTH AT WORLDS.

TONYA HARDING, IN THE LAST AMATEUR PROGRAM SHE WAS PERMITTED TO SKATE BEFORE BEING BARRED BY THE USFSA. STRIPPED OF HER U.S. TITLE FOR COMPLICITY IN THE ATTACK ON NANCY KERRIGAN AT THE 1994 U.S. NATIONALS, HARDING PARADOXICALLY HELPED STIMULATE THE GREATEST BOOM IN FIGURE-SKATING HISTORY. IN ONE OF A SERIES OF DRAMATIC MISHAPS THAT MARKED HER AMATEUR CAREER, HARDING'S SKATE LACE BROKE DURING THIS PROGRAM AND SHE WAS PERMITTED TO SKATE AGAIN LATER. THE THEME MUSIC WAS FROM *JURASSIC PARK*, PROMPTING MANY WRITERS TO REMARK THAT HER AMATEUR CAREER WAS ALSO ABOUT TO BECOME EXTINCT.

superstars. And those superstars help feed television's enormous appetite.

Every major network in North America is involved. Fox might symbolize the new skating world, but it is a minor player. CTV (and to a lesser extent CBC) in Canada and ABC-TV in the United States have always taken leading roles in the sport, and CBS has enjoyed some of its most stunning successes with figure-skating programming.

"The traditional sports press doesn't look upon figure skating as something up there with baseball, basketball, football ... that sort of thing. The fact of the matter is ... it's there," Jay Rosenstein, CBS vice-president of programming, said in the fall of 1993. And Rosenstein was speaking four months *before* the incident that vaulted figure skating into the stratosphere of worldwide publicity.

When Nancy Kerrigan was smashed on the knee by an assailant during a practice session for the U.S. Championships at Detroit in January of 1994, it made instant household names out of the principals: the victimized Kerrigan, a legitimate Olympic medal contender; and her primary American rival, Tonya Harding, who eventually pleaded guilty to knowing that three of her associates, including her husband, Jeff Gillooly, had planned the attack. Harding was later banned for life from amateur competition and seems to be unofficially locked out of the pros.

Christopher Dean, of the legendary ice-dancing duo Torvill and Dean, marveled at the scope of the Kerrigan–Harding affair. He and partner Jayne encountered the media whirlwind surrounding the two American women at the 1994 Olympics, which completely eclipsed all else at Lillehammer. "It was almost good against evil, wasn't it?" Dean said.

But neither of the central characters could fully live up to her role. Harding, never too accomplished artistically, did not relish being the villain, and foisted the role off on her husband and his cronies. And Kerrigan never asked to be Ice Princess, a part for which she was apparently miscast. Still, it was gripping theater, and the world responded. Millions of new viewers tuned in to skating, hoping for more messiness, and many of them became hooked on the more consistent pleasures of the sport: its drama, its grace and athleticism, its judging controversies.

"It is very sad that to make skating popular we needed someone to beat up another one," laments Carlo Fassi, who coached Olympic champions Dorothy Hamill and Peggy Fleming.

The Kerrigan–Harding fiasco was a black eye for the sport of skating, but black ink for the business of skating. Not that the business had ever dealt much in red ink.

"It's undeniable. The incident catapulted ratings beyond the high ratings we already had," said Claire Ferguson, who ended her three-year term as president of the United States Figure Skating Association in 1995 and moved on to the International Skating Union board. "It was a single individual, one incident. But we will be talking about it for decades, as long as we live."

Inadvertently, figure skating had instantly broadened its power base. The sport became a topic of conversation. Talk always began with the Kerrigan–Harding affair, but it soon expanded into discussions about the spectacular technique of Elvis Stojko and whether he should have won the Olympic championship, the innovative work of Philippe Candeloro, the brilliant future of Canadian ice dancers Shae-Lynn Bourne and Victor Kraatz, the number-two-with-a-bullet American Michelle Kwan, the sudden proliferation of professional competitions. And on the grassroots level, membership in the USFSA jumped 25 percent in two years, to more than 125,000. In Canada – where skating had always been popular, achieving mainstream-sport status in the mid-1980s – membership in the Canadian Figure Skating Association continued to climb steadily, to over 180,000 in 1995, representing 1,400 skating clubs.

TV couldn't help but notice. Skating came with a ready-made audience and TV, in turn, made the audience bigger.

"All the networks are doing a lot of figure skating," said Andy Dollas of *Wide World of Sports* on ABC-TV, which was the first network to capitalize on the sport's

KURT BROWNING'S FOUR WORLD CHAMPIONSHIPS ARE A CANADIAN RECORD IN MEN'S SINGLES. HE IS A SHOWMAN WHO IS COMFORTABLE SKATING TO ANY MUSIC. BROWNING WAS THE SUBJECT OF CONTROVERSY AT THE 1996 WORLDS WHEN THE ISU WOULD NOT LET HIM SKATE IN THE OPENING CEREMONIES BECAUSE HE WAS AN "INELIGIBLE" SKATER. IN THE FACE OF MAMMOTH CRITICISM FROM FANS AND THE MEDIA, ISU PRESIDENT OTTAVIO CINQUANTA REVERSED HIS DECISION AND LET BROWNING PARTICIPATE IN THE CLOSING CEREMONIES.

potential when it began televising the World Championships back in 1960. "It's got drama, entertainment. Certainly Tonya–Nancy helped propel things along, but it was building anyway. There's a large audience of women, but it also attracts a lot of men now." In fact, some studies show that where figure-skating viewership once comprised only 20 percent men, it's now up to 35 percent.

The figure-skating broadcasts from Lillehammer were the highest-rated Olympic programming of all time. CBS's coverage of the ladies' technical program drew the sixth-highest rating in TV history, behind such monster events in the 1980s as the final episode of *M*A*S*H** and the conclusion of the *Roots* epic.

ABC's coverage of the 1994 U.S. Nationals received a 14.1 rating (each point represents 924,000 American households), for the women's and pairs finals, and dropped only slightly, to a 10, for the 1995 event, which didn't have the same roster of familiar names.

Going head to head, the 1994 World Championships on NBC outdrew two NCAA basketball games involving perennial favorite Indiana and eventual champion Arkansas, prompting the question "Which is the real March Madness?"

Ironically, Fox helped boost CBS's involvement in skating when it outbid CBS for National Football League rights. Without its longtime Sunday staple, CBS made a full commitment to figure skating, and now it broadcasts six professional competitions on nine Sundays.

A fierce bidding war in Canada landed CTV the Canadian rights to the World Championships for four years, and ABC took a similar prize in the U.S. Both networks also handle their respective national championships.

"Figure skating is extremely important to us," said Doug Beeforth, vice-president of sports for CTV. "It was imperative that we get the rights."

"We'd like to have more skating, but competition rights are out of sight," said Scott Moore, executive producer of The Sports Network, a Canadian cable channel. "There may be too many skating events on TV, showing the same skaters, but no matter what program we put on we attract an audience."

Several demographic polls have shown that figure skating is the most popular sport among American women and their teenage daughters. But the most staggering revelation has come from the Sports Marketing Group of Dallas, which reported that in overall popularity figure skating ranked second in the U.S. behind only NFL football. In another poll, the four skating disciplines – women's, dance, men's, and pairs – ranked second, third, fourth, and fifth behind the NFL, and well ahead of pro and college basketball, college football, Major League Baseball, and the NHL.

Skating offers a crossover between the networks' entertainment and sports departments, and the explosion of televised events has not been limited to competitions. There have been prime-time TV movies about Kerrigan and Harding; about Canadian dancers Isabelle and Paul Duchesnay, who skated for France; and about Baiul's compelling, rags-to-riches life. Stars on Ice, a dynamic, finely produced touring show, featuring Hamilton, Chouinard, Brian Orser, four-time world champion Kurt Browning, Kristi Yamaguchi, Isabelle Brasseur and Lloyd Eisler, and Christine Hough

ONE OF PHILIPPE CANDELORO'S STANDARD SHOW-PROGRAM POSES. THE 1994 OLYMPIC BRONZE MEDALIST FROM FRANCE LOVES TO BARE HIS CHEST AND ELICIT GALES OF APPRECIATIVE SQUEALS FROM THE YOUNGER FEMALE SEGMENT OF THE AUDIENCE.

and Doug Ladret, is taped annually for prime-time television. Orser has had three TV specials and Browning two, including *You Must Remember This*, considered the best skating show ever. Elizabeth Manley, the Duchesnays, dynamic two-time world champion Elvis Stojko, Kerrigan, Toller Cranston, Brian Boitano, Peggy Fleming, Karen Magnussen, Janet Lynn – they've all had their own TV specials. And *Carmen on Ice*, starring Katarina Witt, Boitano, and Orser, won an Emmy, TV's highest award, for all three stars. In one February weekend in 1994, *Nancy Kerrigan and Friends* was shown on CBS,

Fire and Ice (the Duchesnays' story) on CTV, *The Skates of Gold Championship* on ABC, and Kurt Browning's special on CBC. All in prime time. In 1995, one February weekend had the Nancy Kerrigan special *Dreams on Ice* on CBS, *Skates of Gold* on NBC, and *A Promise Kept* (the Baiul story) on CHCH. For a period of thirty-nine consecutive days flanking Christmas 1994, skating in one form or another was on free television at least once a day in the Golden Horseshoe area of Southern Ontario, Canada's busiest TV market.

The incident at Detroit may have galvanized skating's appeal, but there were sparks of interest long before that. The 1988 Calgary Olympics provided two marquee events with marketable catchphrases: the Battle of the Brians, between Boitano and Orser; and the Battle of the Carmens, similar programs skated by world champions Witt and Debi Thomas. Calgary also gave the world at least five skates that rank among the top twenty in competitive history: Boitano and Orser in the men's; Manley in the women's; Ekaterina Gordeeva and the late Sergei Grinkov in pairs; Wilson and McCall in the ice dance.

After Calgary came a period of spectacular jumpers like Stojko, Harding, and Midori Ito, and Browning's popular reign as king of skating. Americans, who have always preferred women's skating, were drawn to the sport by the fact that in 1991, for the first time ever, U.S. women ranked one-two-three, with Yamaguchi winning, followed by Harding and Kerrigan.

Then skating was blessed with an even broader forum, with two Olympics in three years, when the International Olympic Committee decided to separate the Summer and Winter Games for greater exposure.

"Skating has gone through the roof," says influential agent Michael Rosenberg, who lists among his forty clients the athletic Surya Bonaly, British showman Steven Cousins, dance-champion teams Maia Usova and Alexander Zhulin and Oksana Gritschuk and Evgeny Platov, plus world pairs champions Radka Kovarikova and Rene Novotny.

"Skating was always a B-plus sport," he adds. "But the '88 Olympics took it to an A sport. The Tonya and Nancy incident took it to a triple-A sport in one whack of the knee. The evidence is clear in the viewership numbers. Twelve months went by with eighty hours of skating shown on network TV – not eight hours, eighty

NOBODY SAID THIS WAS EASY. ISABELLE BRASSEUR AND LLOYD EISLER, THE 1993 WORLD CHAMPIONS, ARE THE MOST ATHLETIC PAIRS TEAM OF THEIR TIME. THEIR "TRICKS" ARE VISUALLY SPECTACULAR AND OFTEN VERY DANGEROUS.

hours. The numbers have never fallen. And those numbers are followed up by the attendance at ice shows."

Traditional ice shows, offering up lavishly costumed revue numbers, are still going strong in the form of the popular Disney on Ice and a scaled-back Ice Capades, but they are mainly children's attractions. The huge events now are the star-driven tours like Elvis Stojko's autumn caravan across Canada, Stars on Ice, and the Campbell's Soups Tour of World Figure Skating Champions. In each, the focus is on individual performances, with the big names drawing the sellout crowds.

Brian Orser says skating is not only becoming rock 'n' roll, it *is* rock 'n' roll. "That's exactly how we're treated by the audience on tour."

Skating tours mirror rock 'n' roll tours. Bands hit the road to make money and support their albums; skaters hit the road to make money and support their reputations. Stojko, the new king of the blades, says that skating's two distinct elements – competition and entertainment – come directly into play. After seeing the athletes compete on television, audiences can then catch them live, in a less-stressful situation, when the tour comes to their area, "and they say, 'He skated for us.'"

In 1969, Tom Collins, a Canadian-born promoter based in Minneapolis, got involved with what had been a strictly European venture: an International Skating Union tour that paraded winners and up-and-comers around the continent shortly after the World Championships concluded and capitalized on the interest created by television coverage of the Worlds. Collins saw a market for the tour in North America, which had been stricken by Peggy Fleming fever when the American star won the Olympics in 1968.

The first few American tours played fifteen cities. Governed by much stricter definitions of what constituted an "amateur," the featured skaters could usually only pocket about $50 a show. Today there are seventy-six shows in seventy cities, with the season stretching into July and the biggest headliners grossing nearly $1 million from the Campbell's tour alone.

"I never thought that in my lifetime I'd see this glamorous sport in the position it is in now," said Collins. "These people are celebrities. Even though the shows are playing in America, Elvis Stojko, who is a Canadian, brings the house down. Oksana Baiul, who is Ukrainian, tears the place apart. She probably gets the biggest ovations. Everybody knows them. It's like they were all Americans."

In Collins, skating has the right man for the job. Not only does he treat his athletes royally, but he is well-educated in rock touring, the milieu that big-time skating has come to resemble most. His background is in marketing and merchandising for rock cultural icons Crosby Stills Nash and Young, Bob Dylan, John Denver, Neil Diamond, and the Moody Blues, among others.

"It used to be that ice shows were the Ice Follies, or the Ice Capades, or Disney," he says. "But the Tour of World Figure Skating Champions is more like a rock show, because of our sound system and our lights and the fact that we're in town for just one night – two or three, at the most. The production shows could never go into town for one night – they have to move too much equipment."

NOW THAT HE HAS CONQUERED THE MORE DIFFICULT TECHNICAL ASPECTS, SUCH AS A TRIPLE AXEL, BRITISH CHAMPION STEVEN COUSINS – NO RELATION TO ROBIN COUSINS, THE 1980 OLYMPIC WINNER – IS FREE TO DO WHAT HE DOES BEST: ENTERTAIN. OUTFITTED HERE IN A GLITTERING KEYBOARD VEST FOR A JERRY LEE LEWIS NUMBER, "GREAT BALLS OF FIRE," COUSINS ROCKS THE AUDIENCE ON ELVIS STOJKO'S TOUR.

The Campbell's Soups Tour plays to an average of 15,000 fans per engagement, and Collins estimates that no more than 20 percent of those are skating aficionados "who really know what's going on." The rest are casual fans there to be entertained, drawn into the arena by the star factor.

Dovetailing nicely with the expansion of live shows has been the increase in the number of major arenas. As hockey gained popularity in nontraditional areas, 18- to 20,000-seat arenas were erected to keep pace with the interest. The National Hockey League, a six-team endeavor in 1966, now has twenty-six franchises, and each team has a huge stadium, ready to take a touring ice show on an off-night. The minor professional leagues and mid-sized arenas are also burgeoning. All are potential venues for skating shows and competitions.

What was once a thickly drawn line between amateur and professional skating has now been almost wiped away. Formerly ineligible pros were allowed a one-time entry into the 1994 Winter Olympics, but there is widespread support for a completely open Olympics, especially now that the NHL has set the pace by taking part in the 1998 Games at Nagano. Amateurs are now permitted to accept money and tour with the professionals – and learn valuable lessons about showmanship along the way. And the professionals, led by Boitano, Yamaguchi, and Paul Wylie, are maintaining their technical skills, which has led to better, more professional competitions. The 1994 Gold Championship at Edmonton's Northlands Coliseum, for instance, offered a purse of $1.3 million to be split among the six entrants, each of whom had won Olympic gold. Whereas four or five pro competitions used to be the norm, as many as sixteen were crammed into each of the last two seasons.

It's not all rosy, however.

The problem with a brighter spotlight is that it often illuminates what you'd prefer it didn't. Now that the Kerrigan–Harding fiasco has faded, the media are hungering for another compelling story. At the 1995 World Championships, they thought they'd found it in American champion Nicole Bobek.

Like Harding, eighteen-year-old Bobek is not enamored of the rigors of training and does not come from a privileged background – her mother sold ice cream from a cart in Chicago's Lincoln Park to help finance her skating. She, too, is described as a good-time girl, a shock to a nation that fantasizes its women's champion is a cross between Cinderella and Tinkerbell. Bobek speaks her mind, has her ear pierced in five places like many young women her age, and used to wear ten rings at a time, earning her the nickname "Brass Knuckles." When it was revealed that a few months prior to Worlds she had been charged with home invasion, the press went crazy. That the case was officially dismissed seemed to make no difference. Bobek, an elegant skater, is actually quite dissimilar to Harding, but the British press had a field day during the World Championships at Birmingham, England. *The Times* of London mentioned her in the same sentence as Bonnie and Clyde; and *Today*, obviously lobbying for some sequined fisticuffs, ran a headline that screamed "Brass Knuckle Dust-Up."

There was more scandal prior to the 1994 Olympics among the leading teams for the ice-dancing gold medal, Maia Usova and Alexander Zhulin, a married couple, and Oksana Gritschuk and Evgeny Platov. It was revealed to the world that Zhulin

and Gritschuk had had an affair, and during practices at Lillehammer, the on-ice tension was palpable. "The world of ice dancing is almost a microcosm of the real world – politics, drama, and intrigue," said Christopher Dean. "As bad as Tonya–Nancy got, the ethics and power play within ice dancing were probably worse."

Skating has always had its trysts and its intrigues, but until the last few years, there was rarely enough interest from the public for the press to ferret them out.

Many skating insiders fear for the sport because there is no firm hand guiding it. So much has happened so quickly, they argue, that the sport is in danger of collapsing inward on itself. No unified voice speaks for professional skating, and the International Skating Union, which controls the amateurs, has lost its grip on the overall market. The pros, and their television partners, are putting up such stiff competition for talent that the ISU will now offer prize money for its major championships and finally, after years of speculation, has agreed to amalgamate its best autumn international competitions into a Grand Prix circuit called the Champions Series. The ISU is, in effect, bidding for the talent that it created.

Some critics wonder aloud if the market isn't already flooded. Torvill and

A HUNGRY MEDIA IS TRYING TO MOLD NICOLE BOBEK, WITH HER FREE-SPIRITED ATTITUDE, INTO TONYA II. BUT BOBEK IS A MORE COMPLETE SKATER THAN HARDING WAS. HER ELEGANT FINISHING POSE ILLUSTRATES HER MULTIFACETED TALENT. KNOWN FOR CHANGING COACHES, BOBEK DID IT AGAIN IN 1995–96. SUFFERING AN ANKLE INJURY AND UNDERTRAINED AFTER TOURING WITH A PRO SHOW, SHE FINISHED FOURTH AT THE 1996 NATIONALS AND MISSED THE WORLD TEAM.

SONJA HENIE'S POPULARITY WAS UNPARALLELED DURING AND AFTER HER AMATEUR SKATING CAREER. ON TURNING PRO, SHE HEADLINED A TOURING SHOW, COMMANDED A HUGE SALARY AS A MOVIE STAR, AND WAS BESIEGED BY PRODUCT-ENDORSEMENT OFFERS. APPARENTLY, SHE ALSO WAS A BIG FAN OF KOOL-AID.

Dean, for example, had trouble getting good dates in major arenas for their fall tour through North America. TV viewers, it is speculated, will become confused with the myriad of events popping onto their screens out of context. With so many competitions and exhibitions, skaters aren't able to work up enough different routines to satisfy fans, and there has been a great deal of repetition.

But the fears have not yet been borne out in reality.

Corporate sponsorship of USFSA events in 1995 was nearly three times higher than it was in 1994, and in Canada, companies have been clamoring to get involved in the sport since the CFSA created a unique skating–advertising–TV partnership fifteen years ago. Sonja Henie and Barbara Ann Scott, the two skating heroines of the thirties and forties, may have graced the occasional soap or makeup advertisement, but today it's impossible to watch TV or read a magazine in Canada without seeing Browning, Stojko, Chouinard, or Brasseur and Eisler endorsing a product.

Kevin Albrecht of International Management Group, skating's most powerful agency, says that the networks are all screaming for more skating events, not fewer. Since the 1993 national championships and 1994 Canadian Professional Championships drew more than 15,000-plus each night in Hamilton, Ontario, the complexion of big-time skating in Canada has been altered forever. Small sites need not apply. The USFSA was swamped by a record number of bids from U.S. cities wanting to host its biggest events, the 1997 and 1998 nationals and 1998 Worlds.

And Rosenberg points out that the next generation of pro-skating stars – Stojko, Bobek, Kwan, Candeloro, European champion Ilya Kulik – "may be even better than the current one."

The world of skating has changed so radically in the 1990s – when the decade opened, for example, competitors still had to perform compulsory figures at the World Championships – that no one can accurately predict where it will go next. But the sport's inherent dualities are its best safety net against a collapse. What amateur skaters can't provide, the pros can. What competitions don't provide, touring shows do. Men and women can compete together against other men and women, a situation that exists elsewhere only in tennis, and each individual skater has to be both artist and athlete.

Most lasting sports appeal on two levels: the competitive result and the entertainment experience. Figure skating does, too, but it is the only major sport that factors both into its scoring system. Some baseball fans may go to a game because they like the acrobatic form of Blue Jays star Roberto Alomar or the threatening demeanor of Chicago White Sox slugger Frank Thomas, but ultimately, whichever team scores the most runs is the only thing that matters; whether that score was arrived at in an entertaining or a boring manner is irrelevant. Skating competitions, however, reward – or penalize – not only what is achieved, but *how* it is achieved.

"Skating is athletics and it's drama," says 1988 Olympic champion Brian Boitano. "I think skating has always been this popular, but you see it more now because the people who make the ultimate decisions – the networks and sponsors and so on – are realizing just how strong it is.

"I think that when people see it in person, it has so many different dimensions they're awestruck."

TWO

Skating History

The World Figure Skating Championship will open its second century with the 1996 competition at Edmonton, Alberta. Not one of the so-called Big Four championships – football's Super Bowl, baseball's World Series, basketball's NBA championship, even hockey's Stanley Cup – can boast an earlier beginning than skating's annual showcase event.

On February 9, 1896, Germany's Gilbert Fuchs won the premier International Skating Union title. There had been previous competitions – the first known international event was in 1882, and the field included Norway's Axel Paulsen, for whom today's demarcating triple jump, the Axel, is named – but Fuchs's victory over a small entry roster in a one-day tournament in St. Petersburg started a chain of global championships that has been broken only by two world wars and the 1961 plane-crash deaths of the entire U.S. world team.

The history of skating stretches back much further than those turn-of-the-century championships, which were the playthings of the European aristocracy. When early Europeans first took to the ice, it was not about winners' trinkets, but about survival. In order to traverse frozen lakes and ponds, to hunt or to travel to markets, ninth-century residents of northern Europe took flat pieces of wood or hollowed-out elk ribs, looped thin straps of animal skin through holes drilled in the bone, and fastened them to their winter boots. Often the "skater" would use a long stick, similar to a ski pole, for extra propulsion.

During the Middle Ages in Iceland, iron skates made an appearance, and out went the need for poles. Metal skates cut more deeply into the ice, increasing the thrusting power and glide effect severalfold. When, in the late 1500s, the Dutch perfected the iron *schaats*, skating was ready for its first big boom.

Because their vast system of canals, rivers, and inlets froze during the winter, the Dutch had always been pioneers of skating. In fact, they gave skating its patron saint, Lydwina. In the late-fourteenth century, she fell while skating with friends on a frozen canal in her native town of Schiedam and broke her ribs. Thereafter fol-

(TOP) DICK BUTTON WAS KNOWN FOR HIS POWER AND ATHLETICISM. *(BELOW, LEFT TO RIGHT)* ELEVEN-TIME WORLD CHAMPION SONJA HENIE WAS FEATURED ON A SERIES OF COLOR CARDS. BARBARA ANN SCOTT WAS THE FIRST NORTH AMERICAN WOMAN TO WIN A MAJOR INTERNATIONAL TITLE. ULRICH SALCHOW WON TEN WORLD AND NINE EUROPEAN CHAMPIONSHIPS AT THE TURN OF THE CENTURY. ZELJKA CIZMESIJA OF YUGOSLAVIA, THE LAST COMPETITOR AT A WORLD CHAMPIONSHIP TO SKATE A COMPULSORY FIGURE, IS SURROUNDED BY KIBITZING JUDGES. JACKSON HAINES FACED RIDICULE FOR HIS FLAMBOYANT STYLE.

lowed thirty-eight years of terrible diseases for her. She bore them with such a sunny countenance and spiritual outlook that the Catholic Church sanctified her in the late-nineteenth century, just six years before the first World Championship was held. Dutch legend has it that through prayers to St. Lydwina, the townspeople saved Schiedam from the bombing devastation wrought during World War II. That the patron saint of skating gained her reputation by falling down should have amply warned future generations about the vagaries and pains of figure skating.

FROM HOLLAND TO ENGLAND, STIFFLY

The canals were sites not only of commerce but also of social contact and recreation. Speed skating became the sport of the commoners, while "figure" skating – the art of carving fancy patterns in the ice – was the province of the ruling classes. In France, skating had been considered a pastime of the masses, but when members of the court of Louis XVI took to it, it quickly became a pursuit of the nobility. Both Napoleon and Josephine tried their hand – or foot – at skating.

Ironically for a sport that, in this century in North America, has generally been viewed as a feminine pursuit, in many countries in the 1500s and 1600s women were not allowed, or certainly not encouraged, to skate. As late as the middle of the nineteenth century, a German woman was stoned to death for skating.

Before Charles II became king of England, he spent a winter in Holland and was exposed to canal skating. As luck would have it, his return to England coincided with the great "hard frost" of 1662. Skating was thus introduced to Great Britain, and so began that non-icy nation's long and fascinating association with the sport.

The first known skating club was formed in Edinburgh, Scotland, in 1742. By then the stiff British style had already taken hold. Tracing precise figures on the ice was far more important than skating with style and power. The evolution of skates themselves played a role in this. Blades had been attached to wooden soles that were in turn strapped to ordinary boots. But eventually a skating boot was developed, with the metal blades clamped directly to it. Whereas the Dutch started leaning toward long speed skates for quicker canal travel, the British curved the runner and extended it back beyond the heel to facilitate carving figures. Then came "club skates," with the toe piece cut off and the front of the blade rounded, and the heel section rounded and extended even farther. This made more turns possible and rendered skating more elegant ... and therefore more aristocratic. Until the latter half of the twentieth century, figure skating retained that aristocratic nature, if only by virtue of how much it cost to train.

By the time Victoria became queen, the British style was already quite Victorian, with nothing even slightly risqué about it. Skaters maintained a stiff posture, arms held at the sides. Decorum was everything. Figures were expected to be exact – although many were fabulously creative and some people could even carve their signatures into the ice – and precise. This was the birth of compulsory, and we do mean *compulsory*, figures. Artistic skating was not even dreamed of.

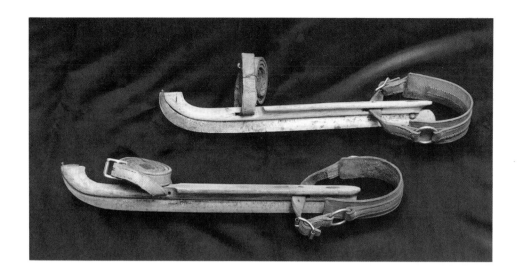

As skating grew in popularity in the nineteenth century, the technology kept pace. Better skates meant greater accessibility to the sport. Early skates, fashioned out of wood and metal, were longer and more cumbersome than later models.

ON TO THE COLONIES

Meanwhile, skating had arrived on the shores of North America in the middle of the seventeenth century via, it is believed, a group of British army officers posted to Halifax, Nova Scotia. They brought with them the British style.

Skating spread quickly throughout the continent, probably because ice covered so much of it. The first figure-skating club in North America was founded in 1849 – the Philadelphia Skating Club and Humane Society. Along with having a strangely hybrid name, it had the unique rule that members had to skate with a length of rope in case they had to rescue other members who had fallen through the river ice.

The Skating Club of New York was formed in 1863, the same year as the famous Christiana Club in Norway. New York and Norway would collide again in skating history some sixty-seven years later when Sonja Henie arrived in the city and immediately triggered the great North American skating explosion.

By mid-century, the Acme Skate Company of Halifax was manufacturing all-iron skates that snapped onto the sole and heel of boots by a small lever. The skates could be electroplated in nickel or gold, and expensive carrying cases were available, endearing the sport to the nouveau riche.

By the 1860s, the first covered rinks had appeared in Quebec City, Montreal, New York, and Toronto. They were really sheds erected over natural ice, but they protected skaters from the elements and boosted the sport's popularity and accessibility.

ARTISTRY IS BORN

North American skating was a landed immigrant, and it brought with it the old, stiff, military ways from Britain, so when the immortal Jackson Haines began strutting his stuff, the continent was not amused. Haines was born in Chicago to Canadian parents. His mother was of Dutch descent, his father of British, so that even at birth he linked the major skating nations of the day.

Toller Cranston, John Curry, the Duchesnays, and others who would initially

GERMAN PROFESSIONAL SKATER CHARLOTTE WAS THE FIRST FEMALE SKATER TO GAIN WIDESPREAD FAME. SHE WAS FEATURED IN THIS FASHION SPREAD IN THE FEBRUARY, 1916, EDITION OF THE AMERICAN MAGAZINE *WOMAN'S HOME COMPANION*.

18   *WOMAN'S HOME COMPANION PICTURE SECTION FOR FEBRUARY, 1916*

Skating is the Newest Fad

More popular than dancing was, and more healthful, also much more fun

Your costume must be shoe-top skirt, vivid sweater, and cap with tassel

JUST suited to an Irene Castle coiffure is this tight little cap of blue wool with button atop. The skirt is tan homespun, and the sweater "chamois" Angora, while scarf is blue, to match the cap.

PRACTICAL and lovely in color is this pretty girl's outfit—emerald-green sweater, white scarf with green border, white cap and mittens, and wood-brown skirt of tweed, cut very wide and short.

Charlotte, who leads the New York Hippodrome ice ballet, started the season's fad for skating

IT'S worth while to learn to skate if you can have a black and silver scarf-toque and a rose homespun suit like the girl at the left,—or a black and white outfit like the girl at the right. Smartest of all is the well-cut black velvet suit and black velvet pompon hat worn by the girl in the oval at the top of page.

suffer low marks more than a century later because of their revolutionary approach, experienced nothing of the kind of artistic rejection that Haines faced. He won what was billed as the Americas Championship in 1863 and again in 1864 in New York, but New Yorkers vilified him. They laughed at two of his inventions: the one-piece boot and the improved blade that made for tighter turns. They thought pretentious his use of the free leg in a preliminary form of the arabesque, and regarded his dancing on ice as too showy.

Haines immigrated to Europe and encountered the same disfavor in Britain, but became instantly famous in Vienna and Stockholm, drawing huge crowds to his exhibitions. What the Americans and Britons found boorish, the Austrians and Swedes found entertaining. Haines was a showman and European audiences loved him. He hired orchestras to accompany him, and by connecting his tracings with bold, twisting skating strokes, he set the precedent that artistry, in the form of graceful movement to music, would be the most important component. How it was done became as important as what was done.

Two of Haines's on-ice inventions, the arabesque (or spiral) and the spread eagle, became the signature moves of, respectively, Nancy Kerrigan and Brian Boitano, American superstars more than a century after his death.

After enjoying spectacular popularity throughout most of Europe and introducing what was called the international style of skating, Haines died at thirty-five from pneumonia he caught while traveling by sleigh from Russia to Stockholm. His tombstone in Gamlarkarleby, Finland, bears the inscription "The American Skating King." His legacy is the unbreakable association between figure skating and performance art. Without him, skating might have stayed two dimensional, a collection of detailed patterns traced temporarily onto a frozen canvas. Or it might have become barrel jumping. Even today, that's the best answer to give critics of the sport who pick on the artistic element: without it, what is left except counting the jumps?

The international style caught on and became synonymous with a number of early champions, including Leopold Frey of Austria, who won that first international skating meet in 1882. A contemporary of Haines was Montreal's Louis Rubenstein. He would play a key role in founding the governing bodies for skating in both Canada and the United States.

Another heir of the Haines style was the flamboyant Swedish star Gillis Grafström, who took over from the first longtime champion and fellow Swede Ulrich Salchow, who also has a jump named after him. Salchow later became president of the ISU. Between them, the two Swedes won thirteen World Championships and the first four Olympic titles, three by the demonstrative Grafstrom. Two of those Olympics, 1908 in London and 1920 at Antwerp, were part of the Summer Games. The British, who invented artificial ice, wanted to show off their improved refrigeration process and so included skating in the 1908 Games, but Stockholm, the 1912 summer site, didn't have an artificial rink large enough to accommodate the competition.

GILLIS GRAFSTRÖM (*LEFT*) AND KARL SCHAFER (*RIGHT*) ON A SPORTS CARD. GRAFSTRÖM WON THREE STRAIGHT OLYMPICS BEFORE SCHAFER FINALLY BEAT HIM IN 1932. SCHAFER WAS ALSO ONE OF THE FIRST SKATERS TO DESIGN INSTRUCTIONAL BOOKS AND FILMS.

MAKE WAY FOR SONJA HENIE

Salchow won the men's championship at the first Olympics and the women's gold went to Great Britain's Madge Syers. The pioneer of women's skating had entered the 1902 men's competition and finished second to Salchow. The next year, the International Skating Union ruled that women were ineligible for the championships, and a separate women's event – which was usually held at a different site than the men's – was introduced in 1906. Syers won that, too.

THE REAL-LIFE RUDY: EVERY YEAR THERE IS A MAJOR STORY IN FIGURE SKATING, AND IN 1996 IT WAS RUDY GALINDO. UNTIL THE 1996 NATIONALS IN HIS HOMETOWN OF SAN JOSE, CALIFORNIA, GALINDO WAS BEST KNOWN AS THE PAIRS PARTNER (FIFTH AT 1990 WORLDS) THAT KRISTI YAMAGUCHI LEFT BEHIND TO PURSUE A CAREER IN SINGLES THAT LED TO THE 1992 OLYMPIC GOLD MEDAL. BUT GALINDO—WITHOUT MUCH FINANCIAL SUPPORT AND SUFFERING FROM THE EMOTIONAL OVERLOAD OF THE DEATHS OF HIS FATHER, OLDER BROTHER, AND TWO COACHES WITHIN A SHORT PERIOD OF TIME—CAME OUT OF NOWHERE TO CAPTURE ONE OF THE MOST EMOTIONAL MEN'S TITLES IN THE HISTORY OF THE U.S. NATIONALS. COACHED BY HIS SISTER LAURA, HE OVERTOOK DEFENDING CHAMPION TODD ELDREDGE TO WIN THE TITLE WITH A LYRICAL INTERPRETATION OF SWAN LAKE IN THE FREE SKATE. THEN, "TO SHOW THAT I WASN'T JUST SOME HOME-ICE FLUKE," GALINDO PUT TOGETHER BACK-TO-BACK EXCELLENT PERFORMANCES AT EDMONTON TO WIN THE BRONZE MEDAL, AS ELDREDGE CAPTURED GOLD—THE FIRST TIME IN FIFTEEN YEARS THE U.S. HAD TWO MEN ON THE PODIUM. NOT BAD FOR A TWENTY-SIX-YEAR-OLD WHOSE CAREER SEEMED HEADED NOWHERE AFTER SLIDES FROM FIFTH TO SEVENTH TO EIGHTH IN THE THREE PREVIOUS U.S. CHAMPIONSHIPS.

Syers was the predecessor of the two women who brought the international style back to North America, which had been without it since Haines left. Irving Brokaw and George Browne, who helped form the United States Figure Skating Association, were proponents of the more artistic style – the U.S. championships in those days consisted partly of endless repetitions of moves like spins and three-turns – but it was the German beauty Charlotte who excited the Americans. She appeared in "Flirting in St. Moritz," a skating extravaganza at New York's Hippodrome playhouse in 1915.

Charlotte – who never used her last name, Oelschlagel – set the stage for the queen of the American skating revolution, Sonja Henie.

Women now had their own World Championships, but there was still an artistic and competitive carryover from the restrictive late-nineteenth century, when females were heavily corseted and wore long, thick skirts, sometimes right down over their skating boots. Henie, who arrived on the scene for the first Winter Olympics at Chamonix, France, in 1924 as an eleven-year-old last-place finisher, changed all that. She wore white skates instead of black ones and skated in short skirts, which enabled her to do the more difficult "tricks," such as jumps and sit spins, that previously only men were trying. By 1927, the blue-eyed blonde Norwegian was world champion, a title she wouldn't give up for ten years.

When New York played host to the 1930 World Championships, she was ready for the city and the city was ready for her.

Most important for skating, she stimulated an interest in the sport that was unparalleled until the 1990s. She liberated women's skating from its previous restrictions, and hundreds of thousands of young North Americans bought skates, inspired by the Henie magic.

POWER SHIFTS WEST

Henie's era was Europe's last great skating fling before World War II. No World Championships were held between 1940 and 1946, and by the time the global tournament resumed in 1947, the balance of power had shifted. Europe had been devastated, its arenas and rinks either bombed out or shut down. With no new skaters being developed, the sport came to a dead stop. But in North America skating had continued, and the United States and Canada produced their first two world champions.

Dick Button probably influenced American skating as much as, or more than, any skater other than Henie, and he's still playing a role: as the first major promoter of professional events and as a TV commentator. He finished second in the 1947 World Championships, then won the next five, plus two Olympics. Followed by brothers Hayes and David Jenkins, Button led an onslaught that resulted in twelve straight world titles and four Olympic crowns for American men. He brought a dynamic athleticism to the sport, jumping higher and longer and skating faster than anyone before him, with the bold pride that is still his trademark. He did the first double Axel, landed the first triple jump – a loop – and helped amend rules, written and unwritten, that said arms should not be raised above the waist. More than a generation of athletic North American male skaters would follow in his footsteps, and from Button's day forth – through the Jenkinses, Donald Jackson, Don McPherson, Tim Wood, Charlie Tickner, Scott Hamilton, Brian Boitano, Brian Orser, Kurt Browning, and Elvis Stojko – Americans and Canadians would capture twenty-eight of the next forty-seven men's championships.

Button's contemporary was Canadian legend Barbara Ann Scott, the first North American to win a World Championship when she triumphed at Stockholm in 1947. She also joined Button as 1948 Olympic gold medalist, heralding the postwar heyday for North Americans, which saw them win twenty-eight titles and sixty-seven medals in men's, women's, and pairs through to the 1960 World Championships.

The adulation heaped on Scott when she won her titles was more like the

BARBARA ANN SCOTT, WHO WON TWO WORLD CHAMPIONSHIPS AND THE 1948 OLYMPICS, WAS THE FIRST NORTH AMERICAN WOMAN TO WIN A MAJOR INTERNATIONAL TITLE. THOUSANDS OF CANADIAN GIRLS ASKED FOR BARBARA ANN SCOTT DOLLS, LIKE THIS ONE, FOR CHRISTMAS.

hero worship bestowed on today's skating icons. She took Canada by storm, prompting a generation of young girls to ask for skates for Christmas so they could be like Barbara Ann.

U.S. skaters had won a dozen straight men's titles and six straight women's, when the next wave of American challengers were killed when their plane crashed near Brussels on February 15, 1961, en route to the World Championships at Prague. It was the first crash of a commercial Boeing 707, and involved seventy-three fatalities, including sixteen-year-old Laurence Owen – the new queen of the ice, who had won the North American Championship only four days earlier – and the other seventeen members of the U.S. team. Owen was the daughter of Maribel Vinson Owen, Olympic bronze medalist behind Sonja Henie in 1932.

The tragedy forced the cancellation of the championships and gutted the U.S. skating ranks. But, stimulated by the immigration of some top European coaches and galvanized by the popular, triumphant reign of Peggy Fleming from 1966 through the 1968 Olympics, the Americans did not take long to regain their position of international power.

As with any plane crash, those who changed travel plans were left to ponder the randomness of life and death. Ron Luddington, a four-time national pairs champion, had just embarked on what would become an extraordinarily successful coaching career. He lacked the money to attend the championship, so he did not board the plane with his students, Pat and Bob Dineen. It was the only time in his first thirty years as a coach and international competitor that he did not go to the Worlds.

The Canadians who would lead Canada's richest World Championship performance the following year, 1962 world pairs champions Otto and Maria Jelinek and men's champion Donald Jackson, often trained with the Americans in New York. They were supposed to fly to Prague with the doomed Americans, but various circumstances prevented it. Jackson had a temperature of 103 and could not leave New York. The Jelineks' parents, already concerned that their children were returning to the Communist country from which they'd escaped a decade earlier, did not find out for several hours that Otto and Maria had taken another plane to Europe.

THE SOVIETS ARRIVE

While the Americans were dominating, then rebuilding, the next great force on the international scene was marshaling behind the Iron Curtain. No Russian had appeared at the World Championships since the Bolshevik Revolution.

Bringing a rich musical and balletical history to the sport, the Soviets were better suited to pairs and ice dancing, which had been finally introduced to the World Championships in 1952. They did not win a men's title until the 1970s and have never won a women's World Championship, although a skater from one of the former republics, the wispy Oksana Baiul from Ukraine, took the 1993 World Championship and the 1994 Olympic gold.

When the Protopopovs captured the U.S.S.R.'s first Olympic skating gold in

DOROTHY HAMILL, LIKE BARBARA ANN SCOTT, WAS IN DEMAND AS A DOLL.

1964, a thirty-year reign was inaugurated in which Soviet/Russian pairs won every Olympic championship and all but four world titles. And when Ludmila Pakhomova and Alexander Gorshkov cracked the British–Czech dominance of ice dancing in 1970, the only breaks thereafter in one Soviet couple after another inheriting the title came with the four fabulous years of Jayne Torvill and Christopher Dean and the 1991 Dean-choreographed triumph of Isabelle and Paul Duchesnay, Canadians skating for France.

Ironically, the dissolution of the Soviet Union into several independent countries has strengthened the pairs division, which had become a shrinking three-country battle between the Soviets, Canadians, and, occasionally, the Americans. The number of entrants, which had dwindled, is on the rise again, thanks to input from the pairs-oriented former Soviet republics.

A QUARTER-CENTURY AFTER THEY BROUGHT A NEW DIMENSION TO PAIRS SKATING, THE PROTOPOPOVS ARE STILL EXHIBITION SKATERS … AND THEY STILL CAN EXECUTE A CLASSIC DEATH SPIRAL.

FIGURES, GONE AND NOT SORELY MISSED

Since compulsory figures arguably cost Donald Jackson one World Championship, Toller Cranston at least one, and Brian Orser two world titles and the 1984 Olympic gold, it seems odd that when figures were abolished from international competition after the 1990 Worlds, Canada argued against the ban.

By the time David Liu, an American resident representing Chinese Taipei, and Zeljka Cizmesija of Yugoslavia skated the last World Championship figures in an arena in Dartmouth, Nova Scotia, in the opening mornings of the Halifax 1990 Worlds, compulsory figures had already become anachronistic. Perhaps it's significant that the last man and woman to skate compulsories came, respectively, from a country that had only six ice rinks and a country that no longer exists.

In Canada, where "patch" – several skaters dividing up the ice to practice figures – was an important part of the sport's economic structure, it was felt that the loss of figures would have a financial impact on coaches and skating schools. Canadian skating officials also pointed out that by encouraging disciplined use of edges, weight shifts, and knee movements, tracing compulsory figures – variations of circles, figure eights, and brackets – developed technically sound skaters. There is still a strong testing program in Canada and the U.S. for developing figures, although in Canada those, too, are rumored to be facing extinction. They'll be replaced by new skill-nurturing programs.

Canadian women skaters such as Barbara Ann Scott, Karen Magnussen, and Tracey Wainman were superb at figures, but in general the men somehow didn't have the same aptitude. One theory, quite supportable, is that Canada developed great free skaters like Jackson, Cranston, Orser, and Browning because Canadians knew they would always need to overcome a deficiency in figures.

There were also the deep historical roots to figures, which after all are part of the sport's name. In the first international competition, twenty-three different figures of varying degrees of difficulty had to be skated before a four-minute free-skate program. For decades, it was impossible to win a World Championship without being able to carve a good figure, then retrace it several times.

But when television began to have an active interest in how the sport was conducted – beginning with the 1960 Olympics and intensified by the Peggy Fleming years – figures came under serious scrutiny. First of all, they were the subject of many judging controversies, if not judging evils, because they were conducted in relative isolation. Until 1968, they were worth 60 percent of the final

OUR TIME HAS NEVER KNOWN ANYONE LIKE HIM. CANADIAN ICON TOLLER CRANSTON BROUGHT A BRILLIANT NEW SENSE OF INTERPRETATIVE SKATING TO A SPORT THAT HAD GROWN SOMEWHAT TECHNICIAN-DOMINATED IN THE 1970S. BUT COMPULSORY FIGURES WERE HIS DOWNFALL, AND THE MOST INFLUENTIAL SKATER OF A GENERATION WAS NEVER RECOGNIZED WITH A WORLD CHAMPIONSHIP.

mark, and by the time the television-friendly free-skating segments appeared on the screen, the winner had often already been decided. This lent a suspicious air to the sport, one that it is still trying to kick.

The long slide of figures into oblivion began in 1968, when they were reduced from 60 percent to 50 percent of the final mark. What clinched their fate was Austria's Trixie Schuba winning the 1972 Worlds, despite finishing ninth in the free skate, because she was so far ahead in figures. When she skated on tour that year and did a figure as one of her exhibitions, a Toronto crowd booed mercilessly.

The following year, the short program (a free skate with prescribed elements) was instituted, and figures fell to 30 percent of the total mark. In their final two years, figures were worth only 20 percent, and where once six figures had to be traced six times, only two had to be traced by 1990.

"It's ironic that it was me to be the last of the men, because I really, really dislike figures," said Liu, one of the most artistic skaters on the planet. "I thought about it before I skated that final loop, knowing that I would be remembered for this."

A WHOLE NEW BALLGAME

The death of compulsory figures radically changed the face of competitive skating. Free skating, which was already on the rise during the 1970s with Janet Lynn, John Curry, and Cranston and which accelerated with Scott Hamilton, Brian Orser, Brian Boitano, and Katarina Witt during the eighties, now became everything. The short program is the first segment of competition. It sets the all-important rankings for the free skate final replacing the seeding mechanism that figures had provided, and it also inherited a make-or-break status. The short program is what now arouses the athletes' greatest anxieties and provides the falls that can knock a contender out of a gold medal.

But the removal of figures has had the desired effect, significantly increasing the interest of television even before the Kerrigan–Harding incident. And now great free skaters can come out of nowhere and win or challenge for major championships. In the days of figures, Oksana Baiul and Ilya Kulik would have languished at the bottom of the heap, "paying their dues" for a few years, before being permitted to enter the upper ranks.

Now, released from the two or three hours of practice a day that figures required, skaters have more time to apply to free skating or to pursue other interests. Purists argue that less time is taken to perfect proper edge-use technique.

In an effort to curb a rising dependence on jumps at the expense of other skating elements, the ISU decided that artistic, or presentation, marks would be used to break ties, whereas previously technical marks were the deciding factor. Someday that may change again if the athletic side of the sport becomes overshadowed by the entertainment elements.

But in the current figure-skating climate, there is no such thing as "too entertaining."

KATARINA WITT, WHO WON TWO OLYMPIC CHAMPIONSHIPS FOR THE FORMER EAST GERMAN REPUBLIC, WAS THE CONSUMMATE COMPETITOR. A MASTER AT SEIZING AN AUDIENCE, SHE WAS ALSO THE MOST PSYCHOLOGICALLY PREPARED WOMAN SKATER OF THE 1980s, AND HER OBVIOUS COOL CAUSED MANY OF HER OPPONENTS TO WILT.

THREE

Judging

igure skating is not defined solely by how fast, how high, how far, or how many. If there is going to be competition, some way of determining winners, other than using finite measurements, must be found. That way is what has come to be known as skating's "necessary evil." Human judging.

Not that the humans are evil. But the process sometimes seems to be, especially to the casual observer.

In theory, judges evaluate a competition according to two general criteria: the content of a skater's program and how that program is presented. Each is assigned a mark, and the competitor with the best marks should win.

Although there has been no shortage of suspect – sometimes outright bad – judging at major international championships, many times the public scorn is not justified. Elite skaters perform technical and artistic elements that are not discernible to outsiders – or even insiders, if they're sitting too far away.

Conversely, sometimes mistakes made by skaters are obvious to the live audience but are missed by some judges because they do not have the right visual angle. (An old choreographic trick is to put the skater's most troublesome section of the program at a point on the rink that is farthest from the judges.)

Although jumps, spins, lifts, and throws always draw the most appreciative gasps from the crowd – skaters call those powerful elements "tricks" – judges try to see beyond the obvious. In the technical section, judges look for height and length of jumps and throws, proper technique, and crisp, clean takeoffs and landings.

Judges also rank the difficulty of different jump combinations. A triple Axel followed by a triple toe loop is a more challenging combination than a triple Lutz followed by a triple toe. The difficulty of jumps varies for skaters, but generally the toe loop is considered the easiest to master and the Axel the most difficult. The Lutz is the second hardest, and somewhere between the Axel and the Lutz and the toe loop lie the Salchow, the flip, and the loop.

THE RAPID RISE OF SHAE-LYNN BOURNE AND VICTOR KRAATZ OF CANADA IS UNUSUAL IN DANCE CIRCLES. AT FIRST JUDGES DID NOT APPRECIATE THEIR INNOVATIVE ANGLES AND REVOLUTIONARY "HYDROBLADING."

Technical proficiency also includes more subtle aspects, such as maintaining the center of a spin and being in control of its rotations; keeping a fluid, deep bend at the knees while stroking; using difficult and varied edges in footwork; shifting smoothly from one element to another.

The artistic half of judging leaves the judges wider latitude. They are instructed during training sessions to critique whether the skaters cover as much ice surface as possible; whether they're in synch with the music and have an interesting, commendable carriage; and whether the character of their music is portrayed through the performance.

THE SHORT PROGRAM

Not only are the marks divided into two parts, but in three of the four disciplines so is the competition. Ice dancing has retained its compulsory dance segment; women's and men's singles and pairs require competitors to skate only a short and a long program.

This opening event is a two-minute-forty-second skate that has been given various titles, from the short program to the technical program and back to the short program again. Rules are constantly being updated, but the purpose of the short program is to show the skater's technical proficiency in a variety of basic elements. The International Skating Union prescribes a set of different elements, usually eight, that each skater must perform somewhere in that 160 seconds. These include jumps, jump combinations, a footwork sequence, and spins for singles; and individual jumps and spins, pairs spins, lifts, a death spiral, and a footwork sequence for pairs.

The competitor chooses the music and it's up to him or her and the coach and choreographer how to demonstrate those elements. World-class skaters try to make their elements as difficult as possible. For instance, a required element in singles is now a jump combination that includes a triple. To have a chance of winning, a female skater probably has to make that triple a Lutz; a male skater must do an Axel. Technical points are deducted for missed or omitted elements, and if an element is failed, it cannot be attempted again. That adds to the incredible stress of the short program, because one botched element can cost a skater a chance at a medal. That disaster befell each of the "Big Three" at the 1994 Winter Olympics: Kurt Browning, Brian Boitano, and Victor Petrenko.

THE LONG PROGRAM

The second part of the competition is the free skate, or long program: four minutes for women and pairs; four minutes thirty seconds for men. The rules are far less restrictive than for the short program, but skaters are limited to doing each kind of jump just once on its own, then once again in combination. Top men's skaters might have a total of eight triple jumps or seven plus a quadruple. Women will usually attempt six or seven triples.

Triple jumps alone do not guarantee free-skate success: the elements of the program must be interesting and varied, and the artistry high. Of course, what comprises artistry is subject to intense argument. Scott Hamilton recalls a time in the 1970s and 1980s when "you didn't dare use rock 'n' roll music, for instance. There were nine

RUSSIA'S ALEXANDER FADEEV, THE DYNAMIC 1985 WORLD CHAMPION, WHOSE PROGRAMS WERE ALWAYS FRONT-END—LOADED WITH BIG TRICKS, SKATED WRETCHEDLY AT THE 1986 WORLDS. THE SOVIET JUDGE MARKED HIM SO HIGH THAT SHE WAS SUSPENDED.

different judges from nine different cultures, and that was in the day of the Iron Curtain, so when we said 'different' cultures it was very different. You couldn't give them music they didn't understand or relate to. Now, as the world has gotten smaller, you can pretty well skate to whatever music you want, as long as it doesn't compromise the integrity of the program. It's an overnight development that only took ninety-nine years."

Compulsory figures in men's and women's competitions were abolished after 1990, but ice dancing has retained its version. Before couples can move on to the more interesting and creative original

(*LEFT TO RIGHT*): Silver medalist Kurt Browning, champion Victor Petrenko, and bronze medalist Elvis Stojko wave from the podium at the 1992 World Championship at Oakland. Stojko, who most observers agreed was robbed by the judges at the Olympics just a month earlier, was vindicated by his first major podium placing and has not looked back since.

dance (short program) and free dance, they have to perform two dances to specified types of music such as tango or waltz. The required dances change from year to year and are announced at the start of the season.

The compulsory dance is an archaic, boring segment of ice-dance competition, and a move is underfoot to eradicate it. Nevertheless, some argue it is a useful event. Because falls in ice dancing are few and far between, there are no obvious mistakes with which to differentiate couples. The extra round allegedly helps judges rank the three-dozen couples who compete. But since the standings rarely change from the compulsories to the end of the competition, that's not much of an argument.

The various sections of competition are factored so that the free skate, or free dance, is the most important. In pairs and singles, the short program is worth one-third and the free skate two-thirds. In ice dance, compulsories count for 20 percent, the original dance 30 percent, and the free dance 50 percent.

READ THE MARKS DOWN, NOT ACROSS

Since judging is subjective, the assumption is that judges will not always agree with each other. So a judging panel must contain an odd number of judges – usually nine at major events – to make sure there won't be a tie. Once an event is in progress, judges are not permitted to speak to one another.

In amateur competition, skaters are marked on a six-point grid, with a 6.0 score signifying a faultless performance. Anything from 5.0 to 6.0 is considered very good, 4.0 to 5.0 good, 3.0 to 4.0 mediocre, and 2.0 to 3.0 poor. Professional competitions have tended to favor a ten-point scoring system, but more and more are opting for the six-point system because it is more familiar to skating's vast audience, who have been reared on the amateur competitions.

The key thing to remember about judging is that each mark given to a skater is important only in relation to the marks given by that judge to other skaters. Once a judge has allotted all the marks, those marks are placed in order. The skater with the highest total marks (adding the technical and presentation marks together) stands first on that judge's card. The skater with the second highest total is second, and so on. Those rankings are called **ordinals**.

A judge's card might look like this:

SKATER	MARK	ORDINAL
A	5.3 (TECHNICAL)	
	5.4 (PRESENTATION)	
	10.7 (TOTAL)	4
B	5.5 (TECHNICAL)	
	5.6 (PRESENTATION)	
	11.1 (TOTAL)	2
C	5.5 (TECHNICAL)	
	5.5 (PRESENTATION)	
	11.0 (TOTAL)	3
D	5.6 (TECHNICAL)	
	5.6 (PRESENTATION)	
	11.2 (TOTAL)	1

This judge thought Skater D was the best all-around: equal to Skater B in presentation, but slightly better technically. So Skater D gets an ordinal of 1 on the judge's card. Skater B gets an ordinal of 2 because the judge felt that skater was equal in technical strength to Skater C, but superior at presenting the material. If a judge has skaters tied in the total mark, the higher artistic mark is used to break the tie in the free skate. In the technical program, the technical mark, logically, is used.

Each judge goes through the same process, and the skater with the majority of first-place ordinals wins that segment of the event. The skater with a majority of second-place (or higher) ordinals is second, and so forth.

For example:

SKATER	JUDGE 1	JUDGE 2	JUDGE 3
A	5.6	5.6	5.3
B	5.5	5.7	5.2
C	5.4	5.4	5.1

Skater A had two first-place votes, and so gets a first-place finish. Skater B had three ordinals of second or higher, and so finishes second. Skater C is third on all three cards.

But when Skater A's marks flash on the arena scoreboard, the crowd will probably boo when Judge 3's mark is read out, because it is lower than the two that went before it. However, Judge 3 actually has Skater A in first place on his or her card. Judge 2, who gave Skater A a higher mark than Judge 3 did, actually marked Skater A in *second* place. Judge 3 is simply a low marker.

There should be more low markers among judges, and then perhaps Elvis Stojko would not have suffered the injustice that he did at the 1992 Olympics. Skating insiders offer all kinds of explanations of why the then lightly regarded Stojko could be the only man in the entire Olympic field to skate a clean short program and a clean free skate and actually drop from sixth to seventh place overall. To the laymen – millions of TV viewers whose only exposure to figure skating was the Olympic Games – that was simply unfair and unforgivable.

What happened to Stojko was elementary: he performed far better than expected and those ranked above him skated more poorly than expected. Stojko skated last in both programs and judges did not "save" enough marks for him.

That was understandable in the short program: judges had given out all the 5.8s and 5.9s, and no marks were left to put him third or fourth, where he belonged. So the only open mark total left him sixth.

But for the same thing to happen two nights later in the free skate was inexcusable. The trouble started fourteen skaters from the end of the event, when the majority of marks given to a middle-ranked French skater were in the 5.0 range. This meant that when better skaters such as Victor Petrenko, Paul Wylie, and Kurt Browning followed and didn't perform up to expectations but were better than the French skater, they had to receive marks in the mid-to-high 5.0s.

When Stojko skated flawlessly, all the upper-level marks had already been taken, and the only gap was at seventh place. In one of the most poorly skated competitions of all time, he skated brilliantly and dropped a spot.

If judges had started out by marking low – remember, the rules define 4.0 as "good" – there would have been more room for Stojko in the third or fourth spot, which he deserved.

"I got boxed in the ears," fumed Stojko's coach, Doug Leigh, who in eleven years at the world level had been generally stoic about judging foibles. "I'm angry. Those judges have got to sleep on it and live with it. We gave them something to judge and they had trouble doing it."

SAVE THE BEST FOR LAST, SORT OF

After the short program, the field is broken into groups – five or six skaters per group in singles, three or four teams in pairs and dance – for the free-skate final. The first group includes the skaters who finished lowest in the previous segment, and the last group comprises the ones who topped the standings after the short program. Within each group, the skating order is drawn by lot.

That random draw often means the eventual winner will skate, and have the title all but wrapped up, before the major challengers get a chance to perform. It also means that skaters with no chance to win (those standing fifth or sixth) could be the last competitors on the ice. At the 1984 Worlds, for instance, Jayne Torvill and Christopher Dean skated second last. It was the final performance of their amateur career and the crowd stood and cheered for minutes. But there was still another couple – fellow Britons Nicky Slater and Karen Barber – to go. They skated brilliantly, but for dramatic purposes the event should have ended with winners Torvill and Dean.

For the U.S. nationals, ABC-TV has succeeded in having the order for the long program changed so that the winner of the short program skates last. This makes for better live TV because the event cannot be over before it's over. Similar appeals to the ISU to change the Olympics and Worlds have so far fallen on deaf ears, but the change is bound to occur.

Yet even under the current world system, medal winners aren't always assured until the end, because of the ordinal system. A good example was the race for the bronze medal in pairs at the 1995 World Championships.

American champions Jenni Meno and Todd Sand had finished fifth in the short program and Germans Mandy Woetzel and Ingo Steuer had finished second. But the Americans skated well in the long, while the Germans faltered. Still, the Germans had built enough of a lead in the short program that they seemed destined to hold onto a bronze, with the Americans likely finishing fifth.

The Americans needed the final pair, Russians Marina Eltsova and Andrei Bushkov, to finish exactly fourth in the long program – ahead of the Germans but behind Meno and Sand. Any other order, and the Americans would not win a medal. Eltsova and Bushkov did exactly as required, and Meno and Sand had an early wedding present (they married that summer).

"As usual," their coach, John Nicks, observed tongue-in-cheek, "the Russians were very helpful."

AMERICANS JENNI MENO AND TODD SAND, ON THE TOM COLLINS'S TOUR OF WORLD FIGURE SKATING CHAMPIONS. IN TUXEDO AND MOCK BRIDAL VEIL, THE 1995 WORLD-MEDALISTS' TONGUE-IN-CHEEK FINALE ROUTINE WAS SKATED TO "GOING TO THE CHAPEL," APPROPRIATELY ENOUGH, SINCE THEY WERE MARRIED ONLY A FEW MONTHS LATER.

VARIED JUDGING PROGRAMS

Some countries such as Canada and the U.S. have challenging training and testing programs for judges who will serve on panels at major and secondary international events. Other countries try to appoint former skaters, who understand the ins and outs of the sport. The ISU itself has seminars for its judges and a review process in which judges are asked to explain themselves after a competition. Each year several judges are suspended or reprimanded for marking mistakes or improprieties.

But that still does not guarantee faultless judging, if there can even be such a thing. Many countries are unable to provide much training for their judges, and as more and more new national associations join the ISU, that could become a greater problem.

One of the biggest concerns is that judges will react to what they're *supposed* to see, not what they're actually seeing. That problem is particularly acute in ice

BRIAN ORSER WON EIGHT CANADIAN NATIONAL CHAMPIONSHIPS, SECOND ONLY TO MONTGOMERY WILSON'S NINE. ORSER, THE SECOND MAN TO DO A TRIPLE AXEL, MADE THE THREE-AND-A-HALF REVOLUTION JUMP IMPERATIVE FOR EVERY OTHER MEN'S CONTENDER, THEN DEVELOPED A SUPERB ARTISTRY TO GO WITH HIS TECHNICAL FAME. AFTER FOUR YEARS ON THE PODIUM, HE WON THE 1987 WORLD CHAMPIONSHIP.

dancing, where there is a wait-your-turn hierarchy. Judges from the Czech Republic, the U.S., Ukraine, France, Russia, and Finland were suspended for "protocol judging" at the 1993 Worlds. They appealed and were reinstated on a technicality. "But the message was still sent," said an ISU official.

Many of the obvious mistakes made in judging are honest ones. The British judge in the 1995 Worlds women's competition thought Canadian Jennifer Robinson had completed a triple Lutz–double toe loop combination in the short program and ranked her fifth. She had doubled the Lutz – which other judges had caught and placed her twenty-second.

The history of figure skating is full of controversies far worse than the outcry that followed Stojko's placing at the 1992 Olympics. One of the reasons the campaign to abolish compulsory figures gained momentum in the 1970s and 1980s was that so much bizarre judging took place during them. There were constant accusations of judges cheating – keeping good free skaters shackled by their standings in figures so they couldn't challenge favored skaters for the title – particularly when the Soviet bloc was at its strongest and most manipulative. Because the figures were contested in empty arenas, early in the morning, and not subject to TV's probing eye, little could be done about the problem.

It was not always just the figures that produced suspicious results.

A Soviet was suspended for her blatant bias during the 1986 Worlds when she gave Soviet skater Alexander Fadeev, the defending world champion, a 5.9 for technical merit after he fell three times. When the rest of the panel had him several points lower, she could be seen dropping her head into her hands.

Judging intrigue dates back to Sonja Henie's first competition, even beyond. There have always been accusations, many of them justified, of power plays within judging panels and part of a coach's job in the 1950s and 1960s was to keep on top of the political developments. One of the most famous controversies occurred in the 1956 Olympic pairs event, when Sissy Schwarz and Kurt Oppelt of Austria won the gold on a 5–4 split over defending world champions Frances Dafoe and Norris Bowden of Canada, a decision ridiculed by everyone in attendance. The Canadians were given two unconscionable third-place votes, which cost them the title. When a similar travesty happened a few weeks later at Worlds, the Austrian coach, Arnold Gerschwiler, apologized to the Canadians. On tour after the competition, the Austrians refused to skate because of the ill-will surrounding them, and later, three judges were given lifetime suspensions.

STILL A PROBLEM

Even with intense TV coverage, the removal of figures, and the collapse of the Soviet bloc, grave questions still persist about judging. At the 1995 World Championships, European champion Surya Bonaly botched her combination in the short program, usually a fatal mistake. But she was given disconcertingly high marks and stood fourth, from where she could mount her attack on a silver medal in the free skate.

The main problem area is still ice dancing, which faces constant threats that it will be removed from the Olympic roster because the final standings are too easy to predict (even though in the past two Olympics the reigning world champions have not won gold). After the 1992 Olympics, Paul Duchesnay went so far as to say that ice dancing should not be a sport, that it is really a performance art.

Many skating observers felt that Canadian ice dancing champions Shae-Lynn Bourne and Victor Kraatz should have won a medal in the 1995 Worlds, when they finished fourth.

"It's not a question of whether it's fair," said Kraatz. "It's the way it is. You have to wait your turn, to take over from someone who's been there longer, who's more mature. And once you're there, you get to stand your ground."

That was meant as a defense of the system, but at heart it is an attack on it.

"A lot of times you question whether the amateur judges actually know what they're seeing," Brian Boitano said during the 1994 fall pro season. "Most of the time I feel much better being watched in the professional competitions by the professional judges."

Professional judging has made great strides in the past few years, and there is some talk of the ISU getting away from the practice of having national associations provide prospective judges. The suggestion is that the ISU, like the NHL or NBA or Major League Baseball, hire and train its own nationality-independent judges and pay them handsomely.

The worst situation for judges is when the skaters place the competition entirely in the judges' hands by skating well below par. Nevertheless, despite the glaring controversies, the potential for human error, and the subjectivity, the surprising fact is that the right skater usually wins. That in itself is a defense of the system.

And, from an early age, competitive skaters develop the philosophy necessary to help them deal with the vagaries of a judged sport.

"You may be the best in your own heart, but not in somebody else's sight," American skater Michelle Kwan said after the 1995 Worlds.

"So all you can do is your best."

Athleticism and Figure Skating

Figure skating's strongest asset is also the source of its greatest struggle: its split personality. Is it a sport or is it an art form?

Skating appeals to hard-core sports fans because it holds World Championships and is the cornerstone of the Winter Olympics. It demands from its athletes coordination and agility; speed, power, and timing; superb conditioning; years of difficult training; and a fierce competitive spirit.

But, with its artistic and entertainment components, skating also appeals to a segment of the population that other sports do not: the large group who go to the arena to see the beauty and elegance, and don't really care who wins.

Supporters of the so-called mainstream sports have always raised a collective eyebrow at the artistic element in figure skating. Sportswriters who parachute in every four years to cover a Winter Olympics become instant critics. Beautiful, graceful, energetic: all those qualities are conceded. But how can anything be a sport, they argue, when it has no objective standards, when human judges, not time clocks or scorecards, decide what the final standings will be? In hockey, the team with the most goals wins; in baseball it's the most runs; in football and basketball the most points. In other sports, the winner is the one who goes the fastest, the farthest, the highest, or the one who throws something the greatest distance.

Competitive skating encompasses many of those elements but also demands that they be accomplished artistically, and to music.

"Skaters are athletes. Period. There is no question about that," says Doug Leigh of the Mariposa Skating School in Barrie, Ontario. Leigh is one of the world's leading experts on technical skills and has coached Brian Orser and Elvis Stojko to World Championships. He has improved the jumping form of several national champions from European countries, including Britain's Steve Cousins, who has now conquered the triple Axel and moved into the sport's upper echelons.

"Even the skaters who are known more as artists [are] athletes first," says Leigh. "They have to be, with what's demanded in the sport now."

Oxygen uptake capacity, one of the critical measurements of athletic

JOSEF SABOVCIK OF CZECHOSLOVAKIA WAS AMONG THE WORLD'S GREAT TECHNICAL SKATERS IN THE EARLY 1980S, AND CAPPED HIS CAREER WITH A BRONZE MEDAL AT THE 1984 OLYMPICS. HE TRAINED WITH BRIAN ORSER IN ORILLIA, ONTARIO, BUT BECAUSE OF INJURIES AND SUSPECT TRAINING HABITS, HE DID NOT REALIZE HIS POTENTIAL AS AN AMATEUR. HE HAS BECOME A SOUGHT-AFTER PROFESSIONAL SHOW SKATER.

performance, is higher among skaters than most other athletes. To get through a free-skate program, a female skater must work, almost always at top speed, for four full minutes, a male skater for four and a half minutes. A hockey player rests after forty-five seconds of effort, although he does repeat the process thirty times in a game. The danger factor in skating is rarely recognized until a Kurt Browning misses almost an entire season with a bad back from the constant pounding of thousands of jumps and landings; or an Elvis Stojko "comes off the bench" with an ankle torn so badly on landing he can barely walk; or an Isabelle Brasseur has trouble skating, even breathing, because of smashed ribs from a pairs throw. There is enough torque in a triple Axel that a botched one can rip a bone apart. Brian Orser suffered three different hairline fractures practicing his Axel.

The psychological requirement – rising to the competitive occasion; "psyching out" opponents; conquering the fear of failure or success; making the butterflies in your stomach fly in formation – is another benchmark for a sport and its athletes.

"Definitely state of mind is part of being an athlete," says Leigh. "And it's a big part of our sport, because you can't skate without your head. You got where you are because you have motor skills. You get where you want to go because of your head."

Katarina Witt was one of the best athletes of her amateur-skating era. She was near the top, but rarely the best, in most of the sport's athletic demands. There were better spinners and better jumpers, and skaters who had better footwork. She probably had more physical strength than most of her opponents, but where Witt had no peer was in the psychological realm. She wanted to win and knew how. One of her favorite ploys during practice sessions or warm-ups at important competitions was to throw one muscular leg over the top of the boards and bend into a powerful stretch, all the while maintaining eye contact with her nearest rival. Unnerved by Witt's supreme confidence, more than one opponent crashed and burned when it came her turn to skate.

"You cannot one-up Katarina. I've always admired that about her," says American Debi Thomas, who beat Witt for the world title at Geneva in 1986, but could not duplicate that feat over the next two years.

Brian Boitano loves competition. It was that passion that fueled his successful campaign to have professionals reinstated for the 1992 Olympics. And Kurt Browning, whose introduction to ice rinks came through the ultra-confrontational sport of hockey, was a master of rising to the moment in winning his four World Championships. When he had the training time and was injury-free, that competitive urge always pushed him beyond his less strong-willed opponents.

Victor Petrenko, Browning's main rival at the time and an elegant skater with all the necessary physical assets, had trouble with the psychological side, particularly in calming his nerves. He almost always wilted during the more revealing long program after dominating the short program. Even when he won his Olympic gold in 1992, Petrenko left the arena after the short program because watching others made him nervous. His free skate deadened as he weakened physically and emotionally in the second half and he was fortunate to win over American Paul Wylie.

THE QUAD SKATE: KURT BROWNING WAS INDUCTED INTO CANADA'S SPORTS HALL OF FAME IN 1994. HE'S HOLDING THE SKATES HE WAS WEARING IN 1988, WHEN HE LANDED THE WORLD'S FIRST QUADRUPLE JUMP. HE DONATED THE SKATES TO THE HALL OF FAME, REMARKING DURING HIS INDUCTION SPEECH THAT THE DIFFERENCE BETWEEN FAILURE AND MAKING HISTORY WAS THE FRACTION OF AN INCH OF BLADE EDGE THAT HELD THE ICE ON LANDING, ENABLING HIM TO COMPLETE THE LANDMARK JUMP.

Browning finally encountered his psychological equal right in his own country. Elvis Stojko, who is deeply involved in two other sports (moto-cross biking and karate), is every bit as competitive as Browning, and by the time they were serious rivals, Stojko was technically superior to Browning.

A LEAGUE OF ITS OWN

Although judging controversies will always cloud figure skating, it is moving deeper into the realm of mainstream sport because it has added more and more competitions. Until the early 1970s, skating was a pursuit mainly of practice and performance. There were opportunities to perform in spring and summer exhibition skates, but there were very few competitions. In an entire year, a skater might have a couple of qualifying tournaments for the national championship, the nationals, sometimes a lead-up competition such as the Europeans or the now-defunct North American Championships, then the World Championships. Bingo, season over. Five competitions in an entire year!

Additional competitions in the form of fall internationals began cropping up in the 1970s as a vehicle for national governing bodies to earn income and for skaters and judges to learn about one another for the coming season. But other than pride

(*LEFT*) ELVIS STOJKO'S ATHLETIC PROWESS IS NOT LIMITED TO FIGURE SKATING. HE ALSO HAS A BLACK BELT IN KARATE AND HAS SINCE MOVED ON TO KUNG-FU. IN THIS PHOTO, TAKEN DURING A KUNG-FU DEMONSTRATION, HE DELIVERS A BLOW TO THE HEAD OF INSTRUCTOR GLENN DOYLE.

(*RIGHT*) ONLY TWO AXELS! ELVIS STOJKO GETS SOME HANG-TIME OF A DIFFERENT TYPE AS HE PURSUES ANOTHER OF HIS ATHLETIC INTERESTS, MOTO-CROSSING. IF HE HAD MORE TIME TO TRAIN, STOJKO COULD PROBABLY RACE COMPETITIVELY IN HIGH-LEVEL EVENTS.

and establishing a pecking order, the Skate Canadas, Skate Americas, NHKs, and the other half-dozen fall internationals had no real standing in the sport. One year the field might be strong, the next very weak. Skaters might drop out at the last moment. In other sports, the fall internationals would be called exhibition games.

The proliferation of professional competitions has altered that. Huge purses are at stake in a dozen pro competitions. To keep pace, the International Skating Union has banded five of its highest-profile fall events, including Skate Canada and Skate America, into a Grand Prix circuit, with a new Grand Prix final. In a sense, the ISU's Grand Prix is competing for stature with its own World Championship, but that has worked in other sports, particularly European soccer.

The Grand Prix was established to give the marketplace more access to the top amateur skaters, but the side effect is that skating now has its own league.

PUSHING THE ENVELOPE

Michael Weiss has not yet competed in a World Championship, but he is already planning ahead. The nineteen-year-old from Washington, D.C., won the 1994 World Junior Championship by landing triple Axels in both his short and long programs, and he has been working on perfecting both a quadruple toe loop and a quad Lutz.

"Skating is still evolving," he explained in *Blades on Ice* magazine. "In another four years, you probably won't need just one quad to be competitive – you'll have to have two or three and use them in combinations. Already you have to do eight triples in a program, just to be up there in the running. What it comes down to is that skating is still very jump-oriented."

There are six basic jumps, defined by whether a toe pick is used to help in the takeoff and which edges of the blade are used in takeoff and landings. The toe loop is considered to be the easiest because the first rotation actually starts before the skater is in the air. The Axel is the most difficult because it is the only one the skater enters while skating forward, and requires an extra half turn. Thus, a triple Axel involves three-and-a-half rotations. The Lutz is rated as the second most difficult followed, in descending order, by the flip, loop, Salchow, and toe loop. For some skaters, the loop is more difficult than the flip.

One sports axiom holds that for success to be appreciated there must also be the potential for failure. In figure skating that comes in the execution of the jumps. No male skater can consider himself a contender for the World Championship without having the triple Axel in his repertoire and landing it consistently. Usually the top half-dozen skaters will have two triple Axels, one in combination with another jump, either a double or triple.

After Vern Taylor landed the world's first triple Axel at the 1978 World Championship, Brian Orser was the only skater to regularly land one until the mid-1980s. Now junior skaters are doing them and looking toward quads.

A tremendous gamble is involved in going for the big jumps. With more and more men doing triple Axels, Orser tried to keep one step ahead of the game by attempting the first triple Axel in combination with another triple jump (toe loop) during the long program of the 1986 World Championships. Orser didn't need that combination because his closest rival, Alexander Fadeev, had fallen several times, but he tried it anyway and tumbled. His program then fell apart, and Brian Boitano became the surprise winner. The next year Orser skated superbly to win the title, while Boitano tried a quad and missed.

Kurt Browning landed the world's first quad, a toe loop, at the 1988 World Championship, then only did three more before abandoning it as too risky to his title chances and not really necessary. But now if you have a quad and don't attempt it, judges sometimes see that as a sign of backing off.

"Skating is a sport," says Stojko, who has tacked a triple jump on the back of his quad. "So you should keep expanding and growing and trying harder things. That's part of who I am as a skater."

Stojko and other cutting-edge jumpers will not predict how far the jumps will go, but quadruple Axels have been mentioned – Stojko has done them in a practice harness – and there have even been whispers that a quintuple jump is not beyond human capability. That won't happen, though, without advances in technology. Skate boots and blades will have to be stronger and more resilient.

Orser was coming to the end of his amateur career when Stojko arrived in Orillia, then home of the Mariposa School. He had been sent there at age thirteen by his coach, Ellen Burka (who was considering retirement), because of Doug Leigh's expertise in building proper jumping technique. Leigh knew from the first workout that he had something special on his hands, but wasn't sure exactly what.

"You can't tell how good anybody is going to be," says Leigh, who also coaches 1995 Canadian world team member Jennifer Robinson. "But you have a chance that they're going to be good at something. Then you start to have an idea of what kind of style they're going to be.

ELVIS STOJKO PERFORMING AN ARABIAN. STOJKO HAD AN UNCHARACTERISTIC FALL ON HIS TRIPLE AXEL COMBINATION IN THE 1996 WORLDS SHORT PROGRAM AND TUMBLED OUT OF THE RUNNING FOR A THIRD GOLD, BUT FINISHED FOURTH OVERALL.

"The two main guys [Orser and Stojko] I've had are two different types. But they are both intelligent about their sport, and very hard-working. They treated *themselves* differently, but they were very similar in training. They both wanted to get the very best out of themselves. Elvis is probably better at the psychology part.

"One guy was always like a colt out of the barn, kind of quick and flashy. Maybe when he was young, not everything was heading in the right direction, but he had a spirit.

"Elvis brought motor skill and power dynamics and desire plus. He has a major no-nonsense attitude. He studies the game a lot and goes out and takes care of business the way it has to be taken care of ... while he's learning."

ELVIS REIGNS

If Orser showed Canadians that they could win, and Browning showed them they could win often, Stojko has shown them that they can win under any circumstances.

The depth and breadth of Stojko's desire and training were evident during the 1995 season, when it seemed certain that he would be forced to miss the World Championships with a serious ankle injury. But Stojko has made a career of reversing setbacks. He trained and waited and learned in the shadow of Kurt Browning, and probably deserved to win the 1990 Canadian title at Sudbury, though it went to a struggling Browning. He stoically accepted terrible judging at the 1992 Olympics. He heard and absorbed criticism of his artistry that peaked with Alexei Urmanov beating him in the 1994 Olympics "because," as one judge explained, "he has better lines." He came back to win the World Championship a month later.

So when Stojko tore the anterior ligament of his right ankle during practices for the 1995 Canadian Championships, he was determined to participate in the Worlds at Birmingham just a few weeks later. Few gave him a chance, especially since he had tried to skate in the short program at nationals and had to bail out. The ankle injury deflected stress onto his knee, which also began to hurt.

Fighting constant pain, Stojko kept on the ice but could not land any triple jumps until just two weeks before the Worlds. But after finishing second in the short program to a vastly improved Todd Eldredge, Stojko opened his long program by nailing a triple Axel–triple toe loop combination. He also attempted the quad and got around four times, but fell on the landing. However, he left his most spectacular moment for the end: he upgraded a planned triple Lutz–double toe combination to a triple–triple, and the title was his on a 6–3 split of judges, with the French judge awarding him a perfect score – 6.0 – for technical merit.

Stojko has repeatedly insisted that he will not let skating rule his entire life. He says he's a figure skater, but also a martial artist and dirt biker, and not necessarily in that order. The danger and speed of dirt biking; the form, concentration, and energy flow of martial arts – all are evident in his skating.

Although he has since turned to the greater freedom of movement of kung-fu and conducted martial-arts demonstrations at the World Wu Shu Championships, he earned his first-degree black belt in karate at the age of sixteen. His father had enrolled him in classes when Stojko was ten because he wanted his small-statured son to be able to defend himself. But it is the mental discipline and focus of the martial arts, not the self-defense aspect, that most attracts Stojko. "It's not just a physical thing, but a mental and spiritual thing. I use it in skating and off the ice. I trust it."

One of Stojko's big thrills, and an indication that he had "arrived," came during the 1994 Olympics, when martial-arts movie star Chuck Norris asked someone to introduce him to the Canadian skater. Stojko had trouble believing that Norris wanted to meet him … he thought it should be the other way around. In 1995, he received an even bigger honor when he, Isabelle Brasseur, and Lloyd Eisler were named recipients of Canada's Meritorious Service Medal by Governor-General Roméo LeBlanc.

Stojko began skating at the age of five, and like most skaters who make it to the top, he showed immediate balance on his skates. Two years later he started his second passionate hobby when his parents bought him a minicycle to ride around the family farm. He now has three motorcycles in his parents' garage, with a fourth belonging to clubmate Steven Cousins. He uses riding on the bike trails to relax, and probably could be a championship competitor if he had more time.

"He said to me once, 'You know I'm really enjoying jumping today,'" Leigh recalls. "Sometimes it's as though he's dirt-biking in the air."

THE RESURGENCE OF TODD ELDREDGE

While Stojko's favorite sports outside of skating are kung-fu and biking, the man he beat for the 1995 world title prefers something a little more serene. Todd Eldredge of Chatham, Massachusetts, says that if he hadn't been a skater, he would have tried professional golf.

With his silver medal, Eldredge reclaimed the bright future that seemed his when he had won a world bronze (1991) and two national championships (1990 and 1991) by the time he was twenty. But a misaligned spinal joint from years and

THREE-TIME AMERICAN CHAMPION TODD ELDREDGE WON THE 1991 WORLDS BRONZE MEDAL, BUT INJURIES AND A COMPETITIVE DOWNTURN KEPT HIM OFF EVEN THE NATIONAL PODIUM UNTIL HE BURST BACK SPECTACULARLY IN 1995, FINISHING SECOND TO ELVIS STOJKO AT THE WORLDS IN BIRMINGHAM. THEN ELDREDGE WON IT ALL IN 1996, WITH A TREMENDOUS LONG PROGRAM IN EDMONTON ON ONE OF THE BEST NIGHTS FOR OVERALL SKATING DEPTH THAT THE MEN'S DIVISION HAS EVER SEEN.

years of twisting and hammering on jumps pained him through the entire 1992 competitive season and pushed him all the way down to tenth at the Albertville Olympics when he missed a routine double Axel in the short program.

The following year, he has admitted, he lost his training focus when he seemed to be getting messages that other Americans – Scott Davis and Mark Mitchell among them – were looked upon more favorably than he was. "All of a sudden, bang, people were picking me apart," Eldredge reflected. "I got to the top and it was all positive. Then it became all negative, and it throws you off." Compounding matters, at the 1994 nationals he came down with a fever and finished fourth behind Olympic-bound Davis and Brian Boitano and world-team member Aren Nielsen – a major disappointment

But Eldredge rebounded spectacularly in 1995. He started the season with a silver medal at the Goodwill Games, then won three straight fall internationals. Along the way he beat two-time American champion Davis, Victor Petrenko, and Alexei Urmanov, the last two Olympic champions, world silver medalist Philippe Candeloro, and bronze medalist Viacheslav Zagorodniuk. His confidence soaring, he took a convincing victory over Davis at the U.S. nationals, although

RUSSIA'S ILYA KULIK WAS ONLY SEVENTEEN WHEN HE WAS THE SURPRISE WINNER OF THE 1995 EUROPEAN CHAMPIONSHIPS WITH A BARRAGE OF EIGHT TRIPLE JUMPS, BUT HE FINISHED ONLY SEVENTH AT THE 1995 WORLDS. KULIK CAME AWAY WITH A SILVER MEDAL IN THE 1996 WORLDS AFTER WINNING THE SHORT PROGRAM, AND MIGHT HAVE TAKEN THE CHAMPIONSHIP IF HE HADN'T REDUCED HIS SECOND TRIPLE–TRIPLE COMBINATION INTO JUST A TRIPLE JUMP.

neither skated well in the long program. The three years between titles was the longest for an American man since 1925, when Nathaniel Niles won after a seven-year gap. Eldredge was also the first American to regain a title after three years out of the medals. Niles was second four times in his nontitle years.

Eldredge, the son of a New England fisherman, started out in hockey skates at the age of five but quickly switched to figure skates because he wanted to jump and spin. Those are still his fortes, although his artistry has been improving in recent years as he overcomes a basic shyness. He says he wants to keep things simple and let his skating do the talking.

Eldredge salvaged his silver medal and put immense pressure on the injured Stojko when he ad-libbed a triple Axel near the end of his free-skate program. He had fallen during an earlier Axel attempt, but had the presence of mind and training to execute a second. (Ironically Stojko, at the end of *his* program, also ad-libbed, adding an extra rotation to a planned triple Lutz–double toe combination.) "I threw the late Axel in because if I did it, I was still in the hunt, and if I didn't, well, I gave it my best shot," Eldredge said. "Elvis skated the best, so he won, as it should be."

Because Eldredge achieved so much so early, some fans assume he must be the sport's senior citizen. But he is only seven months older than Stojko. The battle between the two in the countdown to Nagano should be an interesting one, but there are also several other legitimate contenders, each with the athletic credentials to win. The technical ability of the top ten in the world is so high that the short program could be the most nerve-racking 160 seconds in all of sport. A slight flaw could cost an athlete three or four places in the standings, from which he might never recover.

That lesson was hammered home to seventeen-year-old European champion Ilya Kulik, who came into the 1995 World Championships riding the enormous wave of eight triple jumps he had used to win the European Championship. Nerves got to the young Russian in the short program, and he meekly let a triple Axel–triple toe combination flatten out into a triple–single. He dropped to eleventh and had to fight back to seventh overall.

Alexei Urmanov, Philippe Candeloro, and Viacheslav Zagorodniuk also had trouble during the short program, with only Candeloro rebounding enough to make the podium. As the technical ability and risk taking continue to spiral upward, playing it conservatively is no longer the useful tool it once was. One indication of the more demanding technical level is that the combination jump in the short program must now contain at least one triple. That should prove no problem to the top half-dozen who are beyond such basics. And Urmanov, Stojko, and Zagorodniuk have all successfully landed quadruple jumps.

Two-time American champion Scott Davis, and even Steven Cousins of Great Britain, now that he has a triple Axel, must also be considered in the group of eight who will attempt to crowd their way onto the podium until after the 1998 Olympics. Davis is the antithesis of the European men, in that he tends to do well in the short program, then come unraveled in the free skate. At the 1994 Olympics he was a medal contender after the short program, with a muscular and clean performance, but he dropped to eighth in the final standings. At the 1995 Worlds, he stood third as North Americans swept the top-three short-program spots, with Eldredge first and Stojko second. But again he fell to eighth.

BODY TYPES AND ANGULAR MOMENTUM

When Davis goes into his dizzying spins, he is performing a skill that requires more energy than the most difficult jumps. Spins add to the artistry of a program, but they are actually very technical elements, and far fewer skaters perfect them than master all the triples. Timing, strength, and practice are needed to harness all the forces – particularly centrifugal force – that act on various parts of a skater's body during an arms-folded upright spin.

MICHELLE KWAN, WHOSE STYLE
EMBODIES ATHLETICISM AND
YOUTHFUL ENERGY, WAS FOURTH AT
THE 1995 WORLD CHAMPIONSHIPS
AT THE AGE OF FOURTEEN, AND THE
NEXT YEAR BECAME THE THIRD-
YOUNGEST WORLD CHAMPION OF
ALL TIME, BEHIND SONIA HENIE
AND OKSANA BAIUL. SHE EDGED
DEFENDING CHAMPION LU CHEN
WITH A SUPERB RENDITION OF
SALOME IN ONE OF THE BEST
WOMEN'S FREE-SKATING FINALS IN
WORLD CHAMPIONSHIP HISTORY.

The main physical force in singles figure skating is "angular momentum," which combines two kinds of motion: straight line (or linear) and circular (or rotational). The idea in spins is to maximize the circular momentum.

Jumps are, essentially, spins in the air. Their path is governed by the amount of upward force combined with the force of the straight-line motion and the amount of rotational momentum created by the body movements and the edge of the skate.

"If you're going to rotate in the air, it's no different than the earth rotating on its axis," says Doug Leigh, who loves to talk in similes and metaphors. "You're not just walking through space. So all the curves and angles approaching the jump have to match the flight path of the jump.

"Generally, they're all after the same flight path, but different people are 727s, 737s, or 747s."

The old joke is that the hardest part about skating is the ice. Learning to fall, and living with the constant presence of the tumble, is one of skating's first lessons, and many young skaters never get past it. Leigh calls a fall "an opportunity to learn … give me one more chance and I'll get it." Overcoming that fear is an early step toward becoming a good jumper.

So is acquiring speed. With all that television has done to spread the gospel of figure skating, one of the things that it does not transmit well is the idea of speed. Fans who sit in the seats closest to the ice at a competition are constantly amazed at how quickly and powerfully top skaters get around the ice. That speed comes from proper stroking and edge technique, and is one of the major reasons that skaters spend 75 percent of their time going backward. As Kurt Browning explained, the backward skating motion enables the athlete to cut a much wider swath along the ice than forward skating, allowing for greater pull by the edges and therefore more power. That energy is transferred into speed and vertical motion.

Body shape plays a role in determining how proficient a jumper a skater will become. Females, for instance, tend to plateau, or even regress, in their mid-teens as their body changes shape. It's generally accepted that for both genders narrower hips make for easier rotations.

When skating fans meet their idols off the ice, they're surprised to find how small many of them are. One of the amazing aspects of Brian Boitano is that he has such perfect jump technique despite being much taller than most technically oriented skaters. A lower center of gravity is considered a help in executing the big jumps. Robin Cousins was also much taller than his contemporaries, and six-foot-two (188 cm) Oula Jaaskelainen, the perennial Finnish champion and training mate of Stojko, has landed a triple Axel.

Good jumpers are usually slim, too. "But that doesn't mean frail," said Leigh. "Elvis is so powerful he could rip you apart. But both my big guns [Stojko and Orser] are in the five-foot-seven to five-foot-nine area [170 to 175 cm], which is a good range for jumping. You can, if you work hard enough, program your body to do anything, although there are some people you can't teach to jump. If you have slow-twitch instead of fast-twitch muscles, the odds are against you."

And, like gymnastics, it is enormously beneficial to have a high muscle-to-body-weight ratio.

AMERICAN WOMEN ARE BACK

The muscle-to-body-weight ratio is particularly evident in the recent successes of younger women skaters. Michelle Kwan was a few months shy of her fifteenth birthday when she finished fourth at the 1995 World Championships. That heralds a very bright future, as long as the growth spurts and body changes that hit teenage girls don't interfere with her athletic progress.

Kwan, runner-up to Nicole Bobek in the U.S. Championships, was the 1994 world junior champion when she still had four years of eligibility remaining. She finished third in the long program at the 1995 Worlds, behind Lu Chen and Surya

Bonaly, who also took the top two spots overall. Bobek got the bronze because she won the short program; Kwan was fifth.

The daughter of a father born in mainland China and a mother from Hong Kong, Kwan does a triple Lutz combination, the jump that separates the top female skaters from the rest of the pack. She became the most famous team alternate in history during the Kerrigan–Harding affair, when Harding won the 1994 nationals in Kerrigan's absence and Kwan was second. Harding took legal steps to make sure that, despite a cloud of suspicion over her head, she would be included on the Olympic team with Kerrigan. Kwan remained prepared to compete at Lillehammer if Kerrigan's injuries meant she couldn't or if Harding was barred. She did go to the World Championships a month later in Oakland and finished eleventh. It was a commendable debut for Kwan, but signaled a low point in American skating. Only in 1962 and 1963, the two years after the U.S. world team was killed in a plane crash, had the top American woman at the World Championships finished even as low as eighth.

In 1995, Kwan made a huge leap up the standings and, despite her ninety-pound (40 kg) build, had the power and timing to land seven triple jumps. Many fans thought she should have won a medal. "Maybe my artistic is not enough for them," Kwan said. "Maybe they thought I was too young. I think that has a lot to do with it, but I don't really care. I did my best and I was excited afterward and I didn't care where I finished."

Kwan's coach, Frank Carroll, indicates that as she matures, Kwan's programs will have "a feeling that has more depth to it, more female expression." A strong athleticism will carry her in the meantime. Carroll says one of Kwan's assets is that she's fearless. She's willing to try the triple Axel, which only two other women – Midori Ito and Harding – had landed in competition. It is not yet ready for use in a program, however.

Carroll, who has coached dozens of international stars, is one of Nicole Bobek's seven ex-coaches, most of whom grew frustrated with her cavalier attitude toward training. Kwan's rapid ascension has brought a new excitement to women's skating in the U.S., and she and Bobek should have some interesting confrontations on the road to Nagano. They differ in skating style, age (Bobek is three years older), and approach.

"Nicole is someone who likes to have fun," said training mate Todd Eldredge. The two are coached by Richard Callaghan in Bloomfield Hills, Michigan. It has been too easy for the media to latch onto Bobek as Tonya Harding's successor as skating's bad girl. If she weren't a figure skater, Bobek might be considered a pretty average teenage girl of the mid-1990s, with her flock of pierced earrings, a little brush with the law, a smoking habit, and a propensity for speaking her mind.

"I'm free-spirited. I'm open. I don't hide much," Bobek says. But some within the sport are telling her to do exactly that – hide a bit of herself – advising her that as a champion, she must act like one … or at least somebody's idea of one.

However, during the 1995 season, skaters who had known Bobek earlier in her career found her far more serious about her sport, no longer indifferent to, or abusive of, her immense talent. "When she lands her jumps now, it's like 'Here I am.' It's controlled, not her normal wildness," said a former training partner.

BECAUSE SURYA BONALY'S ATHLETIC BACKGROUND IS VARIED — SHE WAS WORLD JUNIOR TUMBLING CHAMPION AT AGE TWELVE — AND NOT LIMITED TO SKATING, SHE LACKS SOME OF THE BASIC COMPONENTS OF STROKING AND EDGE WORK THAT ARE SECOND NATURE TO MOST OF HER CONTEMPORARIES. SHE IS A STRIKING FIGURE ON THE ICE, WITH POWERFUL JUMPS, BUT SHE DOES LITTLE OF NOTE BETWEEN THOSE JUMPS. ON TOUR, HOWEVER, BONALY IS ONE OF THE MOST POPULAR SKATERS WITH FANS AND IS ALWAYS GRACIOUS AND ACCOMMODATING, DESPITE A REPUTATION FOR POOR SPORTSMANSHIP. THAT REPUTATION DEVELOPED AFTER SHE ANGRILY YANKED OFF HER SILVER MEDAL ON THE PODIUM AT THE 1994 WORLD CHAMPIONSHIPS, FOR WHICH SHE FELT SHE, INSTEAD OF YUKA SATO, SHOULD HAVE WON A GOLD. HERE SHE IS PICTURED DOING ONE OF THE MOST SPECTACULAR SHOW MOVES — THE BACK FLIP. HER VARIATION IS THAT SHE LANDS ON ONE FOOT.

TWO GREAT JUMPERS

If Kwan and Bobek continue in their quest for the podium at the 1998 Olympics, they'll encounter two of the most athletic women who have ever laced up skates: perennial runner-up Surya Bonaly of France and Midori Ito of Japan.

Bonaly is one of the most compelling women in skating history, but she is not really a skater. She is an athlete who could probably be world class in a number of sports, but happened to choose figure skating. She has improved her connecting steps and her speed, but Bonaly is still primarily a jumper, and doesn't have the subtle use of edges and the flow that come with literally growing up in a rink. Her jumps are spectacular, but they are telegraphed – even an outsider can see them coming.

Originally, legend had it that Bonaly was born in the Réunion Islands, a tropical French protectorate. However, it was later revealed that she was born in Nice, France. She was adopted by Suzanne and George Bonaly, who owned a farm near Nice, and Surya – the name means "sun" – grew up surrounded by animals. In fact, she says that after her career is over she'd like to become a veterinarian.

Suzanne Bonaly was a physical education teacher until she interrupted her teaching career to oversee – those close to the sport consider that too mild a verb – her daughter's career. Mother and daughter have developed a private sign language between them that enables them to communicate what they don't want others to hear. Surya was introduced to sports at a very early age when she accompanied her mother's students to gym and swim meets. By the time she was twelve, she had won the World Junior Tumbling Championship, which was open to gymnasts up to the age of eighteen.

Bonaly has never won the World Figure Skating Championship, but she has finished second three successive years. She had intended to turn professional after the 1994 season, but the French association, which wanted to keep its strong team together, threatened not to accept any later application for reinstatement of her amateur status. Her agent, Michael Rosenberg, had already lined up twelve professional appearances for her, and by remaining amateur, Bonaly lost $1 million, by Rosenberg's estimation.

Controversy has often swirled around Bonaly. At the 1994 Worlds, upset that she was beaten by Japan's Yuka Sato on a split decision, Bonaly at first balked at climbing onto the podium beside Sato, then tore off her silver medal only moments after receiving it. "When I stood on that podium, I was just trying to say, 'It's not fair.' I wanted the judges to know I thought the scores weren't right," Bonaly said later.

Two years earlier, during practice sessions for the Albertville Olympics, Bonaly did a back flip close to Midori Ito, unnerving the Japanese champion just as she was about to start the formal run-through of her program. Chief referee Ben Wright told Bonaly that she couldn't do the back flip, a jump that is illegal under amateur rules. That prompted an angry outburst by Bonaly's mother before a gathering of perplexed skating media.

When coaches and judges were insisting that skaters could not function efficiently if they took part in competitions too often and too close together, Bonaly exploded that myth by entering five autumn internationals in the 1992 season and winning four of them. Add to that the Europeans, Worlds, and the French nationals, and it could be argued that Bonaly paved the way for a Grand Prix circuit. She is always a threat to win the World Championship because of her superior jumping ability, and says she still wants to be the first woman to land a quadruple in competition.

Ito already has that pioneer status. She was the first woman to land a triple Axel in competition, when she won the World Championship at Paris in 1989. She seemed poised to join fellow 1989 winner Kurt Browning as a multiple titlist into the nineties, but never won another World Championship.

After taking a silver medal at the 1992 Olympics, Ito joined the professional

(LEFT) JAPAN'S MIDORI ITO WAS THE FIRST WOMAN TO LAND A TRIPLE AXEL, AND ONLY TONYA HARDING HAS SUCCESSFULLY COMPLETED ONE SINCE THEN. ITO TOOK ADVANTAGE OF A LAST-CHANCE WINDOW FOR PROFESSIONALS TO REINSTATE THEIR AMATEUR STATUS AND COULD BE A SERIOUS THREAT IN THE 1998 OLYMPIC CHAMPIONSHIP. IN HER RETURN TO AMATEUR COMPETITION AT THE 1996 WORLDS, SHE SHOWED COMPETITION JITTERS. SHE MISSED HER TRIPLE AXEL AND FINISHED SEVENTH OVERALL. A CHANGE OF HER COMBINATION JUMP IN THE SHORT PROGRAM RUINED HER CHANCES OF 1992 OLYMPIC GOLD. SHE VALIANTLY RALLIED IN THE FREE PROGRAM TO EARN THE SILVER MEDAL.

(RIGHT) 1994 WAS THE YEAR OF TONYA, NANCY, AND OKSANA, BUT THE WORLD CHAMPION WAS YUKA SATO OF JAPAN. SATO'S REIGN WAS SHORT-LIVED AS SHE JOINED THE PROFESSIONAL RANKS FOR THE AUTUMN SEASON.

KRISTINA CZAKO IS STILL DEVELOPING HER STYLE. HERE SHE TRIES A BIT OF COQUETRY ON FOR SIZE.

ranks, but announced in early 1995 that she wants to make a comeback for the 1998 Olympics in her native country. "I have come to realize the charm surrounding amateur figure skating, something I did not notice before," Ito explained in her typically humble manner.

Ito hated the compulsory figures because she was not cut out for the quiet, businesslike precision they required. She was all pent-up energy and bursting fast-twitch muscles. After winning in 1989, she finished second to Jill Trenary in 1990 because she had been tenth in figures. But that was the final year for the dreaded tracings. Some called the death of the figures the Ito Rule, and it was assumed that she would regain dominance. Injuries and timing got in the way.

With all the stress and thumping of her big jumps, Ito had always suffered from pain in her ankles and feet, but in 1991 she also had a medical problem that did not result from skating. She underwent two surgeries for glandular cysts in her jaw and missed valuable winter training time. During the warm up for the original program at Worlds, she collided with another skater and suffered several bruises. Then followed one of the most famous incidents in World Championship history: Ito jumped out of the rink! Always one to skate too close to the boards, Ito came down from a triple Lutz and suddenly disappeared out the gap cut into the barrier to make room for TV cameras. She charged back onto the ice, but finished fourth as the Americans swept the medals.

At the 1992 Olympics, she made a rash, title-costing decision in the original program. At the last minute she changed her mind about her combination and switched from the triple Axel to the triple Lutz. She crashed, and managed only a fourth-place standing. She fought back in the free skate to take a silver medal, with the only triple Axel ever landed by a woman in Olympic history.

Japan hasn't had many professional competitions, so Ito has spent most of her professional career skating exhibitions. She has, like Brian Boitano, maintained a disciplined training regimen, and in 1993 became the first woman to land a triple Axel in a professional event. Sometimes she even does them in her touring shows.

"MORE ATHLETE THAN ARTIST"

Three-time Canadian champion Josée Chouinard also joined Ito in reapplying for amateur status, but in Chouinard's case the choice was easier.

"After a few more years it would have been much harder," said Chouinard, who was always touted as a world medalist but never finished higher than fifth. "Six months out isn't that long."

She was motivated to return to the amateur ranks by several factors. She saw Lu Chen win the world title in 1995 without a triple–triple combination; she had trained and skated well on tour, and won the inaugural Canadian Pro Championship in late 1994, taking home $50,000; the 1996 Worlds are in Canada; and she has not fulfilled the dream of winning a World Championship medal.

All through the nineties, Chouinard had what skating people call "the complete package": she could jump, she had excellent footwork, her programs were superbly crafted by Sandra Bezic, and she had good looks and charisma. But there was no consistency in her performance level. In 1993, she was a disaster at the divisional championships, and confessed through her tears that she was considering quitting then and there. Two weeks later she gave the performance of her life to win her third Canadian title, and a prolonged standing ovation from 17,000 fans. Had she skated exactly that way at Worlds she would have medaled, but instead she tightened up, fell, and finished ninth. Same thing at the 1994 Olympics.

"I know the perception is that in the past she's had some 'choking' moments," her coach, Louis Stong, conceded when Chouinard's decision to return was announced. "But I feel a lot more confident in Josée now. She's had some very good moments in the pro competitions."

One of those moments is a triple Lutz combination, which, if landed, will stand her in good stead at the world level. Because her downfall, so to speak, has usually been a critical tumble that sets off a domino effect of mistakes, Chouinard's inherent athleticism has taken a back seat to her audience appeal.

"I'd say I'm more of an athlete than an artist, and I know that will surprise people," says Chouinard. "I'm good at the artistic side, but I think the technical part came more naturally to me. I developed the artistic side because I loved the crowd, and that's why people think I'm more artist than athlete. I think I have both, and that put me apart from those who were better technically.

"I can remember landing triples easily as a young teenager. But I needed to *work* on the artistic, so I had to think about it. My technical part came to me easier, so if I got nervous like you do in competitions, I didn't know how to do the technical under stress."

Other women who should have added the necessary audience rapport and artistic sense to their native athleticism by the time the 1998 Olympics arrive include Canadian challengers Susan Humphreys, Netty Kim, and Jennifer Robinson. Elena Liashenko of Ukraine, ninth-place finisher at the 1995 Worlds, excels at the triple Lutz combinations. Kristina Czako of Hungary had a terrible 1995 Worlds, finishing twenty-third, a drop of eleven places, but has a barrage of triple jumps and will be only nineteen years old at Nagano.

THE FORERUNNERS

Athleticism has been, in turns, promoted and suppressed in skating history, but the acknowledged groundbreaker was Dick Button. He introduced the world to the triple jump, and to a double Axel, when he began a postwar American grip on the men's championship that lasted a dozen years. Donald Jackson dashed and leaped to the 1962 world title, initiating the tradition of daring Canadian men's skaters, who were forced into being innovative by terrible results in the compulsory figures. He executed the first triple Lutz, a jump so far ahead of its time another wasn't seen at the world level for twelve years. Jackson's torch was picked up by

JOSÉE CHOUINARD COMING OFF THE ICE IN TRIUMPH AFTER THE SKATE OF HER LIFE AT THE 1993 CANADIAN CHAMPIONSHIPS. HAD CHOUINARD BEEN ABLE TO MATCH THAT PERFORMANCE AT ANY OF HER WORLD CHAMPIONSHIPS, SHE WOULD HAVE COME HOME WITH THE MEDAL THAT STILL ELUDES HER.

fellow Canadians Ron Shaver, Vern Taylor (who landed the first triple Axel in 1978), Brian Orser, Kurt Browning, and Elvis Stojko.

Shaver's impact on skating is underrated because he never won a world medal and took just one Canadian Championship. But he was on the ground floor of a revolution that has led to Stojko and the possibility of perhaps even a quintuple jump by the turn of the century. Shaver recalls that at his first World Championship appearance in 1972, when he finished eighth, "I did a triple Salchow, triple toe, and triple loop, a few of each except the loop, and I was the only one at the World Championship with three triples. The world champion [Ondrej Nepela] did a double Axel, and not very well, and Sergei Chetverukhin, the number two guy, did a double Axel. Neither did triples. Skating, technically, was pretty stagnated at that time largely because of the figures."

Bonaly, Midori Ito, and the rest of the current crop of female triple jumpers are the on-ice heirs of Sonja Henie's athleticism. Petra Burka followed the lead of fellow Canadian Donald Jackson and initiated the women's attack on the triple jump. Burka is widely credited with landing the first triple jump at a women's World Championship with her 1965 triple Salchow.

American Linda Fratianne, the 1977 and 1979 world champion, was a graceful, acrobatic performer who forced triple jumps into the repertoire of any women's gold-medal hopeful. Switzerland's Denise Biellmann upped the stakes when she landed the first triple Lutz at the 1978 Europeans. She was succeeded by American Elaine Zayak, whose record six triples landed her the gold medal at the 1982 Worlds. Zayak did only two different triples – the toe loop and Salchow – in winning her title. That championship was the most error-plagued women's competition of the decade, and the ISU instituted a series of new rules, one of which limited to two the number of the same kind of triples that could be used in a free-skate program.

"THE" BATTLE

The coronation of the new era of athleticism was the royal rumble of the 1988 Olympics – the celebrated Battle of the Brians. Brian Orser and Brian Boitano had rounded into crowd-pleasing artists, but it was their athletic superiority that separated them from the rest of the field. The only skater in the early part of the decade to routinely land a triple Axel, Orser had, by the late eighties, pushed the envelope to include two Axels in his long program, and the other contenders had to follow suit. Boitano won the brilliant Olympic skate-off, largely because he did his second triple Axel and Orser did not.

No two looked better in the air than the Brians, but they were different in their style. Orser was exciting and daring, Boitano proud and seamless.

"In practice I stand by and watch Brian Boitano jump," says his choreographer, Sandra Bezic. "And me, who's been around this sport forever, I'm blown away."

Artistry and Figure Skating

The Great Debate does not limit itself to figure skating, but it sure spends a lot of time on it.

"What is Art?"

"That is the million-dollar question," says renowned choreographer Sandra Bezic, who would rather create art than define it. So would most skaters. "And that's the problem with judging … what is the yardstick? It is tough to judge artistry, and everyone in figure skating is extremely opinionated on what art is."

Which do you prefer, Monet or Picasso? Bach or Led Zeppelin? *Swan Lake* or *The Godfather?* They are all, in somebody's view, the pinnacle of art.

When all else fails, when all other assessments are inadequate, when something without precedent forces the issue, figure skating almost always drops into this safety net: "artistic" equals "classical." So Alexei Urmanov, with his traditional, and pleasing, body lines from his Russian ballet heritage, wins the 1994 Olympic men's gold over the modernistic, martial-arts-as-dance performance of Elvis Stojko. Or a respected judge in a professional competition is overheard saying that the hilarious stripper routine of Isabelle Brasseur and Lloyd Eisler has no place in a competition, while 15,000 members of a standing ovation loudly beg to differ.

TOLLER CRANSTON IS REFERRED TO AS THE MODERN PIONEER OF ARTISTIC SKATING.

Competitive figure skating has two objectives: to execute as difficult a routine as possible and to perform that routine so it is most pleasing to the eye. In the rulebook, both technical merit and artistry are given equal weight, except when two athletes are deadlocked; then the more artistic one is supposed to win. In truth, though, artistry cannot truly emerge unless the skater is already technically proficient. It's tough, for instance, to portray a carefree butterfly if you're worried you'll kill yourself on a triple Lutz combination.

Figure-skating artistry cannot be just what appeals to mass audiences, because, like TV sitcoms, the lowest common denominator would eventually prevail. But the entertainment factor cannot, and must not, be ignored, or competitive skating loses its relevance. It may be a sport first, but it's a performance art a close second.

Art is generally defined as the production, through the use of skill, of something beautiful. Then the problem becomes, "What is beauty?" The answer could

ELVIS STOJKO AS BRUCE LEE: THE 1994 MARTIAL-ARTS THEME PROGRAM, "DRAGON", PROPELLED THE NEWLY CROWNED CANADIAN CHAMPION OUT OF ATHLETE-ONLY STATUS AND INTO THE REALM OF ARTISTRY.

well be, "It's in the eye of the beholder." Competitive skating agrees, in principle. The skills are well defined; the eye of the beholder belongs to the nine judges.

Judges and skating officials should not determine what art is, only how well that art is interpreted. If Elvis Stojko is creating an image of Bruce Lee, the martyred martial artist and movie star, how believable is that image? The only way it should be compared with, say, a program that interprets Beethoven's "Moonlight Sonata" is in whether the portrayal is more believable. Which skater made us understand and feel what he was performing? If it is Stojko, then he should get the higher artistic marks, irrespective of whether he has the body shape to perform the "Moonlight Sonata." He doesn't, so he chooses another artistic vehicle.

Figure-skating audiences are like theater audiences. They check their cynicism at the door; they *want* to believe in what the skater is trying to portray. Hardly anyone goes to a rink to see failure: this is not Evel Knievel or the Hell Drivers, where the crash is the big thing. Skating fans yearn to be pulled onto the ice with the skater. So a broad definition of artistry is "the ability to get the audience to willingly suspend their disbelief."

There will always be a place, perhaps the most-honored place, for classical interpretation in figure skating. But in the past quarter of a century – particularly the past five years – the boundaries of skating artistry have expanded more quickly than officials can keep pace. Skaters are simply better performers now, with more to say and more tools to say it with.

Like young actors, young skaters are influenced most by what they see on TV, not at the ballet or at Broadway shows, although both are still popular choices for competitive programs. And another brand of music – rock 'n' roll and its derivatives – is no longer new music. It is older than the parents of many skaters.

Television is a driving force in figure skating – a sometimes Faustian pact that has its assets and liabilities – and it loves the innovative and canonizes the different. More and more television coverage for the sport means a better stage for those who can somehow stand out from the crowd.

THE SINGLE THEME

One of the leading proponents of the new skating creativity is France's Philippe Candeloro, who thrust himself into the public eye during the 1994 Winter Olympics. It was one of those fortuitous forks in the skating road, where people come into the building talking about one thing and leave talking about another. The men's event was supposed to be a pitched battle among three proven veterans: Kurt Browning, the four-time world champion seeking Olympic redemption; and Victor Petrenko and Brian Boitano, the returning pros and previous Olympic champions. But it quickly became a tale of the passing of the torch as Elvis Stojko, Alexei Urmanov, Scott Davis, and Candeloro initiated the new era right in the middle of the short program. The two most intriguing fresh faces were Stojko and Candeloro.

With defiant Gallic flair, Candeloro skated both the short and long program to the same theme music, the first skater ever to do so at a major level. As a tribute

TWO-TIME AMERICAN CHAMPION SCOTT DAVIS IS BETTER KNOWN AS AN ATHLETE THAN AS AN ARTIST. BUT HE IS ALSO THE BEST SPINNER AMONG THE WORLD'S ELITE MALE SKATERS, AND THE SPEED OF HIS ROTATIONS IS VISUALLY EFFECTIVE. HERE, HE IS CAUGHT MID-AIR IN A DEATH DROP.

CARYN KADAVY OF THE UNITED STATES WON THE BRONZE MEDAL AT THE 1987 WORLD CHAMPIONSHIPS IN CINCINNATI, BUT HER CAREER WAS AFFECTED BY A SERIES OF ILLNESSES AND INJURIES. SHE IS ENJOYING SUCCESS IN PRO COMPETITIONS BECAUSE OF HER GRACEFULLY CLASSIC ARTISTIC STYLE.

to his Italian-born father, he selected music from *The Godfather* movies, portraying the young Don Corleone in the short program and the older don in the free skate.

"It is a new style of choreography. I just thought it was the right kind of thing to do for my kind of skating," said Candeloro, who won the Olympic bronze, then took silver at the Worlds a few months later. The Godfather single-theme pro-

grams evolved after he had skated to another movie score, *Conan the Barbarian*, the previous season. It was the "Conan" program that, in retrospect, was the turning point of his career. Previously, Eric Millot and others were always viewed as France's hopes for the future. "Yes, that is true," Candeloro said. "The judges started to see with the ["Conan"] program that I could be much more than just a jumper."

Ironically, like Stojko, Candeloro had been viewed as a one-dimensional skater, who relied strictly on power and speed and paid little or no attention to linking the elements with style and continuity. Guilty as charged, he says. "When I first got my choreographer, I did not do what she said. Until I was at least fifteen, I did not want to do my choreography – I just wanted to skate and jump. I hated it. I was worried that my friends, who are all hockey players, would tease me. But then I started to feel the choreography and understand it."

The change did not come overnight, but by his twenty-second birthday, the day of the short program at the Lillehammer Olympics, Candeloro had the feel just right, and mesmerized the audience. Two nights later, France was celebrating its first men's Olympic skating medal in twenty-two years.

Candeloro is one of those rare skaters who was not inspired by a skating role model of an earlier generation. There are no Toller Cranstons or Robin Cousinses in his memory bank. He had never heard of Brian Boitano or Brian Orser until, as the host country for the next Olympics, France invited him to skate in the closing ceremonies of the 1988 Calgary Olympics. "I didn't even watch skating on TV – I sometimes found it too boring," said Candeloro, who could never be accused of that. "I wanted to do my own skating, be my own person, so I didn't have any skating heroes."

In fact, when he first took to the ice at the arena in the Paris suburb of Colombes, as part of a school skating program when he was seven and a half, he was upset because only figure skates were available and he wanted hockey skates. After two weeks, André Brunet, who became his coach, suggested to his parents that his obvious talent would be better served by private lessons. He passed all the available tests within six months, then began combining skating lessons with academic lessons at the arena, which has now become part of France's national training center.

Like his rival Stojko, Candeloro had his triple Lutz under control by the age of thirteen, and the triple Axel in his arsenal two years later. And, like Stojko, he developed a passion for motorcycles. It was a motorcycle accident that caused him to miss the 1992 Olympics. A broken foot cost him a month of valuable training time, and although he was able to skate in the French Championships – and, he says, skate well – he was left off the French team for Albertville. "That really hurt. I felt I should have made the team," he said. "But maybe that made me skate harder, because I was angry and sad." And maybe that same anger and sadness found itself into the Godfather routines.

As with all signature programs, it may be difficult for Candeloro to expand his style and subject matter beyond the Godfather. It is so tempting to stay with the first heady successes. In a few cases, such as Victor Petrenko's tired, third-time-around 1992 Olympic free skate, repeat programs do come out on top, but only if the rest of the field is not up to par. For the most part, judges and audiences want a skater to give them a new look every year in at least one of the short or long programs. Candeloro himself said he skated "with no emotion" at the 1995 European Championships, when he continued the Godfather saga in his programs, and did not win a medal. He did rebound a month later to win a bronze medal at the World Championships.

The concept of a single-theme program is not new. Thematic classical music – *Swan Lake, Romeo and Juliet,* even "Flight of the Bumblebee," for example – has always been a staple of world-class skating. Except for a few great artists such as Cranston and John Curry, however, in competitive programs skaters usually gave the music a limited, superficial interpretation.

The real breakthrough came at the St. Ivel competition in Richmond, England, in the fall of 1982, when Jayne Torvill and Christopher Dean unveiled their new free dance, taken from the West End musical *Mack and Mabel*. It told the animated story of silent film star Mack Sennett's pursuit of Mabel Norman. The program received three 6.0s – perfect scores – for the reigning world ice-champions, elevating them to a new artistic plane.

The concept didn't gain immediate acceptance by other competitors, however. For one thing, Torvill and Dean already had the credibility of being world champions, which gave them a certain leeway to experiment. For another, they were self-demanding masters of the technical aspects of their discipline. Their new creativity expanded on their technical skills, rather than substituted for them. To skate in character requires an unshakable belief that your technical elements will not fail you. Few dance teams, and no pairs or singles skaters other than Scott Hamilton, could offer that entire package in the early 1980s.

The judges were not unanimous in their approval of unified themes. Some of them felt that acting was the province of professional skating. Americans Judy Blumberg and Michael Seibert, for instance, missed a bronze medal because one judge said that their *Scheherazade* music, by Rimsky-Korsakov, wasn't suitable for competition, that it was too showlike.

But by the time of the 1988 Calgary Olympics, competitive skating's true watershed event, both marquee contests pitted single-theme programs against each other. Brian Boitano and Brian Orser were technically sound and artistically secure enough to present theme programs. Both, coincidentally, skated to military music. And Katarina Witt and Debi Thomas each chose to portray *Carmen* in their battle for the women's gold.

PAINT A PICTURE

Today, in the second half of the 1990s, it has become almost de rigueur for the top skaters to paint a recognizable picture during their programs.

Even skaters regarded more as athletes than entertainers are better choreographically. Todd Eldredge had enormous success with his "Charlie Chaplin"

(*BELOW*) DENISE BIELLMANN BECAME SWITZERLAND'S FIRST WORLD CHAMPION IN 1981 AND IS BEST-KNOWN FOR THE STUNNING BIELLMANN SPIN, AND AS THE FIRST WOMAN TO LAND A TRIPLE LUTZ. BUT IN RECENT YEARS, SHE HAS PAID MORE ATTENTION TO CHOREOGRAPHY AND HAS COME UP WITH AVANT-GARDE ARTISTIC MOVES, RESULTING IN SEVERAL VICTORIES IN PROFESSIONAL COMPETITIONS OVER LARGER MARQUEE ATTRACTIONS.

(*ABOVE*) NATHALIE KRIEG SHARES NOT ONLY NATIONALITY WITH DENISE BIELLMANN, BUT ALSO THE SWISS HERITAGE OF GREAT SPIN TECHNIQUE.

program because it enabled him to hide his normal shyness behind the persona of the great comedian.

Elvis Stojko, the two-time world champion, has worked incessantly with Uschi Keszler to unearth a style that fits his shorter, more muscular lines. His 1994 martial-arts program was his artistic breakthrough and he successfully followed that up with Christopher Columbus. Stojko's choreographer, the former German champion who turned Brian Orser from a jumper into a consummate showman, speaks a skating language all her own, based on vectors and energy flow. Stojko grasps the concept completely. "My style is definitely not classical," he says. "It's not quite this and it's not quite that. It revolves around motion, not movement. They are two different things. Motion is never ending. Movement is from one place to another."

Ukraine's Viacheslav Zagorodniuk, whose jumping ability pushed him onto the world stage, used his 1995 free skate to play the apprentice in an animated version of Paul Dukas's *The Sorcerer's Apprentice*. And 1994 Olympic champion Alexei Urmanov, who is capable of big jumps and has landed a quadruple in competition, leans heavily on his long, elegant lines, portraying classical themes. Even with all the new artistry, classical lines still go the farthest in covering up any technical problems.

Rules on theatrical costuming and illegal moves have been more strictly enforced to make sure that the skater, not the props, interprets the music. Candeloro's visually effective trademark spin, in which he ends up spinning on his knees without his skates on the ice, has sometimes caused marks to be deducted. Candeloro, who was also penalized for too much theatricality in his Conan costume, continues to accent the sit spin, which was developed by accident when he made a mistake on a normal spin.

WHERE HAVE ALL THE SPINNERS GONE?

Although Candeloro has woven the knee spin into his on-ice persona, the current group of top amateur skaters are not as a whole memorable spinners. The best all do passable spins, of course, but no Ronnie Robertsons loom on the horizon — something that troubles longtime skating observers. Robertson, American

Olympic silver medalist in the mid-1950s, is acknowledged as easily the fastest and best spinner of all time.

Spins are an effective visual tool, athletically demanding but artistically important, particularly as a dramatic ending or as a spectacular segue from one set of moves into another. At one time spins were far more crucial to a successful free skate, but the explosion in jumping prowess seems to have relegated them to a back seat.

Scott Davis, two-time U.S. champion and seventh in the world in 1995, is considered the best male spinner in amateur competition. Growing up in Great Falls, Montana – where, he says, the winters are so long you have to skate – Davis

ALEXEI URMANOV OF RUSSIA, WITH HIS FLOWING COSTUMING AND BALLETIC LINES, EXEMPLIFIES THE CLASSICAL STYLE THAT IS STILL CONSIDERED THE HEART OF ARTISTIC SKATING BY MOST JUDGES.

DAVID LIU RISES OUT OF THE MIST
DURING SKATE CANADA 1991 AT
LONDON, ONTARIO. LIU, WHO
HAS REPRESENTED BOTH THE
UNITED STATES AND TAIWAN
INTERNATIONALLY, IS AN
EMOTIONAL ARTISTIC PERFORMER
AND WAS THE LAST MAN TO SKATE
A COMPULSORY FIGURE AT A
WORLD CHAMPIONSHIP, IN 1990.

wore thick glasses. But he would achieve such speed on his spins that the glasses would fly off (he eventually switched to contact lenses).

There is absolutely no doubt about the best female spinner in the world. Nathalie Krieg extends the line of Swiss skaters who have forged their reputations from a spin in which the hands hold the free-leg skate over the head. It is called the Biellmann Spin, after 1981 world champion Denise Biellmann. Outside the Centre Sport des Vernets in Geneva, where the 1986 World Championships were held, stands a statue of Beillmann doing the spin.

Ever since Krieg was a junior, she has attracted larger audiences than her world standing would dictate, simply because people want to see her spin. A Biellmann Spin builds in increments, until the skater ends up with one leg extended well over her head, both hands reaching back to grab the back post of the skate. Because of the extreme back arch required to do the spin well, few skaters can execute the full Biellmann Spin, although some use less-difficult variations of it. Both Krieg and Biellmann seem almost double-jointed in the mid-back when they perform the spin. The effect is mesmerizing. At top speed the skater looks like a tulip, or a vibrating tuning fork, and audiences never fail to respond.

Biellmann has caught a second wind as a competitive skater. On the expanded pro circuit in 1994 and 1995, she piled up several wins and second-place finishes with quick footwork, her always-strong technical skills, and a new approach to artistry honed by more than a decade of professional touring. "I never paid much attention to choreography," she said during intense practices for the Canadian Professional Championships in Hamilton. "But I came to see the value in it. I keep in shape, and I work very hard at keeping my skills up." And, of course, there is always call for the Biellmann Spin, which was developed from a spin invented by yet another Swiss skater, Karin Iten, ten years before Biellmann's world title.

Like Biellmann, Krieg is able to keep centered in her spins – the pivot foot rarely moves from its anchor spot – while other skaters, even medalists, sometimes drift three or four feet. This helps the speed and duration of her rotation. She reportedly had one spin timed at three minutes and twenty seconds while she changed positions within the spin. Unfortunately, Krieg has been unable to translate her prowess at spinning into a mastery of triple jumps.

Lagging behind in triple jumps has also proven costly to Canadian artist Sebastien Britten. When Britten is able to land his jumps, his flair and on-ice *joie de vivre* take over and he can hold an audience in the palm of his hand. His spins are elegant, his body line classical, and he has an excellent sense of dramatic presentation, which enabled him to finish eighth in the 1994 World Championships. But a disastrous short program the following year cost the native of Brossard, Quebec, dearly and he finished only seventeenth overall at the 1995 World Championships.

David Liu, who moved to the U.S. when he was six but represented Chinese Taipei, gave up skating when he was thirteen to study on scholarship at the School of American Ballet Theater in New York and didn't resume the sport until he was sixteen. That hiatus proved to be both a strength and a drawback. Losing perhaps the most important years for a skater to develop technically, he had trouble landing the triple jumps in competition that would have put him into the upper bracket. Conversely, he has a sense of performance that any of the top skaters in the world would love to borrow.

ARTISTRY GROWS FROM WITHIN

There are as many ingredients to successful artistry as there are successful artists. Among the most crucial to skaters are flexibility; a strong desire to be watched; the ability to play to and off a crowd; a well-developed musicality and sense of rhythm; confidence in your coach, your choreographer, and your technical skills; and no fear of looking foolish. Good artists take chances.

OKSANA BAIUL POSSESSES AN IMPRESSIVE ARRAY OF ARTISTIC STRENGTHS, NOT THE LEAST OF WHICH IS HER FLEXIBILITY, ILLUSTRATED BY THIS VARIATION ON A LAYBACK SPIN.

TANJA SZEWCZENKO. THE YOUNG
GERMAN HAS A STRONG ON-ICE
PERSONALITY AND EXEMPLIFIES THE
NEW WAVE OF SKATERS WHO,
BECAUSE THEY'RE EXPOSED TO
BIGGER CROWDS MORE OFTEN,
DEVELOP ARTISTRY MUCH MORE
QUICKLY THAN DID PREVIOUS
GENERATIONS.

Younger skating fans will not remember that Brian Orser, who became the most expressive skater of his graduating class in 1988, was once regarded as purely a leaper because of his pioneering work with the triple Axel. Inside was an artist trying to get out, but he was sometimes embarrassed about it. However, an exhibition program skated to the "Theme from *The Pink Panther*," in which he prowled around the ice like a cat, removed his inhibitions, and he worked many of the artistic phrases into his 1984 Olympic programs. He won the first of two Olympic silvers, and eventually became known as much for his artistic interpretation as for his technical skill.

Most elite skaters have spent so much time stroking around the ice to music that their sense of rhythm is acutely developed. But some rise above even that crowd, usually because they are technically proficient.

The best choreographers recognize this automatically. Among her scores of choreographic credits, Sandra Bezic has created programs for Kurt Browning, Brian Boitano, Katarina Witt, dozens of other professionals and the entire Stars on Ice tour. She says that only a few skaters can handle the precise timing of a big trick as an artistic element. "Generally speaking, I won't put a jump that's difficult for a skater in a crescendo of music, because at a stress level, it's hard to hit an exact note. But Brian Boitano will hit any note you want."

Boitano is a prime example of a skater who is not a born entertainer, yet has carved out – with the help of Bezic and his coach, Linda Leaver – his artistic niche. He usually skates with a self-confident detachment that borders on nobility.

Sarah Kawahara of Los Angeles is one of the most sought-after choreographers in North America, along with Bezic and Uschi Keszler. She says that the key to successful choreography is extracting a skater's talents, some of them hidden talents, and amplifying them. Kawahara is a contemporary of former Canadian champion Ron Shaver. Both grew up near Hamilton, Ontario, and both skated professionally for Ice Capades. She has designed programs for Surya Bonaly, Dorothy Hamill, Robin Cousins, Charlie Tickner, John Curry, and Scott Hamilton, among others.

"The absolute essence of artistry is to translate your personality and your inner being," says Hamilton, who has no trouble doing exactly that. "When you look at the skaters who have done well and created an interest – from Dick Button to Oksana Baiul – all of them have not strayed very far from who they are. Dick Button was power, John Curry was ballet, Toller Cranston is abstract, Robin Cousins is a stage actor.

"Me? I like being the center of attention. The aim is to find something within yourself that you can translate through music and movement. That is our art."

No skater in the 1990s has understood this so thoroughly as Oksana Baiul.

THE ARTIST FROM THE UKRAINE

Usually, heartfelt artistry is not the province of young skaters. They have not experienced enough of life to deeply feel and convincingly project emotions the way a more mature skater can. Michelle Kwan, fourth at the 1995 World Championships, will likely become a superior artist, and is already moving in that direction, but she is still barely into her teens.

The one exception is Baiul.

Not since Sonja Henie has skating experienced a Sudden Impact like that made by the waifish Ukrainian. When, at fifteen, she became the second-youngest world champion (after Henie), winning at Prague in 1993, it was only her fourth major skating competition.

Just in case anyone thought she was a mere flash in the pan, she overcame Nancy Kerrigan's steamrolling momentum and her own injuries to win the Olympic gold the next spring, cementing her standing as the best female skater of her time and one of the best in history. She won the title on a 4–4 split in first-place votes, with the ninth judge, from Germany, tying the two. But a 5.9 artistic impression to Kerrigan's 5.8 broke that tie and gave the decision to Baiul.

Baiul's appearance in the final was in doubt until the day of the free skate because of a freak collision in practice the previous day with Germany's Tanja Szewczenko that sidelined the German hopeful and left Baiul with stitches in her leg and strained ligaments and muscles in her lower back. Although the confrontation was accidental, Baiul's injuries were nearly as serious as Kerrigan's had been. In fact, the lingering back problems kept her out of the World Championships a month later.

Her presence of mind in inserting a triple that she had missed earlier at the very end of her Olympic free skate won Baiul the gold and was a reflex decision beyond her years. But most things about Baiul are beyond her years. She is possessed of an artistry uncommon among teenagers. Her ballet training is evident in the way her hands and lower free leg sway like foliage. Her spectacularly large eyes enable her to project emotion to the far corners of an arena.

She has been described as a fawn, a swan, and a madonna for her supple, fluttering interpretations of classical music, but Baiul can just as readily give you gyrating youth-culture pop.

Baiul emerged into the spotlight from a cold and lonely youth. When she was just three, her father deserted the family in the northern Ukrainian city of Dnepropetrovsk. She loved the ballet, but her mother, a French teacher, enrolled Oksana in skating because she was considered overweight for ballet – a laughable thought today. Eventually she got her dance lessons, but by then she had shown an aptitude for skating.

Her grandmother, with whom she and her mother lived, died in the early 1980s, and in 1990, when Baiul was just twelve, her mother died of ovarian cancer. Alone in the world, she moved into a tiny room at the local skating club, but two years later her longtime coach, Stanislav Karatek, moved to Canada to teach, leaving Baiul on her own again. Karatek's father, a Ukrainian skating official, set her up with Galina Zmievskaya, who coached Victor Petrenko, Viacheslav Zagorodniuk, and Petrenko's brother Vladimir. So Baiul moved 300 miles (480 km) south to Odessa to stay with Zmievskaya and her family. She and Victor Petrenko

(*ABOVE*) 1992 OLYMPIC
CHAMPION KRISTI YAMAGUCHI
HAS THE MIX OF ATHLETIC
ACCOMPLISHMENT AND DELICATE
ARTISTRY THAT THE INTERNATIONAL
SKATING UNION WANTS TO SEE IN
ITS LEADING SKATERS. YAMAGUCHI'S
FEATHERY TOUCH ON THE ICE
CONTRIBUTES TO HER ELEGANT
STYLE.

– who married Zmievskaya's daughter Nina – developed a brother–sister relationship, and Petrenko used income from his tours in America to pay for Baiul's training expenses. "She had no blades, no boots, no fabric for costumes," Petrenko
recalled. "But she had talent. What she has done is unbelievable. I saw her for the
first time in the summer of 1992. She was really a nobody then in skating, and as
soon as I saw her first step, I could tell right away that she would be good. As a
skater, you can tell."

It was only a few months before her first major competitions that she mastered the triple Lutz and flip, establishing the technical base that would free her to exploit her natural artistry.

GRACE AND POLISH UNDER FIRE

Sometimes artistry is best portrayed by pure skating. Pairs legends Ekaterina Gordeeva and Sergei Grinkov achieved the elegance of simplicity. As an amateur, Nancy Kerrigan trained diligently to become a strong technical skater, but the lasting image fans have of her programs is her tour across the ice in a powerfully disciplined arabesque. It is basic beauty. The same applies to Boitano and his proud spread eagle.

Janet Lynn of the U.S. embodied beauty and emotion on the ice, and during world tours in the early 1970s, she was always paid the ultimate compliment: she was so entrancing to watch that most of the other skaters on tour would gather in the runways every night to see her performances. She never won a World Championship, but partly because she didn't, the rules were changed to diminish the importance of compulsory figures and increase that of free skating.

There are other skaters, such as 1995 world champion Lu Chen and Olympic and two-time world champion Kristi Yamaguchi, whose delicacy in performing difficult tricks ultimately became their trademarks. Their programs are created around this gracefulness, because a softness of touch never goes out of style. Hamilton, for instance, has always had gentle landings and he's benefited in several ways: he hasn't suffered the career-threatening knee injuries that bigger, heavier-landing skaters have incurred; and the lightness is readily translated into surface speed, one of his strongest artistic assets as he skips across the ice, his skates apparently never touching it.

Lu Chen's gracefulness in her skating was obvious even when, at fourteen, she appeared for the first time at the World Junior Championships and finished third. Chen gave China both its first Olympic figure skating medal (bronze, 1994) and World Championship. Her ascent to the world title was incredible, considering that when she was growing up, not a single indoor rink existed in China. Sports are in her genes. Her father was an ice hockey player for the Chinese national team, and later managed the ice rink where Chen learned to skate; her mother excelled at table tennis, one of China's favorite sports. To this rock-solid athletic heritage she added a finesse through years of ballet training.

Finish and polish eventually come to all world champions, at least in the current era; otherwise they never ascend to the top of the podium. Kurt Browning forced his way onto the world scene as a raw bundle of energetic jumps out of Caroline, Alberta. He was an engaging personality, who sharpened his wit and his skill in the shadow cast by Brian Orser. He landed the world's first quadruple jump during Orser's last amateur competition in 1988 and became world champion a year later, before Canadian officials had even stopped worrying about how they would replace Orser.

At that time Browning was just a diamond in the rough. Now he's the

IN 1995 LU CHEN BECAME CHINA'S FIRST WORLD CHAMPION. SHE FINISHED SECOND IN 1996 TO MICHELLE KWAN, BUT MANY FELT HER ELEGANT FREE SKATE WAS SPECTACULAR ENOUGH FOR A SECOND TITLE. SHE HAS BEEN CHOREOGRAPHED BY TOLLER CRANSTON (1995) AND BY SANDRA BEZIC (1996).

diamond itself. No skater has made the transition from athlete to artist as definitely as he has. His speed, power, and jumping potential are still there, but Browning is an entertainer. He has an innate understanding of music and characterization that has emerged over the past few years. Louis Stong, his Toronto-based coach, marvels at the variety of interpretations Browning is comfortable with, and has yet to discover a role or a rhythm Browning cannot master. If he were a singer, Browning's range would stretch from the aria to the yodel.

In 1993, he unveiled the most memorable free-skate program of his era. Casablanca, in which he played a cool Humphrey Bogart, was a program he could not have skated a few years earlier. Casablanca was a triumph of theme, mood, character, countermovements, and dramatic pauses.

When Marijane Stong suggested the song "As Time Goes By" from the movie *Casablanca*, Bezic thought it was perfect, because by then Browning had become an actor on ice. "I wanted to find that special mood, a moment to build the program around, that would sum up the program in one second," said Bezic. "And that moment comes when he flicks the cigarette away."

American Christopher Bowman, nicknamed "Bowman the Showman," was every bit the actor Browning was when their amateur careers intersected. In fact, in another sport each of them might have been labeled "hotdogs." But Bowman didn't have Browning's technical grounding, and lacked the drive and direction Browning brought with him out of the foothills of Alberta.

Germany's Norbert Schramm, who adopted techno-rock as a skating persona and won the silver medal at two World Championships in the early 1980s, was unable to expand that artistic style, and had already begun a slide in the standings when he suddenly retired during the compulsory figures at the 1984 Worlds. Elvis Stojko, on the other hand, broadened a choreographic style similar to Schramm's and has won two successive world titles.

Katarina Witt could be classified as an athlete because of her superior competitive drive, or as an artist because she can sell a program. Her Carmen in the 1988 season, and later in a feature-length movie, was a brilliant interpretation of an old standard. And in the 1994 Olympics, long after dozens of younger competitors had surpassed her technically, Witt entranced the live audience with her haunting interpretation of "Where Have All the Flowers Gone?" It was her tribute to the tragedy-stricken people of Sarajevo, where she had won the first of her two Olympic golds.

Czech Petr Barna, who has always been in the upper echelons of skating but has never made a big splash, had the technical prowess to become the second skater after Browning to land a quad, yet it is his musical sense that separates him from others. His Amadeus drew a perfect score for artistry at the 1991 World Championships. That was the first 6.0 ever given to a man in the short program, which is such a nerve-racking two and a half minutes that skaters usually pull inward instead of pushing themselves outward toward the audience.

The following year Barna won a bronze medal at the Olympics and revealed

AMERICAN CHRISTOPHER BOWMAN NEVER DID THINGS ROUTINELY. NICKNAMED "BOWMAN THE SHOWMAN" FOR OBVIOUS REASONS, HE LOVED THE SPOTLIGHT AND WAS A CHILD ACTOR IN SEVERAL TELEVISION SERIES. DESPITE STRONG ATHLETICISM AND, AT THE TIME, UNPARALLELED PRESENCE ON THE ICE, HIS IRREGULAR TRAINING HABITS WERE A PROBLEM. HE NEVER AGAIN ROSE TO THE LEVEL OF HIS SILVER MEDAL AT THE 1989 WORLD CHAMPIONSHIPS. IN A BIT OF TRUE BOWMANESQUE DRAMA, HE ENDED HIS AMATEUR CAREER BY LIMPING OFF THE ICE AFTER HE CRASHED INTO THE BOARDS DURING THE 1992 WORLDS, JUST MOMENTS AFTER THIS PICTURE WAS TAKEN.

something of what he had been going through in the former country of Czecho-slovakia before the Iron Curtain fell. Money given to skating officials in his country was never used as intended: for better costuming, more lessons and choreographic help, travel perks – all the extras that elevate good skaters into great ones.

The elegant Czech is now carving a good professional career for himself.

Britain's Steven Cousins has a beaming smile and an arresting on-ice presence that demands that those in the seats pay attention to him. He has moved into the world's top ten (he was eighth in 1995), but will almost certainly enjoy more success as a pro than as an amateur because of his showmanship.

Paul Wylie excels as a professional skater, with his ability to combine artistry and technical skills. Never a U.S. champion, and somewhat of an afterthought on the 1994 U.S. team, he came into his own in his final two days as an amateur, appearing out of virtually nowhere to win the silver medal at the Albertville Olympics. And many felt he should have received the gold.

SHOWSTOPPER: BRITISH CHAMPION STEVEN COUSINS IN THE MIDDLE OF THE SPLITS DURING THE ELVIS STOJKO TOUR. COUSINS CAN CONTROL A CROWD WITH A SHIMMY AND A SMILE, AND, NOW THAT HE ALSO HAS CONTROL OF HIS TECHNICAL ELEMENTS, HE HAS JOINED THE WORLD'S ELITE.

FORMER CANADIAN CHAMPION
AND CURRENT TOURING-SHOW
PROFESSIONAL KAREN PRESTON
POSSESSES A REGAL, CLASSIC
ELEGANCE THAT EVOKES IMAGES OF
LEGENDARY ACTRESS GRACE KELLY.
BUT PRESTON, A SUPERB SKATER
WHEN SHE WAS ON, ALWAYS HAD
TROUBLE INVITING THE AUDIENCE
"IN" DURING HER AMATEUR CAREER.

CRANSTON AND CURRY

One of the great oversights in figure skating history is that the sport never found a way to make Toller Cranston world champion. Competitive figure skating should boast, "He was ours." Instead, Cranston's only major competitive trinkets are bronze medals from the 1974 World Championships and the 1976 Olympics. Yet, since Jackson Haines, no other skater has influenced on-ice artistry more, and for a longer period of time, than the dramatic Canadian.

Cranston is often referred to as the modern pioneer of artistic skating, so it seems strange that a man who, in 1994, could be named Skater of the Century by so influential a body as the German Skating Federation would not have taken at least one world title. But, like so many Canadian men before and after him, Cranston disliked, and did poorly at, compulsory figures. The skater who would have won had figures not been included was known as the free-skating champion. Cranston took that honor in both 1974 and 1975 with his dramatic abstracts on ice.

Opinionated and fearless, Cranston is a Renaissance man in skating and in life. A renowned artist whose paintings fetch high prices, he also writes, choreographs, and still skates professionally, nearly twenty years after retiring from the amateur ranks. His often critical observations as a skating commentator led to his removal from CBC skating broadcasts, a dismissal the courts later found to be unlawful. Yet it was Cranston who set the standard for TV skating specials. His "Strawberry on Ice" drew 2.3 million viewers in 1982, long before skating Hardinged its way into prime time. The one-hour special has since been sold to almost fifty countries, a record for a CBC variety program, and it won the San Francisco Film Festival's Best TV Program award in 1983.

Those who break with tradition, as Cranston most surely did, often find huge hurdles in their path in the form of judges who have trouble accepting new ideas. If these pathfinders persist, if they can take the rejection, if they can afford the time that the public and judges require to adjust, eventually they will prevail. Cranston reaps the rewards of his amateur career from a distance. When the current generation of skaters is asked which skater has most influenced them, he is cited far more often than anyone else.

The 1976 Olympics were a milestone for the Cranston school. In addition to Cranston taking the bronze medal, the late John Curry gave Great Britain its first Winter Olympic gold since a two-man bobsled team came in first in 1964, and only its third Olympic skating gold ever (Madge Syers won the women's event in 1908, Jeannette Altwegg in 1952).

Curry saw his first ice show at the age of six, then gravitated toward the ballet. His father preferred something a little more "masculine" for his son and suggested ice skating, instead. Like Torvill and Dean, he bobbed and weaved through public skating sessions at the local arena. Eventually Curry moved from Birmingham (site of the 1995 Worlds, which honored his memory after he died of AIDS the previous year) to London to work as an underpaid bank clerk and study under famous Swiss coach Arnold Gerschwiler. He also worked with "finishing" coaches Gustave Lussi and Carlo Fassi in the United States. His training expenses were financed by a then-secret benefactor, U.S. industrialist Ed Moser, who also provided financial help for the other 1976 singles gold medalist, Dorothy Hamill.

Like his contemporary Cranston, Curry met with resistance to the artistic temperament. Many observers said that he would never win a title because his graceful arm and hand movements would antagonize the judges. The Eastern Europeans in particular, it was predicted, would not find his skating masculine enough.

After finishing second in the European Championships at Copenhagen, Curry finally said out loud what others had been only whispering. He accused the Eastern Europeans of ganging up on him and focusing on Soviet Vladimir Kovalev. According to James Cootes's *Olympic Report '76*, Curry began to read and hear that certain judges felt his balletic style was "not right for the ice," and that other judges, after he had spoken up, encouraged skaters from their country to make rude remarks about the gentle nature of Curry's program.

Curry did make some concessions by rearranging his choreography so that the jumps became featured elements. His previous best was one World Championship bronze medal, but at Innsbruck in 1976, he struck Olympic gold with what Cootes called "a performance of such dexterity and sheer perfection never before seen in an Olympics."

Four years later, another artistic Briton, Robin Cousins, repeated Curry's achievement and took the Olympic gold at Lake Placid without having first won a World Championship.

THAT'S ENTERTAINMENT

"Talent, artistry, athleticism, and work ethic," says Sandra Bezic. "Those are the four components of great skating … and luck is the fifth. I think the combination of it all is very rare, and always has been.

"In any great champion, there is a personality that is developed. The presentation of personality is what makes it artistry. I think Scott Hamilton is someone you always want to watch. His performance is something. You can't call Scott a great 'artiste,' compared to John Curry. Scott is an entertainer. But both are equally exciting to watch."

Hamilton says that artistry, while only one-half of the formal equation, is what gives skating its enormous popularity, "because you can go to a competition and like the seventh-place skater the best, because that's the one whose style touched you the most."

While Hamilton is capable of many different styles, his routines almost always have a current of humor. He calls his back-to-back wins at Hamilton and Edmon-

THE LATE JOHN CURRY, WHO DELIVERED THE PERFORMANCE OF HIS LIFE TO WIN THE 1976 OLYMPIC GOLD, WAS A CONTEMPORARY OF TOLLER CRANSTON. THE BRITON AND THE CANADIAN COUNTERED THE ATHLETIC TIDE OF THE 1970S WITH ARTISTIC, BALLETIC INTERPRETATIONS THAT WERE UNMATCHED BY THEIR COMPETITION.

ton in the pro circuit's first big season a "victory for short, bald guys everywhere."

"Kurt Browning says that there is a line that a sense of humor reaches, and beyond it is going too far and, well, sometimes I cross it," Hamilton says with a laugh. "What makes skaters special is that what they do comes from within them.

"I try to show audiences and fans who I am. If you ever see me skate to *The Afternoon of a Faun* and it's not meant to be funny, take me out and shoot me."

SIX

Skating as One: Pairs and Ice Dancing

One of skating's unique strengths is that it teams men and women in the same high-profile events.

Golf, cycling, skiing, and track and field have high-level competition for both genders, but usually in separate events. Only tennis, with mixed doubles, has men and women on the same team competing against other mixed-gender duos. Yet mixed doubles are usually an afterthought, a wouldn't-it-be-neat-if-we-teamed-up sideshow to the main event.

No other sport offers big-time, prime-time competition the way figure skating does with pairs and ice dancing.

Pairs skating in the nineteenth century had been little more than singles skating with the couple holding hands, still a component of the discipline today. It wasn't until late in the century that men and women were the partners. Men often skated with men and women with women — what today is known as "similar pairs" in low-level competitions or shows when there are not enough boys or girls to go around.

At the beginning of the twentieth century there was little difference between the two disciplines. In the early years of international competition, pairs was often called hand-to-hand skating and was really dancing on ice. But at the 1924 Winter Olympics, British pair Mildred and T. D. Richardson introduced "shadow skating," which is the art of performing identical movements or elements a few feet apart. Then Andrée Joly and Pierre Brunet of France, world and Olympic pairs champions, put in large lifts, as opposed to the tiny ones — much like the small ones permitted under current dance rules — pairs had used before World War I.

MARINA KLIMOVA AND SERGEI PONOMARENKO. THE EXPRESSIVE, ROMANTIC, AND DRAMATIC ICE DANCERS OVERCAME INTERNAL RUSSIAN POLITICS AND THE MOMENTUM OF FRANCE'S POPULAR CHAMPIONS ISABELLE AND PAUL DUCHESNAY TO WIN THE 1992 OLYMPIC TITLE. THE MARRIED COUPLE NOW LIVE IN CALIFORNIA, AND HAVE ADDED COACHING AND CHOREOGRAPHY TO THEIR RÉSUMÉ, WHICH ALSO INCLUDES PROFESSIONAL TOURING.

In Europe in the first half of this century, roller dancing was more popular than ice dancing. When the sport made the successful transition to the ice with its inclusion in the 1952 World Championships, the long tradition of ballroom, ballet, and roller dancing gave the Europeans a head start they have never relinquished.

Traditionally, pairs and dance both present the female partner to the audience. Both are about intimacy (dance more so), and unity and common purpose. But ice dance hinges on rhythm and subtlety, pairs on power and speed. Dancers never lose contact with each other, even in the brief moments when they're not touching; a pairs program is all about powerful separations and evocative reunions.

A MAN AND A WOMAN

Pairs and ice dancing celebrate emotional and physical interaction between men and women. Like actors, the couple must project convincingly to the audience and judges whatever relationship the program has cast for them – more often than not one of love's many incarnations. So for an entire season of practice, exhibitions, and competitions, a couple may find themselves acting out a love relationship, five or six hours a day, five days a week. That's a lot of emotional contact, and for ice dancers the contact is even more intense than for pairs, because they spend so much time cheek to cheek.

Many times, the constant togetherness spills over into an off-ice relationship. The results can be uplifting, or disastrous, or somewhere in between.

Scores of world-class pairs and dance teams have married. In fact, many of the earliest pairs teams were singles skaters who were married to each other. Marriages were common among dance and pairs teams from the former Soviet Union.

Just before the 1992 Olympics, Isabelle Brasseur and Lloyd Eisler, Canada's gold medal pairs hope, revealed that they had been partners not only on the ice, but off it, as well. For a year and a half they had been boyfriend and girlfriend, but two years before the Olympics had decided to call it quits, not because they had lost romantic interest in each other but because they felt their professional relationship was more important.

"It just came down to the fact that we were just spending so much time together," Eisler said then. "Maybe it was starting to affect our skating – maybe it wasn't. We didn't know for sure, but it was sort of understood between the two of us that this would make our skating better."

Cooling off a romantic relationship is difficult enough without having to go to work every day and hold hands with that person for several hours. It helped that Brasseur and Eisler were close friends.

"At first it was very difficult for me," said Brasseur, who was only nineteen at the time. "We made the decision for professional reasons. But you don't stop the feeling. We're probably best friends now. We're always going to be there for each other."

Brasseur and Eisler did not skate well at those Olympics but did come away with a bronze medal, Canada's first Olympic pairs medal since 1964. They won the World Championship the following year and skated brilliantly to take a second Olympic bronze in 1994, behind reinstated professionals Ekaterina Gordeeva and Sergei Grinkov and Natalia Mishkutienok and Artur Dmitriev. Brian Orser and Brasseur and Eisler are the only Canadians with two Olympic figure-skating medals.

American pairs champions Jenni Meno and Todd Sand became enamored with each other during the 1992 Olympics, in which each of them competed with different partners. Meno skated with Scott Wendland, finishing eleventh, and Sand paired with Natasha Kuchiki, finishing sixth at Albertville after winning a bronze at the 1991 Worlds. Both pairs trained under world-class pairs coach John Nicks at Costa Mesa, California.

"In the beginning it was very difficult," said Sand, who earlier in his career had represented Denmark in men's singles at the World Championships. "All four of us had been kind of close. I knew my partnership was going to end [after the 1992 Worlds] and Jenni was unsure about her future." Meno and Sand found they had the same goals, including skating to classical music, and joined forces on the ice. They won the national title in 1994, finished fifth at the Olympics, and, increasing their speed through exhaustive training, had an outstanding 1995 season. They received a rare six perfect scores for artistic impression in winning the nationals, then took the bronze medal at the 1995 Worlds, rising from fifth after the short program. During the Lillehammer Olympics, they got engaged, and they married during the summer of 1995. "I see an extraordinary closeness between them," reporters were told by Nicks, who joked that he would be choreographing the wedding. "Often during my instructional periods with Todd and Jenni I feel like an intruder."

That closeness has worked for Meno and Sand and countless other pairs and dance teams, among them former U.S. dance champions Liz Punsalan and Jerod Swallow; Gordeeva and Grinkov; Marina Klimova and Sergei Ponomarenko; and the Protopopovs. As Phil Hersch, respected skating writer for the *Chicago Tribune* points out, seven of the last nine Olympic pairs gold medals were won by Russian husband–wife tandems. And the last U.S. pair to capture an Olympic medal, Jill Watson and Peter Oppegard, who took bronze in 1988, were romantically linked at the time.

Watching Gordeeva and Grinkov in the 1993–94 season, when they reapplied for amateur status and won the Olympic gold, you couldn't help but notice their feeling for each other. They teamed up to win the World Junior Championship when she was just twelve and he was sixteen, and four years later they took their first Olympic title at Calgary. They married in 1991, and a year and a half later their daughter, Daria, was born. The maturity and closeness that longtime togetherness, marriage, and parenthood had given them were apparent when they returned from the pro ranks, which they had joined after the 1990 Goodwill Games. They had long since outgrown the Mutt-and-Jeff designation. Instead people were calling them the greatest of all time, their elegant programs "seamless."

But on November 20, 1995, Grinkov died of a heart attack while he and his wife were practicing in Lake Placid for the 1996 Stars on Ice tour. "He loved her so much," said a distraught Barbara Underhill. "It was so evident, everytime they touched, every time he looked at her. He didn't speak much English but you could tell … this went beyond language."

Perhaps the most obvious example of love on the ice was the 1992 Olympic ice-dance championship won by the lithely sensual Klimova and Ponomarenko. The lyrical dancers from Moscow are the only skaters to have won gold, silver, and bronze Olympic medals. They edged out fan favorites Isabelle and Paul Duchesnay,

JENNI MENO AND TODD SAND DEMONSTRATE THE HEIGHT AND STRENGTH REQUIRED IN PAIRS SKATING. SAND CONTINUES TO MOVE ACROSS THE ICE AS HE SUPPORTS MENO, WHO REVOLVES ABOVE HIM.

CHRISTINE HOUGH AND DOUG
LADRET WON JUST ONE CANADIAN
PAIRS CHAMPIONSHIP (IN 1988),
BUT HAVE HAD SPECTACULAR
PROFESSIONAL CAREERS WITH THEIR
FLEET, SULTRY ROUTINES.

Canadian siblings skating for France, with a smoldering long program that, Ponomarenko said, "could only be skated by husband and wife. It could not be skated by
Paul and Isabelle, because they are brother and sister."

As their music ended, Ponomarenko hugged his wife and said, "I love you,
Marina."

TRUST AND TOGETHERNESS

Ice dancers must have a subconscious connection to their partners, permitting
them to synchronize a program that may contain as many as two thousand separate movements. For pairs, with the potential of serious injury to both skaters, trust
is an important ingredient. In both disciplines, verbal and nonverbal communication are absolutely essential.

"You can't control romance, but I strongly discourage dating or any romantic
links if I can," said noted pairs coach Kerry Leitch, who has overseen the amateur
careers of three world pairs medalists, a stableful of national champions at three levels, and Christine (Tuffy) Hough and Doug Ladret, who are establishing a reputation as one of the most dynamic touring-show pairs. "I really encourage our pairs
to have a rapport, but we stress that it's a business relationship. It tends to be
different in each case. In Tuffy and Doug's case, for instance, it's always been a strong
bond. Not love as such, but it's very strong. Most of the successful pairs have that
bond. Most of the unsuccessful ones don't."

Hough and Ladret teamed up in the spring of 1984 and skated in an international event before they had even qualified for Canadians. They won the national
title in 1988, but thereafter took a back seat to Brasseur and Eisler. They did not

have strong side-by-side jumps, a fairly frequent Canadian pairs shortcoming, but were always crowd favorites. The Albertville audience booed when they were given low marks for presentation in their 1992 Olympic long program. The French crowd had fallen in love with the pair during their sultry, bluesy short program, which had been designed with their impending professional career in mind.

"I guess if you're paired up together when you're both seventeen, you're going to have hormones, but Doug and I are eight years apart," says Hough. "We're one of the few pairs teams who are as close as we are who have never been involved with each other. We laugh about it when we think about it. It'd be like kissing your brother or sister.

"I think from the time you pair up, you have to have something in common that you want. You have to have compatibility and you have to *care* about the other person. There is a lot of compromise. It's very similar to a marriage, and you don't have to have the physical part. You can't just walk away from something that bothers you – you have to deal with it."

If the personal relationship doesn't work out, that doesn't always mean the skating partnership has to dissolve. Elena Valova and Oleg Vasiliev were three-time world champions and 1984 Olympic gold medalists. They divorced a few years ago, but until 1995 still skated together professionally.

One of the great public intrigues in skating history occurred in the early seventies and revolved around the unbeatable and fiery Irina Rodnina, who teamed with Alexei Ulanov to win the 1972 Olympic pairs championship and four world titles. But when Ulanov fell in love with Ludmila Smirnova, the Rodnina–Ulanov team was doomed. The 1972 Olympics had the bizarre spectacle of Rodnina and Ulanov winning the gold medal, with Smirnova and her partner, Andrei Suraikin, finishing second, and Ulanov and Smirnova having been married only weeks earlier.

Rodnina then held auditions for a new partner – an unusual situation, since generally the male partners are the ones in demand (just look in the Partners Wanted classified ads of any skating magazine). Alexander Zaitsev was chosen, and Rodnina went on to win another six World Championships and two Olympic titles with him. They also married, although they later divorced. Ironically, in their first two World Championships together, Rodnina and Zaitsev defeated Ulanov and Smirnova, the runners-up both times.

ELENA VALOVA AND OLEG VASILIEV. THE RUSSIAN 1984 OLYMPIC PAIRS CHAMPIONS CONTINUED SKATING TOGETHER PROFESSIONALLY EVEN THOUGH THEY HAD DIVORCED, BUT THEIR SKATING PARTNERSHIP BROKE UP IN 1995.

THE ESSENTIAL INGREDIENTS

When other dancers tried to imitate the legendary Jayne Torvill and Christopher Dean in the mid-1980s, but did not have their technical skills or innate dance sense, ice dancing seemed to be moving closer to pairs. The ISU noticed, and tightened ice-dancing rules. Some, including Torvill and Dean themselves, said that there was too much clamping down.

Reading the rulebooks on pairs and ice dancing is a quick cure for insomnia. Essentially, the difference between the two disciplines is that pairs has identifiable moves such as lifts, throws, and parallel individual jumps and spins, and dancing has none except lifts, which should not be performed above the shoulder. Ice dancing promotes rhythm, precision of strokes and edges, and interpretation of the music. Pairs revels in the spectacular and the dangerous – one of its important elements is the death spiral, evoking images of something tragic. Ice dancers need more years together to acquire the harmonious moves and erect upper body designed to make the difficult footwork appear easy and natural.

Dance has been under fire ever since it became an Olympic sport in 1976. It has regularly been threatened with the loss of Olympic status. The discipline pricks outsiders on two main issues: sporting components and judging.

Because ice dancing has no throws or jumps, the falls that occur so regularly

NO ONE HAS STRETCHED THE BOUNDARIES OF ICE DANCING AS FAR AS JAYNE TORVILL AND CHRISTOPHER DEAN, UNQUESTIONABLY THE BEST DANCE PAIR OF ALL TIME. THEY EVEN REVERSED THE ACCEPTED PRINCIPLE THAT THE MALE SUPPORTS AND SHOWS OFF THE FEMALE PARTNER. DURING THIS UNUSUAL SEGMENT FROM THEIR ORIGINAL DANCE AT THE '94 OLYMPICS, IT WAS DEAN WHO REVOLVED ON ONE EDGE AROUND THE ANCHORED, SUPPORTIVE TORVILL.

in the other three disciplines are not common in dance. To the layman, falls are the failures that offer some measure of the athletic demands of a sport. Additionally, to people who do not understand edges or angles, dancing seems like something you might do at a local nightclub. Put on the skates, put on the tunes, and let's party. The judging is a more serious problem, and dance panels are constantly being monitored and admonished for "protocol" judging, which is placing couples in the predicted order. One year at Worlds, the only change in standings from the first compulsory dance to the free dance was a flip-flop of seventeenth and eighteenth places. Paying dues has long been a dance tradition, and the hierarchy usually doesn't vary without retirements or a leading couple falling severely out of favor — and the latter is rare. But there is some evidence that this has been changing in recent years, with the rise of the Canadian couple Shae-Lynn Bourne and Victor Kraatz; Finns Susanna Rahkamo and Petri Kokko jumping from thirteenth to sixth between 1989 and 1990; the Duchesnays' World Championship in 1991; and Gritschuk and Platov's win in the 1994 Olympics.

(LEFT) SUSANNA RAHKAMO AND PETRI KOKKO AT SKATE CANADA IN 1992. THE FINNS, WHO HAD BEEN FAN FAVORITES FOR YEARS, FINALLY WON THE SILVER MEDAL AT THE 1995 WORLD CHAMPIONSHIPS.

(RIGHT) GRITSCHUK AND PLATOV DURING THE FREE DANCE OF THEIR 1995 WORLD CHAMPIONSHIPS VICTORY AT BIRMINGHAM, ENGLAND. THEY WON AGAIN AT EDMONTON IN 1996, BUT MANY FEEL THE SECOND RUSSIAN TEAM, ANJELIKA KRYLOVA AND OLEG OVSIANNIKOV, WILL CHALLENGE THEM IN 1997.

PULLING IN THE NUMBERS

Yet for all its public warts, ice dancing is in no real danger of disappearing, because it attracts huge audiences. And huge audiences translate into money. When Jayne Torvill and Christopher Dean were ruling the event in the early 1980s, it was always the first event to be sold out at the World Championships. In the U.S., which has never produced a world champion in the discipline, ice dancing is second only to the women's event in popularity.

Pairs skating, on the other hand, is not as admired in the United States. It ranks fourth in popularity among the disciplines, and even the best pairs do not generate many extra ticket sales to live shows. What those pairs do, however, is bring audiences back. So shows that plan to visit the same arena year after year make sure that their pairs combinations are top-notch. Stars on Ice does entrance and exit polls of their customers, and discovered that while skaters such as Brasseur and Eisler are not the acts mentioned on the way in to the arena, they're often the ones talked about on the way out. Those people will be back to see those pairs – as well as whatever big-name singles skaters are in town – when Stars on Ice returns the following year.

"One of the reasons that pairs is not so popular in America, I think, is that for so many years we from Russia have been winning it," said Ekaterina Gordeeva. "So the people who win are not familiar to people here."

During the 1992 Olympics, Evy Scotvold, Nancy Kerrigan's coach, said that the reason probably lies as much in the longtime U.S. fascination with the star system. The country is founded on the celebration of the individual, and young American skaters want to be *the* star, not share billing, even with one other person. That is probably true on the fortune-and-fame level, but even singles skaters like to work in tandem occasionally, because it takes them back to their earliest days at the arena. One of the most popular exhibition acts ever, both with audiences and the principals themselves, was a pairs routine performed by training mates Kerrigan and Paul Wylie. On tours, male and female soloists often team up for routines.

Canadians have no ambivalence about pairs skating. They love it. Its simple, rough-edged power and lurking danger somehow appeal to the national psyche.

Even more to the point, Canadians have always been good at it, and usually seem to be on or around the podium. Their nine pairs titles may pale against the twenty-six won by the Russians/Soviets, but it is the third highest total of any nation – the Americans have won only twice. The discipline is in a bit of a trough in the mid-nineties with the retirement of national symbols Brasseur and Eisler, and it is hard to determine if there is medal potential among the current senior crop, led by supple national champions Michelle Menzies and Jean-Michel Bombardier, and including Jodeyne Higgins and Sean Rice; Allison Gaylor and David Pelletier (who also competes in singles); and Kristy Sargeant and Kris Wirtz.

But even if that group cannot duplicate the successes of Brasseur and Eisler, Canada has a strong development system. Preston Figure Skating Club continues to turn out good young pairs teams with strong individual elements, but it is no longer the only choice for a Canadian interested in a pairs career. Mariposa, home of Elvis Stojko, has a program strong enough that Bombardier and Menzies moved there from Montreal. And the rise of Quebec skating since the mid-eighties, mirrored in the innovative pairs teams that have emerged from that province, shows the strong training available there.

BOURNE AND KRAATZ KINDLE CANADIAN HOPES

Ice dance has also grown everywhere, particularly in Quebec. Shae-Lynn Bourne and Victor Kraatz started their partnership in Montreal, where they skated under coaches Eric Gillies and Josée Picard from the time they first got together as a team in 1992 until the autumn of 1994, when they left to train with Klimova and Ponomarenko in California. A few months later they were on the move again. Retaining coach-choreographer Uschi Keszler, they also spent time training in Lake Placid with coach Natalia Doubova.

Bourne and Kraatz, Canada's brightest dance hope since Tracy Wilson and the late Rob McCall, bronze medalists at the 1988 Olympics, made their world debut in 1993. They placed fourteenth, jumped to tenth in the 1994 Olympics, then sixth in the World Championships a month later. In 1995, they moved up another couple of notches to fourth. That's a rapid rise within ice dancing's rigid hierarchy, an indication that another breakthrough may be right around the corner.

"The Canadian couple have real potential. I'm sure they will be champions," says Christopher Dean – fittingly, since Bourne and Kraatz are often compared with Torvill and Dean.

Before skaters make a big move up in the international rankings, there is usually one signpost of an imminent burst into the spotlight: they draw a knowledgeable crowd to practice sessions.

For Bourne and Kraatz, that signpost came in their second practice at Hamar – skating venue for the Lillehammer Olympics – a few days before the 1994 Olympic dance championships opened. The other skaters in their session had gone to their

(ABOVE) ISABELLE BRASSEUR AND LLOYD EISLER REALIZE THAT THEIR WORLD CHAMPIONSHIP DREAM HAS FINALLY COME TRUE SECONDS AFTER THEIR FREESKATE AT THE 1993 PRAGUE WORLDS. THE NORMALLY SELF-COMPOSED EISLER BREAKS DOWN IN TEARS AS HIS PARTNER SUPPORTS HIM. THE PAIR DEDICATED THE PERFORMANCE TO BRASSEUR'S FATHER, WHO HAD DIED ONLY A FEW MONTHS EARLIER.

(OPPOSITE) BARBARA UNDERHILL AND PAUL MARTINI TRIGGERED A WAVE OF NATIONAL PRIDE WHEN THEY WON THE 1984 WORLD CHAMPIONSHIP AT OTTAWA AFTER A DISASTROUS OLYMPICS. THEY BECAME EVEN BETTER PROFESSIONAL SKATERS THAN AMATEURS. THIS IS A POSE FROM THEIR MOVING "YESTERDAY" PROGRAM, CHOREOGRAPHED IN TRIBUTE TO BARBARA'S LATE DAUGHTER.

(LEFT) One of the signature moves of Isabelle Brasseur and Lloyd Eisler. The move they maintain across the ice expresses protective tenderness in the middle of a classical program. When the Canadian pair first joined forces, they were known more for their powerful bursts of athleticism than for gentle moves like this one.

(RIGHT) Michelle Menzies and Jean-Michel Bombardier won the Canadian pairs championship in 1995, and again in 1996.

dressing rooms, but the Canadians remained on the ice, experimenting with a new style of skating they call "hydroblading." Bent low to the ice as they skated, at an angle more acute than seemed physically possible, Bourne and Kraatz looked like cats ready to pounce. It was a slinky, revolutionary style that only skaters with the best edges and the softest knees could work. People casting an eye back over their shoulders as they were leaving the arena stopped in their tracks. Almost in unison they returned to their seats, sensing they were witnessing something different. The next day, four times as many people attended the practice, and several European television networks requested interviews – fanfare out of proportion to the team's eventual tenth-place finish.

Many of the skaters – Brasseur and Eisler, Elvis Stojko, Menzies and Bombardier – who have worked with choreographer Uschi Keszler used some form of hydroblading in their practices and a few had incorporated it into their competitive routines. Bourne and Kraatz, though, brought it to the world, and on the World Tour of Figure Skating Champions in 1995 several pairs and couples were imitating them. The team is trying to alter dance's strict adherence to maintaining a totally erect upper body, and expand the horizontal plane of the discipline.

Bourne started out as a pairs skater, which brings a different approach to their ice dancing. "We want to show that it's athletic, that there are risks," she says. This is another parallel to Torvill and Dean. When she was fourteen, Jayne Torvill won the British Championship for pairs with partner Michael Hutchinson. The Duchesnays were also pairs skaters early in their career.

Kraatz was born in Germany, then lived in Switzerland, where he was Swiss junior dance champion, until moving to Vancouver Island when he was fifteen. He and Bourne teamed up almost by accident in the summer of 1992 when the manager of the Boucherville Arena in Montreal and Picard herself suggested they skate together for a few minutes when each was looking for a new partner. It was apparent from the beginning that they had good lines, and both were athletic and driven. "There is a softness to their knees that is so rare," said Doug Leigh, the coach of Stojko and Brian Orser. "And to have two of them with it is amazing." A few months later they had won two internationals (Grand Prix International and Nebelhorn Trophy) and were receiving overtures from both the German and Swiss

KYOKO INA AND JASON DUNGJEN WERE U.S. PAIRS SILVER MEDALISTS FOR THREE STRAIGHT YEARS FROM 1994–96 AND HAVE IMPROVED THEIR WORLD STANDING FROM TWELFTH TO EIGHTH TO SIXTH GIVING THE U.S. TWO PAIRS IN THE TOP SIX FOR THE FIRST TIME IN EIGHT YEARS. INA STARTED SKATING AT AGE FOUR AND COMPETED FOR JAPAN FOR TWO YEARS, WINNING THE JAPANESE NATIONAL JUNIOR TITLE AT AGE FOURTEEN. SHE WAS FOURTH AT SENIOR NATIONALS AS A SINGLES SKATER IN 1995. PARTNERING HIS SISTER SUSAN, DUNGJEN WON THE U.S. JUNIOR PAIRS TITLE IN 1983 AND WAS SECOND AT THE 1984 JUNIOR WORLDS.

federations, since they would have been eligible to skate for both. But they dethroned reigning champions Jacqueline Petr and Mark Janoschak at the 1993 Canadian nationals in Hamilton and were on their way.

In the fall of 1994, while on Stojko's tour, they met Ponomarenko and Klimova. They had already become disenchanted training in Montreal, sensing they needed a new direction. And a rift was developing between their coaches and choreographer. Although the triple Olympic ice-dance medalists had never coached, Bourne and Kraatz decided to move to Lake Arrowhead to train with them.

"We came to the [1995 Worlds] to show the judges we've improved technically and I think we did that," said Kraatz, after the couple finished tied for fourth in the compulsory dances, then claimed fourth overall. "And what we do is different from everybody else. I think the judges are seeing that. We want to move up gradually and be in contention for first place in 1997. The ultimate goal is that in 1998 we want to be first. Anything that comes before that is a bonus."

The other leading North American couples must also wait their turn, and their move up the ladder will be much slower. U.S. champions Renée Roca and Gorsha Sur were tenth at the 1995 Worlds, after being eleventh in 1993 and missing the Olympic year with an injury. That qualified a second American team for the 1996 Worlds, but U.S. fans are concerned that Roca and Sur, particularly in 1993, were not getting a fair shake from the judges.

A EUROPEAN SPECIALTY

Christopher Dean says that ice dance is "the poor cousin" of singles skating among North American competitors, but in European countries it's a different story. The Russians and British took to it immediately, simply transferring what they had learned at the ballet barre or on the ballroom floor to the arena. The art form was taken seriously at all levels. But it seems that only the most creative or, sometimes, controversial North Americans over the past quarter of a century have made it to the top of the ice-dance ladder: Judy Blumberg and Michael Seibert from the U.S.; the Duchesnays; Wilson and McCall; and now Bourne and Kraatz.

Only the Canadian-developed Duchesnays were able to make the big score, winning the 1991 Worlds – and they were skating for France at the time. After the 1985 national championships, when they were edged 5–4 for second place behind another brother-sister couple, Karyn and Rod Garossino, the Duchesnays saw nothing but roadblocks in Canada. They applied to skate for France (their mother is French and Paul was born in France) and were quickly welcomed, giving that country an entrée into the small inner circle of leading skating nations. The Duchesnays' programs, choreographed by Dean – married to Isabelle at the time – were visually stunning and full of creative moves and countermoves; the skaters were *the* crowd favorite, and their Jungle Rhythms and Missing I and II routines are among the most memorable programs of all time.

In Canada, the Duchesnays and Garossinos were ranked well behind Wilson and McCall, who lifted Canadian ice dancing up by its bootstraps. They, too, left their original coach, Olympic champion Bernard Ford, after getting a firm foothold on the international scene. They, too, faced Russian domination. Many observers felt that Wilson and McCall should have won either the 1988 Olympics or the World Championship, or both. Their speed and daring use of edges were unparalleled in their era, and there was no emotion they could not yank out of an audience. They deliberately varied their short programs and free dances year after year, so that when their amateur career ended in 1988, they had the most extensive portfolio of their skating generation. When the ISU rewrote ice-dancing rules several times in the 1980s, Wilson and McCall, not champions Natalia Bestemianova and Andrei Bukin, were held up as the prototype of what the ISU was aiming for.

Lynn Copley-Graves in her detailed book *The Evolution of Dance on Ice* calls McCall and Wilson's Charleston "the best ever," and when McCall died of AIDS in 1991, the world was robbed of all the innovative programs that had not yet gone from his mind to the ice.

Wilson and McCall were a team of two extremely strong, engaging personalities, whose forte was making people laugh. Not every dance had to be a Greek tragedy. Their heirs in that sphere are the popular Finns Susanna Rahkamo and Petri Kokko. When they finally made the podium in 1994 after years of trying, their contemporary style and ability to see the unusual angle or humor in everything were legitimized. Their polka one year was from *The Addams Family* movie; they parodied ice dance itself in 1991; in 1990 their free dance showed the seedy underside of street life. "It took a long time to get the character, because I didn't have any practice," Rahkamo quipped of her role as a prostitute. Because of their controversial programs and costuming, Rahkamo and Kokko had rarely been rewarded for their subtly excellent technical skills. But their bronze in 1994 was the first world medal ever for Finnish dancers, and they stepped up to silver the next year. Their free dance, skated to the Beatles tunes "Yesterday" and "A Hard Day's Night," drew a prolonged standing ovation, while the reception for winners Oksana Gritschuk and Evgeny Platov was decidedly more cool.

Gritschuk and Platov subscribe to different stylistic schools: he to the classical, she to rock 'n' roll. They both had success with other partners before teaming up in 1989: Gritschuk was world junior champion with Alexander Chickow; Platov

ELIZABETH PUNSALAN AND JEROD SWALLOW WON THEIR FIRST U.S. ICE DANCE CHAMPIONSHIP IN 1991, THE SAME YEAR THEY WERE MARRIED, BUT LOST THEIR TITLE TO RENÉE ROCA AND GORSHA SUR IN 1995. THEY TRIUMPHED AGAIN IN 1996, AND MOVED UP TO SEVENTH IN THE WORLDS. THEY ADMITTED THAT THEY HAD WRITTEN LETTERS AGAINST AN ATTEMPT TO SPEED UP SUR'S CITIZENSHIP BID IN TIME FOR THE 1994 OLYMPICS, WHEN ONLY ONE U.S. TEAM WOULD QUALIFY FOR LILLEHAMMER.

ISABELLE AND PAUL DUCHESNAY IN ONE OF THE MOST FAMOUS MOVEMENTS FROM THEIR LANDMARK "MISSING" PROGRAM, WHICH WON THEM THE 1991 WORLD CHAMPIONSHIP. FRUSTRATED BY CANADA'S INDIFFERENT APPROACH TO THEM, THE DUCHESNAYS SWITCHED THEIR ALLEGIANCE TO FRANCE IN THE MID-1980S. WHEN THEY FINISHED SECOND AT THE 1990 WORLD CHAMPIONSHIPS IN HALIFAX, THE AUDIENCE CHANTED IN UNISON "SIX, SIX, SIX" AFTER THEIR FREE SKATE. THROUGH 1995, NO ICE-DANCE TEAM REPRESENTING CANADA HAD EVER WON THE WORLD TITLE.

was sixth in the 1989 Worlds with Larisa Fedorinova.

Gritschuk and Platov were upset winners at the 1994 Olympics. Many in the audience thought dramatic silver medalists Maia Usova and Alexander Zhulin were better, and a large block of fans favored Torvill and Dean. Gritschuk and Platov, though, have dazzling speed. Yet their free dance at the Olympics lacked convincing feeling and contained, many felt, such illegalities as prolonged separations and two-footed skating. Gritschuk's earlier affair with Zhulin, who is married to Usova, cast a shadow over the competition. "That's all water under the bridge now," said a friend of both couples. "They're skating on the same tour, but it will always be tense." Dean and others felt that the victory by Gritschuk and Platov signified a victory for their coach Natalia Linichuk over rival Natalia Doubova in ice dancing's notorious internal wars. Both women now live and coach in the U.S., Doubova in Lake Placid, New York, and Linichuk in Newark, Delaware.

After the 1995 championships, Gritschuk and Platov and Rahkamo and Kokko said they would retire from amateur ranks, leaving bronze medalists Sophie Minotte and Pascal Lavanchy from France and Bourne and Kraatz as the top two seeds, although Gritschuk and Platov later decided to stay on.

But the French and Canadians are not immune to pressure from those below them. Anjelika Krylova and Oleg Ovsiannikov of Russia and Tatiana Navka and Samuel Gezolian of Belarus could threaten, and there are other strong couples in Russia who have yet to qualify for a World Championship. Yet Gritschuk and Platov were the only Russians to reach the podium in 1994 or 1995 after the country swept the medals in 1992 and 1993.

Russians or Soviets have won every Olympic dance gold except 1984. Four World Championships by Torvill and Dean and one each by the Duchesnays and Hungarians Kristina Regoeczy and Andras Sallay were the only non-Russian triumphs in twenty-six years.

MAIA USOVA AND ALEXANDER ZHULIN PERFORMING IN THE GALA AT THE 1994 OLYMPICS, IN WHICH THEY FINISHED SECOND TO BITTER RIVALS OKSANA GRITSCHUK AND EVGENY PLATOV.

RADKA KOVARIKOVA AND RENE NOVOTNY AT THE 1993 WORLDS. THE CZECHS WERE THE HARD-LUCK COUPLE OF PAIRS SKATING FOR SEVERAL YEARS, MISSING MEDALS AT THE EUROPEAN CHAMPIONSHIPS (TWICE), AND AT THE 1992 OLYMPICS BY ONE-TENTH OF A MARK, BUT THEY FINALLY GOT THEIR REWARD BY WINNING THE 1995 WORLD CHAMPIONSHIP.

THE KING AND QUEEN OF ICE DANCE

There can be little doubt that Torvill and Dean are the greatest ice dancers of all time. Although their retirement from the amateur world in 1984 brought an ISU clampdown on technical rules they had broken, or at least stretched beyond recognition, they left behind an artistic legacy that is unchallenged. Ice dancing continues to develop, sometimes a little too recklessly, but the envelope of creativity is being pushed in many directions. And without that push – directly attributable to the Torvill and Dean reign of 1981 to 1984 – there can be no art.

"I would like to think we had a little to do with that," says Dean.

At the height of their popularity, Torvill and Dean were the monarchs of figure skating, mirroring the status of another British royal pair of the same period, Prince Charles and Princess Di. But Torvill and Dean came from much humbler beginnings.

Training in Nottingham, better known as the city Robin Hood's tormentor was sheriff of, they often had to practice during public sessions at the dark local arena or rent the ice after midnight. Torvill might still be laboring at clerical work in the offices of Norwich Union and Dean as a police cadet had the Nottingham City Council not decided to pay their training expenses. What the world would have missed if police work had had more of a hold on him! "Yes, but there would have been some rather creative arrests, don't you think?" Dean says, laughing.

Although they won their first World Championship in 1981, the real arrival of Torvill and Dean – and a turning point in skating history – came later that year when they unveiled Mack and Mabel, their radical-departure free dance, at the St. Ivel competition in Richmond, England. Full of innovative moves and lifts, it set the stage for theme choreography and earned them their first three 6.0s, including one from the Soviet judge, a revealing sign of acceptance and resignation.

Bolero, which opened with the skaters on their knees for thirty seconds, mesmerizingly swaying, is considered their signature piece, and their 1995 professional tour lifted its curtain with five dance couples reprising that opening. They won the 1984 Olympics with Bolero, and during their then-final week of amateur skating at the Ottawa Worlds a month later, they harvested a total of twenty-nine 6.0s in the compulsories, short program, and long program.

After mounting several tours, they decided to reinstate for the 1994 Olympics. Their ten-year absence was the longest of any of the returning pros. They won the European Championships, but only because of a judging split. Their program was considered too conservative, which they thought was required under the new rules.

They returned to training and revamped 60 percent of the program for Lillehammer, just two weeks later, and arrived looking older and haggard because of the pressure of the redesign – this is a couple who used to spend a whole day on one five-second segment – the food poisoning Dean had contracted, and the "Cold of the Century" Torvill had caught. But they improved as the week went on, and in the free-dance final, many observers thought their Let's Face the Music program was the best.

Said Dean: "What we were guilty of was listening too hard to the powers-that-be. Maybe we should have done what we would be happy with. Even with that … there was this 'who do they think they are?' feeling. We got a great reaction from the people in the building that night. We didn't feel in any way that we'd lost."

They also got hundreds of faxes and letters of support, including telegrams from Gene Kelly and Julie Andrews, telling them they were the real winners.

In the end, rightly or wrongly and despite their brilliance, Torvill and Dean's time as Olympians had passed.

PAIRS: THE RUSSIANS AND EVERYONE ELSE

Pairs skating did not have the exact equivalent of Torvill and Dean, but it did have the Protopopovs and Irina Rodnina. And as in ice dance, the Russians have had a firm grip on the gold.

When Czechs Radka Kovarikova and Rene Novotny shook off a history of disappointments to win the 1995 World Championship, they were just the fifth winners in thirty-one years to call a country other than the Soviet Union or Russia their home.

The Russians have not only been good, but they have also had a mystique that has made them better, although with the fall of the Iron Curtain and more communication between East and West, some of that forbidding aura of invincibility has faded. "I remember all the times I walked into a rink and they scared me,"

MAXI HERBER AND ERNST BAIER AT THE 1936 OLYMPICS.

(LEFT) ELEGANCE AND PASSION HIGHLIGHTED ANY PROGRAM BY EKATERINA GORDEEVA AND THE LATE SERGEI GRINKOV, THE HUSBAND-AND-WIFE TEAM FROM RUSSIA WHO WON THE 1988 AND 1994 OLYMPICS. GRINKOV DIED SUDDENLY DURING A PRACTICE FOR STARS ON ICE, AT LAKE PLACID IN NOVEMBER, 1995.

(RIGHT) GORDEEVA AND GRINKOV OPEN UP THEIR LONG PROGRAM AT 1993 SKATE CANADA, THE FALL INTERNATIONAL THAT MARKED THEIR RETURN TO "AMATEUR" SKATING AND THE FIRST STEP TO RECLAIMING THEIR OLYMPIC CHAMPIONSHIP.

said Canadian pairs skater Christine Hough.

The Russian domination began at Colorado Springs in 1965 when Oleg and Ludmila Protopopov graduated from three years of silver medals to win the gold. Artistic and maturely elegant, the Protopopovs were dethroned by Alexei Ulanov and Irina Rodnina after three years at the top of the podium. The Protopopovs may have passed the baton to Rodnina and Ulanov, but not the style. The tiny Rodnina and her two partners (Alexander Zaitsev was drafted in 1973) brought athleticism and speed to the discipline. And Rodnina upped the stakes in the side-by-side jumps to a double Axel, well beyond the leaping powers of any other female pairs skater at the time. Now it's a must for any top pairs team and is often the jump that scuttles hopes of victory when one of the partners misfires.

Rodnina and her partners were the forerunners of a parade of pairs in which the man was tall and muscular and the woman short and slight. That enabled teams to perform more spectacular lifts and monster throws in which the woman would sometimes travel more than twenty-five feet (8 m) in the air. No wonder injuries among female pairs skaters are now so common and, Rodnina aside, men often partner two or three women in their careers. Of course, Rodnina did not take part in the big throws that were becoming the vogue.

When Rodnina retired in 1980, no pair dominated until Ekaterina Gordeeva and the late Sergei Grinkov put the title under lock and key beginning with the 1986 World Championship. Before G and G, as they came to be known, there were six different pairs champions in seven years. The only double winners were Elena Valova and Oleg Vasiliev, in 1983 and 1985. They also interrupted G and G's four-victory reign with a win at Budapest in 1988, after Gordeeva and Grinkov had won the Olympics. Valova and Vasiliev came out of relative obscurity to win gold at their first World Championships in 1983 at Helsinki with a shocking development: side-by-side triple toe loops, while most pairs were struggling to get up to a double Axel. Martini and Underhill, who had skated so well that many Canadians anticipated them stealing the gold, got bronze instead, Canada's first pairs medal in nineteen years.

Because of their effort at Helsinki, Underhill and Martini went into the 1984 Sarajevo Olympics as Canada's only hope for a gold medal in skating. But it was a terrible week for them in Sarajevo, punctuated by a dispiriting spill Underhill took on the throw double Axel. They fell apart and finished seventh. Deflated, they returned home and pondered retiring rather than risking, they said at the time, further humiliation at the World Championships, which would be held only a few weeks later before a partisan crowd in Ottawa.

Underhill and Martini turned in the performance of their lives. Somehow competitions at Ottawa Civic Centre are always packed with the most knowledgeable skating fans anywhere, and when Underhill came down triumphantly on the demon throw double Axel less than a minute from the end, the audience exploded. They knew the Canadians had won.

Underhill and Martini weren't equal to some of the other pairs in some of the shadow skating elements, such as side-by-side jumps, but through years of success, failure, and growing up together, they understood completely what it meant to be a pairs team. They won just two world medals, but they may be the best pair of all time when professional skating careers are factored in. Their level of trust and timing enabled them to do more difficult elements and be even better pro skaters than they were amateurs. With time, they became superb skating broadcasters – perfect complements for each other at the microphone as they are on the ice.

After Underhill and Martini turned professional in 1984, Canada went only three years (1987, 1988, and 1995) without a world pairs medal. Katherina Matousek and Lloyd Eisler, Cynthia Coull and Mark Rowsom, Cindy Landry and Lyndon Johnston, and Isabelle Brasseur and Eisler all got to the podium. Brasseur and Eisler made it five times, with two bronze, two silver, and the 1993 gold.

Coached by Josée Picard and Eric Gillies in the dynamic skating atmosphere in Montreal, Brasseur and Eisler are unique in so many ways, yet typical in a couple of others. They started as a rag-doll pair (she is about a foot shorter than him); he had had three other partners, to her one; and he was seven years older than her. The height difference remained, but became a nonissue because they developed unison and strong lines and because their pairs tricks were so spectacular. Their triple lateral twists, throws, and lifts were huge, and they also performed the most difficult death spiral: the forward-outside.

The Canadians overcame Eisler's severe knee injuries and their nerves in big competitions, and evolved from tricksters into complete artists. They are natural comedians on the ice, and one of their show numbers, in which Brasseur dresses up

MANDY WOETZEL AND INGO STEUER OF GERMANY, WHO'VE ENDURED SEVERAL ACCIDENTS AT MAJOR INTERNATIONAL CHAMPIONSHIPS, DEMONSTRATE EXTENSION AND UNISON.

as a Chaplinesque gentleman and Eisler as a gaudy stripper, brings audiences to their feet and new meaning to the term "pairs tricks."

A BUMPER CROP OF PAIRS

The thrill of victory for Brasseur and Eisler in Prague was also the agony of defeat for Czech hopefuls Kovarikova and Novotny. They had hoped to use their home-ice advantage to become the first Czech world pairs champions. Instead they discovered the reality that has affected so many others on home ice: the increased weight of your country's hopes and expectations. They fell on their Axels and finished fourth, a drop of two places from the previous year, when their silver medal was the first medal by a Czech pair since 1958.

They had won silver at the 1992 Worlds after being edged by Brasseur and Eisler for the Olympic bronze in a narrow 5–4 judging split.

Kovarikova, the tiny beacon of composure, is sixteen years younger than her tall, graceful partner. They finally made up for all their heartbreak in competition when they decisively won the 1995 World Championship over defending champions Evgenia Shiskova and Vadim Naumov.

Shiskova and Naumov, a veteran pair with superb lines and creative lifts, are leaders in some of the technical elements, such as side-by-side triple loops, but do not have the foot speed of some other leading pairs, a serious drawback.

Marina Eltsova and Andrei Bushkov, like the Czechs, have had some financial aid from American supporters and are a threat to win future championships. They have, however, been hampered by inconsistent results, injuries, and the return of professionals Gordeeva and Grinkov and Mishkutienok and Dmitriev, which knocked them off the 1994 Olympic team.

But the hard-luck team of pairs skating is the German duo of Mandy Woetzel and Ingo Steuer, who have been together only since the end of the 1992 Olympics. Already they are the most star-crossed couple in skating.

Their crash during the short program of the 1994 Olympics was replayed again and again on network news shows. Woetzel caught a toe pick in the ice, slammed her chin and chest violently on the rink, and slid toward the boards. The startled Woetzel, coming out of a hand-to-hand spiral, barely avoided skating right over his partner. They were forced to

withdraw from the competition, but a month later they got through the same program safely, to finish fourth at the World Championships. In a burst of humor, Steuer lifted up Woetzel, tenderly cradled her to his chest, and carried her off the ice, just as he had in Hamar. The previous year the pair had won a silver medal at the European Championships despite an accident during training in which Steuer's lips were cut by Woetzel's skate. That autumn, during practice for Skate Canada, Woetzel nailed Steuer again, this time with an elbow to the jaw during a lift. He fell backward and suffered a concussion when his head struck the ice.

Woetzel and Steuer are one of about half a dozen world-caliber pairs who can include side-by-side triple jumps in their programs, but even without their accidents, they've had irregular results: a world silver medal in 1993, fourth in 1994, and fifth in 1995, when a clean long program would have won them at least a bronze.

Depending on who remains eligible and who decides to forego the grind of amateur competition pairs could be the hardest discipline to predict.

But the most intriguing confrontations might not be on the amateur level at all.

There was every reason to believe that the pairs division of professional competitions would have been equal, or even superior, to that in the amateur ranks for the next few years. Underhill and Martini had made a trimphant return to the competitive circuit; Kovarikova and Novotny had turned pro; and Gordeeva-and-Grinkov vs Brasseur-and-Eisler had already become a pitehed battle where the real clash was one of styles rather than ability.

But skating, and Gordeeva, were robbed of Grinkov's quiet grace when he died of a heart attack in November, 1995.

"We were competitors," said a grieving Eisler. "But we were friends. We have all lost a great guy."

NATALIA MISHKUTIENOK AND ARTUR DMITRIEV WON THE 1992 OLYMPIC GOLD AND, RETURNING FROM PRO RANKS, TOOK SILVER AT LILLEHAMMER IN 1994, WHEN MANY THOUGHT THEY PERFORMED A BETTER FREE SKATE THAN GOLD MEDALISTS AND FELLOW REINSTATED PROS EKATERINA GORDEEVA AND SERGEI GRINKOV. MISHKUTIENOK AND DMITRIEV DISBANDED THEIR PARTNERSHIP IN 1995, AND HE BEGAN TRAINING WITH OKSANA KAZAKOVA. AFTER STANDING FOURTH IN THE SHORT PROGRAM AT THE 1996 WORLDS, THE NEW PAIR FELL APART DURING THE FREE SKATE, TO FINISH FIFTH, AND PROBABLY COULD HAVE BEEN LOWER.

SEVEN

The Great Skates of All Time

One thing figure skating has not done well is develop its legends. Baseball and basketball, for example, unleash floods of statistics on the sporting public and have mythologized the heroes of their game for generations. A youngster in North America could not grow up without hearing about the Bronx Bombers, the Shot Heard 'Round the World, the Greatest Game Ever Played, or the Sultan of Swat.

But who is skating's Babe Ruth? Its Wayne Gretzky or Gordie Howe? Its Michael Jordan?

Ask a hundred different skating fans and you'll get a hundred different replies. One might answer, "Dick Button, Oksana Baiul, Katarina Witt, and Torvill and Dean." Another could say, "Ulrich Salchow, the Protopopovs, Kurt Browning, and Peggy Fleming." Still another might respond, "Elvis Stojko, Sonja Henie, Scott Hamilton, and Gordeeva and Grinkov."

"In skating, I don't think you can compare people from different eras," says Scott Hamilton.

Hamilton is right. Was Ulrich Salchow a lesser champion than Elvis Stojko just because he didn't attempt any triple jumps? No one in Salchow's time did. Was Trixie Schuba a better skater with her two titles than Jill Trenary with her one? Hardly.

Still, if a sport's great and not-so-great moments are celebrated – even embellished a little – that can add depth and texture to its history. Legends, myths, and statistics give a sport points of reference, even if they're not reliable or entirely fair.

Entire books are written on the terrible mistakes that have occurred in baseball's World Series. Every American football fan can tell you that the Greatest Game Ever Played is considered to be the 1958 NFL title game; in hockey that distinction is usually given to the 1975 New Year's Eve game between the Montreal Canadiens and the Soviet Red Army; in baseball it was game six of the 1975 World Series between the Cincinnati Reds and the Boston Red Sox.

Until the past few years, skating did not have the wide audiences that the other sports enjoy, so such comparisons have not been necessary. But recently, the United

BOLERO WAS THE DEFINITIVE PROGRAM IN THE AMATEUR CAREERS OF JAYNE TORVILL AND CHRISTOPHER DEAN AND WON THEM THE 1984 OLYMPICS. THE STUNNING INTERPRETATION, REVOLUTIONARY BECAUSE IT WAS SKATED TO A SINGLE MUSICAL WORK, BEGAN WITH THE COUPLE ON THEIR KNEES, SWAYING TO RAVEL'S HYPNOTIC MUSIC. WHEN THEY RETURNED TO THE OLYMPICS AT LILLEHAMMER TEN YEARS LATER, THEY RESURRECTED THE FAMOUS PROGRAM FOR THEIR EXHIBITION PERFORMANCE, AS A TRIBUTE TO WAR-TORN SARAJEVO. BOLERO'S OPENING SEQUENCE WAS ALSO A CORNERSTONE OF THEIR PROFESSIONAL TOUR IN 1994–95.

States Figure Skating Association began including in its publicity packages lists of "firsts" and "youngests" and "mosts" because there have been so many requests for comparative statistics from the growing media horde who cover the sport.

Skating fans should automatically recollect that Sonja Henie's ten consecutive titles were the most for a female singles skater, that Irina Rodnina owns the most pairs golds. But how about Surya Bonaly, who, if she finishes second one more time without taking gold, will become the all-time runner-up at the World Championships? Regine Heitzer of Austria, second three times behind Sjoukje Dijkstra from 1963 to 1965 is tied with Bonaly for taking the most silver medals without winning a world title. Jimmy Grogan of the U.S. holds that record in the men's division, with four seconds, two behind Dick Button and two more behind Hayes Jenkins. Brian Orser, who had finished second to Scott Hamilton, Alexander Fadeev, and Brian Boitano threatened to match Grogan, but finally took gold in 1987.

Then there's Ludmila Smirnova, who had the misfortune to be of the same era as Rodnina and finished second five straight years, the first three with Andrei Suraikin and the final two with Rodnina's old partner Alexei Ulanov, who had fallen in love with Smirnova.

When Kristi Yamaguchi, Tonya Harding, and Nancy Kerrigan of the U.S. finished one-two-three at the 1991 World Championships, it was duly publicized as the first time one country had swept all three women's medals. But few took the time to mention that that has happened three times in men's and ice-dance competition and twice in pairs, because the statistics were not readily available.

FAMOUS FIRSTS

Skating has been weak at recording its historic moments. Pioneers in jumping are not officially recognized. This is partly because it's usually not who does the jumps first but who does them best that's most important. As the technical envelope continues to be pushed, more attention is being paid to who does what first.

In 1978, for instance, CTV officials called ISU members into their broadcast truck to see replays of Canadian Vern Taylor's triple Axel. After several viewings, it was determined that he had landed the jump cleanly without touching his free foot down.

"That's true," says Ben Wright of Boston, one of the world's most respected skating officials and historians. "But I'd prefer to think of Brian Orser as doing the first one, because he did it right, and did it often." Likewise, most skating fans assume Petra Burka did the first triple jump by a woman when she landed a triple Salchow in winning the 1965 Worlds. But many observers insist that Jana Mrazkova of Czechoslovakia clearly landed a triple Salchow at the 1959 Worlds.

THE FIRSTS: (For a skater to be eligible, he or she must have landed the jump in a major competition: a national championship; Worlds; Europeans; North Americans; Olympics.)

MEN:

Single Salchow: Ulrich Salchow (Sweden), 1909

Single Loop: Werner Rittberger (Germany), 1910

Double Lutz: Dick Button (U.S.A.), 1947

Double Axel: Dick Button (U.S.A.), 1948

Triple Jump (a triple loop): Dick Button (U.S.A.), 1952

Triple Lutz: Donald Jackson (Canada), 1962

Triple Axel: Vern Taylor (Canada), 1978

Triple Axel combination (triple Axel–double toe loop): Brian Orser (Canada), 1985

Quadruple Jump (a quadruple toe loop): Kurt Browning (Canada), 1988

Quadruple Jump combination (quadruple toe loop–double toe loop):
    Elvis Stojko (Canada), 1991

WOMEN:

Double Jump (a double Salchow): Cecilia Colledge (Great Britain), 1936

*Triple Jump (a triple Salchow): Jana Mrazkova (Czechoslovakia), 1959

Triple Lutz: Denise Biellmann (Switzerland), 1978

Triple Axel: Midori Ito (Japan), 1989

Quadruple Jump: Not yet accomplished

*Some insist Petra Burka of Canada was the first woman to do a triple jump (a
    Salchow in 1965), but many witnesses saw Mrazkova land hers in 1959.

SONJA HENIE AT THE 1932 OLYMPICS.

CHOOSING THE BEST

If skating experts have found it difficult to determine who did the first this or that, they have certainly never agreed on the best of anything. So selecting the best competitive performances of all time would be nearly impossible. But what's to stop us from trying? If nothing else, it makes for a good discussion.

"The thing is, if you're choosing the best, it has to be when the skater does their best at the best possible time," says respected British/American skating writer Sandra Stevenson. "Most don't skate well at the Olympics, although John Curry skated the performance of his life to win ... as did Brian Boitano.

"And you have to consider other things, such as Janet Lynn when she skated to [*Prelude to the*] *Afternoon of a Faun* at the U.S. nationals. She never did as well when she got to the Worlds, but that performance was just mesmerizing."

To qualify for a Best Skate, the performance has to take place at a major event: a national championship, Worlds, Europeans, or Olympic Games. A number of factors go into such a decision: the technical and artistic level of the performance; the pressure under which it was skated; the competitive scenario; whether it was a landmark in skating history; how the audience reacted.

You might look at the list that follows and see that the performance you found most memorable isn't on the Top Ten of All Time, or even given an honorable mention. Such is the danger of lists.

In reality, a larger, more complete list needs to be done. There are probably twenty-five performances that should be in the Top Ten. Scott Hamilton, for instance, may be the best male skater of all time, but he is not listed. His best achievement is his entire career, and his best amateur performance was really a series of three – the figures, short, and long of the 1983 U.S. Championships. Brian Orser, for his sensational 1988 performance at Worlds, and Barbara Ann Scott should be mentioned. Ronnie Robertson should probably be there for his 1956 Olympic free skate, and surely there should be room for Dorothy Hamill, Peggy Fleming, and Janet Lynn.

And no one is around to plead for Ulrich Salchow, Jackson Haines, or Gillis Grafström.

"And for me, any one of maybe six Toller Cranston skates should always be included," says broadcaster and former world pairs silver medalist Debbi Wilkes. Many of Cranston's greatest performances were exhibition skates.

The same list done five years from now might be completely revamped to include professional championship skates, which are gaining in stature, or a winning performance from the new Grand Prix circuit. Victor Petrenko, for example, in winning the 1994 Challenge of Champions in Japan, delivered one of the most marvelous programs of the year at any level.

Even at a glance, three things about the list become obvious: many of the performances are by Canadians, which could, admittedly, reflect the bias of the author; most of them are from the so-called modern era, when free skating became more important as figures were phased out; and the 1988 Olympics provided several great skating events of all time. In every discipline at Calgary there were at least two outstanding performances among the top skaters.

And so, here is a very subjective list of **Ten Skates for the Ages**, plus five honorable mentions.

1. DONALD JACKSON, CANADA: WORLD CHAMPIONSHIPS, PRAGUE, MARCH 15, 1962

That Donald Jackson was in Prague at all was a matter of good fortune. The previous year, the Worlds had also been scheduled for Czechoslovakia but were abruptly canceled when the Boeing 707 carrying the entire U.S. skating team crashed over Belgium, killing everyone on board. Jackson, who was training in New York with several American team members that spring, was supposed to be on that plane. But while winning the North American Championships, he developed a dangerous fever and was bedridden, which forced him to miss the doomed flight.

No Canadian had ever won the men's World Championship, but Jackson had come close two years earlier in Vancouver when he lost to France's Alain Giletti by just one-tenth of a point. In that era, there was no short program and six compulsory

figures were worth a total of 60 percent of the final mark. Jackson was a notoriously inconsistent practitioner of figures, and in both the 1960 Worlds and Olympics, where he won bronze, poor performances in figures had left him too great a gap to make up with his dazzling free skating, which was clearly the best in the world at that time.

After the first day of competition at Prague, it looked to be the same story all over again as Jackson made a horrendous error on his fourth figure and fell thirty-five points behind the favorite, figures expert Karol Divin, a gentle, kind Czech who was skating in front of hometown fans. The final two figures were traced the next morning, with the free-skate final scheduled for the evening and 18,000 spectators ready to cram into Fucik Sports Hall.

Heading into the free-skate final, Jackson trailed Divin by a whopping forty-five points. Divin skated four spots before the Canadian and rang up scores in the 5.7 range. It would take a nearly perfect score for Jackson to win, but as his coach, Sheldon Galbraith, told him, "There is room at the top." That became one of the most famous sentences in Canadian skating history.

IN 1962, DONALD JACKSON BECAME THE FIRST CANADIAN MAN TO WIN A WORLD CHAMPIONSHIP, BUT IT TOOK WHAT IS OFTEN CALLED "THE GREATEST SKATE OF ALL TIME" TO OVERCOME CZECH KAROL DIVIN'S MAMMOTH LEAD.

Galbraith had originally tried to talk Jackson out of attempting the triple Lutz. It had never been done before – not many triples of any kind were being landed – and Jackson himself, in hundreds of practice tries, had nailed it perfectly only a handful of times. But the twenty-one-year-old was determined to include the Lutz and had already mentioned it to several people. Everyone, including the judging panel, was expecting at least an attempt. A few seconds into Jackson's five-minute program, they all got their wish.

The Lutz, because its mid-air rotation is counter to the skater's on-ice motion, requires a buildup and exact timing. A skater has plenty of time to think and get nervous during the lengthy approach. The crowd grew silent as Jackson started his long entry. He planted his left foot, took off, and came down cleanly on the left foot, completing a jump that wouldn't be seen again at a world competition for twelve years. Although Divin was the local hero, the audience exploded and Jackson had to skate to his accompanying music, from *Carmen*, by memory because he couldn't hear it for a few seconds. He did one more triple jump, ten double jumps, and ten single jumps, all connected by sizzling footwork, and ended with a dazzling spin.

The week had been an emotional one for Czech skating fans. Maria and Otto Jelinek, who had fled the country with their family when the Communists assumed power, had returned to Czechoslovakia for the first time. Representing their new country, Canada, they had won the pairs gold the previous night. Czechs Eva and Pavel Roman would go on to win the dance title. Karol Divin had led the men's competition after figures … and now this. The crowd gave Jackson a fifteen-minute standing ovation, and Jackson received seven perfect scores, which stood as a record until Jayne Torvill and Christopher Dean arrived.

While the final results were being tabulated, Divin searched out Jackson and told him that if his point total fell short, he would give the Canadian his gold medal because Jackson was the real champion. "It's true. I would have done that," Divin said twenty years later when the two got together again in Orillia, Ontario, where Divin was helping a young Brian Orser with his figures and Jackson was offering input on Orser's free skating. "That was the greatest display of skating I'd ever seen, and have still seen. I would not have wanted to take that championship that day."

Divin didn't have to worry. Jackson's point total was high enough, and he became Canada's first men's world champion. Divin, unfortunately, never did win a World Championship. His best finish thereafter was a bronze in 1964.

The World Championships would not return to Prague for another thirty-one years, and in a wonderful bit of symmetry, 1993 was the first year since Jackson's gold that Canada won two World Championships. Kurt Browning recaptured his men's title with the most outstanding artistic program of his era – Casablanca – and Isabelle Brasseur and Lloyd Eisler were emotional winners in the pairs event. They had duplicated the victories of Jackson and the Jelineks.

2. JAYNE TORVILL AND CHRISTOPHER DEAN, GREAT BRITAIN: WINTER OLYMPICS, SARAJEVO, FEBRUARY 15, 1984

If that Dudley Moore–Bo Derek movie *10* had been about figure skating, it would have been called 6 and would have starred Jayne Torvill and Christopher Dean, because, by the time they reached Sarajevo for the Olympic title that was their due, they rarely received a mark that wasn't perfect, or close to it.

Few athletes – Babe Ruth, Wayne Gretzky, and Michael Jordan come to mind – have ever dominated and defined their sport so thoroughly as Torvill and Dean did during the early 1980s. By the 1981–82 season, when they launched the historic theme program Mack and Mabel on an unsuspecting skating public, Torvill and Dean had no peers. Ice-dancing competitions were that in name only. Torvill and Dean were, in reality, competing against no one but themselves and their own legendary feats. They were a royal family of two.

Perhaps because each of their final three free dances of that era – Mack and Mabel, then Barnum and Bailey in 1983, Bolero in 1984, even their original short program of 1984 to a *paso doble* – were technical and creative masterpieces, the principals themselves disagree on which was their best. Torvill thinks it was Barnum at Helsinki in 1983, because she had been injured and they had rallied to overcome that and meet their own, and the world's, high expectations. In the same rise-to-the-occasion vein, Torvill also cites their 1994 comeback Olympics, in which their Let's Face the Music program underwent a major overhaul just two weeks before the Games. "We were under tremendous pressure and skated very well. It finally came together," she recalls.

Dean, however, says that the 1984 program was their finest, because "Bolero launched us into what we're doing today."

Indeed, in their major international tour of 1994–95, the performance began with several couples, one by one, reprising the famous opening scene of Bolero: facing each other on their knees, bathed in flowing purple and swaying in a mystical counterflow. As soon as the first few strains of Ravel's brilliant score came over the loudspeaker, the audience reacted in instant recognition.

At Sarajevo, Torvill and Dean captured the audience with that mesmerizing opening, and as the music increased in tempo, tension, and sensuality, so did their skating, building toward the crashing climax.

"Usually I don't get a chance to see too many skates because I'm taking care of my own skaters," said Brian Orser's coach, Doug Leigh. "But that is one I'll absolutely remember. They really brought something to the table."

And the judges' table brought something to them: a dozen perfect scores, running their career total to 107 6.0s, with the World Championships still to go.

"It was so brilliant," praises Canadian coach Ron Shaver, "that it was not even within the realm of figure skating."

3. BARBARA UNDERHILL AND PAUL MARTINI, CANADA: WORLD CHAMPIONSHIPS, OTTAWA, MARCH 22, 1984

British journalist John Hennessy expressed it best when he wrote: "I can only guess what it felt like to be Canadian in the Ottawa Civic Centre on the night of March 22."

Few moments in Canadian sport have been as electrifying as the four minutes of the final free skate of Barbara Underhill and Paul Martini's amateur career. Until then, they had had a checkered, perplexing career, full of inspiring accomplishments and equally deflating disappointments.

The greatest of those disappointments had occurred only a month before the Ottawa Worlds. After winning a bronze medal at the 1983 World Championships behind Soviet newcomers Elena Valova and Oleg Vasiliev – who took the gold medal many Canadians thought should have gone to Underhill and Martini – the five-time national champions arrived at the Sarajevo Olympics with high aspirations, carrying their country's only realistic hope for a gold medal in skating. They had missed the Canadian Championships because of Underhill's ankle injury, but that had healed and was behind them.

However, their Olympic medal dreams were dashed the first night. Underhill fell heading into a required sit-change-sit spin and they finished sixth in the short program. Never recovering emotionally, they dropped to seventh overall when the long program was flawed by a weak throw triple Salchow and an ugly overrotation on the throw double Axel.

They made brave promises about returning to Canada to prepare for the Worlds with great determination, but when they began practicing again, they found they were emotionally flattened by what had happened in Sarajevo. It was the most difficult moment in their career, and both admitted later that they were within minutes of packing it in.

The media paid attention to them, but not as much as they had in Sarajevo, and not as much as they did to Torvill and Dean, who were in the final week of their fabulous amateur career, or to Brian Orser, who was just coming into his salad days. Besides, Canada had not won a World Championship in any discipline in eleven years and had not struck pairs gold since the Jelineks, twenty-two years earlier.

The Ottawa Civic Centre is probably the best skating venue in Canada. The rink is small enough (10,000 capacity audience) to always be filled for major events, and with one side of the roof angular (because of the seats of the outdoor football stadium overhead), sound magnifies many times beyond its source. Ottawa is not only the capital of Canada, but that night it was the capital, too, of pairs skating. Present were Frances Dafoe and (since deceased) Norris Bowden, Barbara Wagner and Bob Paul, and Otto and Maria Jelinek – the only Canadian pairs to win the World Championship.

When Olympic champions Valova and Vasiliev, skating before Underhill and Martini, had a good, but not overwhelming, free skate, the audience sensed the Canadians could overtake them. Underhill and Martini burst onto the ice, opening with a soaring triple twist and continuing through spins, side-by-side jumps, and a clean throw triple Salchow.

About thirty-five seconds from the end, Martini lifted Underhill and propelled her into the throw double Axel, the one that had crumpled at Sarajevo. Underhill twisted the two-and-a-half rotations as she traveled the thirty feet, then landed on one blade and flung her arms triumphantly in the air. The entire audience were yanked to their feet, screaming, because they knew the Canadians had won. Dafoe, a judge, had tears running down her cheeks. In the stands, a fourteen-year-old named Christine Hough, who had quit skating, decided at that moment she would return to the sport. Eventually she performed in some of the same professional shows as Underhill and Martini.

"I remember the last thirty seconds. They were so excited," recalls Sandra Bezic, who had choreographed the Canadians' program. "They could have gone down if they had caught an edge because of their excitement. Everyone was on their feet, yelling and clapping. I kept screaming at the top of my lungs, 'Keep thinking, keep thinking!'

"It was very special, not just because of the performance, which was great, but because everyone in the entire building knew the history."

4. BRIAN BOITANO, U.S.A.: WINTER OLYMPICS, CALGARY, FEBRUARY 20, 1988

Brian Orser and Brian Boitano should probably be paired as entries 4-A and 4-B, but it was the American who came up with the slightly better performance to win one of the greatest skate-offs in Olympic history. None of the 20,000 people in the audience that night – the largest crowd to see an Olympic skating event – went away feeling they hadn't got more than their money's worth.

Skating had never seen a marquee event of the magnitude of the Battle of the Brians. It was, in fact, a watershed week in the sport's history, the beginning of a boom in popularity that has accelerated at a breakneck pace in the 1990s.

As usual in an Olympic season, the event had been previewed a few months earlier, at Skate Canada. Orser won five of the seven judges in that fall international, and although the Canadian remarked he hadn't skated to his potential, Boitano said he would gladly accept the same performance at the Olympics. As it turned out, both had improved dramatically by the time the Olympics in Calgary rolled around three months later.

Orser had chosen a military theme, to the music "The Bolt," and Boitano, coincidentally, had also decided on a military approach, to the music from the movie *Napoleon*.

Until 1988, Boitano had described himself as a "technical robot," with jumps more fundamentally sound than anyone's in the game. At his debut World Championship in 1983, he became the first skater ever to successfully land all six possible triples at Worlds, and he won the 1986 world title when he skated flawlessly, while Orser and defending champion Alexander Fadeev struggled with their jumps. Orser took the gold the following year in Cincinnati, setting up the all-time rubber match in Calgary.

Although Boitano had always been a superior technician, his programs often appeared detached and without spirit. He recognized that flaw himself and enlisted the aid of Toronto choreographer Sandra Bezic. That provoked a reaction in the Canadian media, who did not understand the nature of figure skating and assumed a Canadian would not work for another Canadian's U.S. rival. But Orser understood. "Completely," he said. "Skating is a business."

Bezic made the difference.

"When Brian lost the Worlds in '87, in the first thirty seconds of his program, I was completely taken by his physical power," Bezic said. "But his program worked against that physical power. He was trying to be an entertainer. As I got to know him, I realized he was not comfortable working the room, but I also realized his immense desire. Not a day went by when he didn't drink, eat, and breathe the Olympics. I used that power and desire, and we came up with Napoleon."

It was the perfect vehicle for Boitano's jumping style and five-foot-eleven (180 cm) statuesque physique.

"That's the best skate I've ever seen," said 1992 Olympic champion Kristi Yamaguchi. She has several seconders, including Scott Hamilton, who ranks John Curry's 1976 program and Boitano's Olympic victory the best.

Boitano finished second in compulsory figures; Orser was third. Then Orser was brilliant in the short program, with Boitano right behind him. As predicted by months and months of hype, the Battle of the Brians was a virtual tie, and would be determined by the free skate.

Boitano skated first in the final group and Orser third. Both were superb, but Boitano was slightly better. He landed a second triple Axel – or appeared to, because replays showed a slight flaw – but it was made at a point on the ice farthest from the judges. Only one year before, Orser had become the first skater to include two triple Axels in the same program. However, this time, tiring, he decided not to attempt the second one. That and a miscue on the triple flip were enough to cost him the title. Against any other skater, in any other Olympics, he would have had enough to win. But not when Boitano skated as he did.

Even though Orser received a 6.0 for artistic impression, the judges were split 5–4 in favor of Boitano. Orser actually won four judges outright to Boitano's three, but the Danish and Swiss judges had them tied and each gave Boitano the higher technical mark. Technical marks were used to break ties at the time, so the two judges were, in reality, saying that Boitano was better.

Orser later wrote he appreciated the fact that Boitano sought him out in their empty dressing room and with compassion told him, "What can I say?" then turned to the Canadian team psychologist and summarized the entire stressful season: "This has been so, so hard."

"The best skate I've seen? I'd have to say Brian Boitano in 1988," Orser commented a few years later. "I have absolute respect for that. And to be honest, ever since then, there hasn't been a performance like that in competition."

5. OKSANA BAIUL, UKRAINE: WINTER OLYMPICS, LILLEHAMMER, FEBRUARY 25, 1994

The spotlight glared so brightly on Nancy Kerrigan and the terrible time she endured leading up to the Lillehammer Olympics that all other skaters, except Tonya Harding, were left in the shadows.

But Baiul had suffered a few tribulations of her own. Her lonely early years as

AT AGE FIFTEEN, OKSANA BAIUL BECAME THE YOUNGEST WORLD CHAMPION SINCE SONJA HENIE WHEN SHE CAME OUT OF NOWHERE TO WIN THE 1993 TITLE. HER PRESENCE OF MIND IN INSERTING AT THE END OF HER OLYMPIC FREE SKATE A TRIPLE SHE HAD EARLIER MISSED WON HER THE GOLD AT LILLEHAMMER, BY 0.1 OVER NANCY KERRIGAN.

an orphan from northern Ukraine were documented in a made-for-TV movie. And the day before the free-skate final, she was injured in a terrible collision with German champion Tanja Szewczenko during practice. Baiul suffered a gash in her lower right leg that took three stitches to close, and wrenched her back badly enough that it continued to bother her months later.

"You had to be there and know all the arguments going on about whether or not she would actually skate in the final," recalls Michael Rosenberg, who was Baiul's agent at the time. "Where Tanja's skate went into her leg, it was extremely painful and hard for her to walk on."

Baiul was the second-youngest woman ever to win a World Championship when she arrived, virtually out of nowhere, to take the 1993 title. Her artistic sense and rapport with the crowd are her two biggest assets, but she is solid technically, as well.

And she can think on her feet. A few days before the women's final, Elvis Stojko had rearranged his program to incorporate a triple Axel combination to compensate for the triple Axel he had missed earlier. It was not given much credit by the

NANCY KERRIGAN, IN THE SHORT
PROGRAM AT THE 1994 OLYMPIC
GAMES. TWO MONTHS AFTER THE
INFAMOUS ATTACK THAT
THREATENED HER VERY PARTICIPATION
AT LILLEHAMMER, SHE REBOUNDED
TO CAPTURE THE SILVER MEDAL,
AND NEARLY THE GOLD.

judges, but it did prime them for a similar decision by Baiul at the end of her free skate. Just seconds before her program concluded, she threw in an unplanned triple combination, knowing that she had not built up enough technical points to over-take Kerrigan. That was just enough to put her even with the talented American and give her the Olympic title.

The judges' decision was as close as it had been for the Battle of the Brians, the other momentous singles skate-off of this half-century. Four judges – all from Com-munist (China) or former Communist countries – had Baiul first in the free skate. Four other judges preferred Kerrigan's work. The ninth judge was two-time world champion Jan Hoffmann, who had the women tied in total score. He had Kerrigan ahead by a tenth of a point in technical merit and Baiul ahead by a tenth of a point in artistic impression. New rules adopted earlier in the decade, designed to promote artistry, gave Hoffmann's first-place ordinal – and the gold medal – to Baiul.

6. NANCY KERRIGAN, U.S.A.: WINTER OLYMPICS, LILLEHAMMER, FEBRUARY 25, 1994

Had Nancy Kerrigan skated under the same rules as Brian Boitano when he won the 1988 Olympics, she would have been the winner at Lille-hammer. Technical merit broke ties in the eighties; presentation marks break them in the nineties. There is, however, the counter-theory that judges pick the winner by what they see, then apply the rules accordingly.

No matter how you feel about Kerrigan's manner or her com-portment before and after the Olympics under the unprecedented media glare that no one could possibly have prepared her for, it is impossible not to admire what she did at Lillehammer. No skater has ever been subjected to as much scrutiny as Kerrigan, unless it is Tonya Harding, the woman she will unfortunately forever be linked with in skating history.

Yet Kerrigan skated through that enormous burden as if it were papier-mâché. She did all that any athlete can do when the Big Event comes, which is put herself in a position to win. That she didn't win really came down to the preferences of individual judges and the extraordinary resiliency and charisma of Oksana Baiul.

It is important to remember not only the attack at the U.S. nationals in Detroit, for which Harding's then-husband and two associates were later convicted, but also the physical and psycho-logical damage it inflicted. It was questionable at first whether Ker-rigan's injured knee would allow her to skate again. Enormous effort – swimming, weight lifting, and riding the exercise bike – got her on the ice in time for the Olympics just seven weeks later. The emotional terror was not dealt with as easily. Just after the attack, it was assumed that she had been stalked by an unknown "admirer," and later it was suspected that the attack was connected to a rivalrous teammate. It will be impossible for Kerrigan ever to feel totally safe again. No matter how big ($10 million U.S.) her contract with Disney, it was a terrible price to pay.

Yet Kerrigan's competitiveness and technique, particularly her trademark extended spiral, carried her to within one-tenth of a point of a gold medal that most Americans felt she should have won.

DICK BUTTON HAS PROBABLY HAD MORE INFLUENCE ON HIS SPORT, PARTICULARLY IN THE U.S., THAN ANY OTHER SKATER. HIS TRIUMPHS AT THE 1948 OLYMPICS STARTED A NORTH AMERICAN DOMINATION OF MEN'S SINGLES THAT HAS RARELY ABATED.

7. DICK BUTTON, U.S.A.: WINTER OLYMPICS, ST. MORITZ, SWITZERLAND, FEBRUARY 5, 1948

By the time he was twenty-two, Dick Button had won seven national titles, five World Championships, and two Olympic gold medals, and had run out of chal-lenges to conquer in amateur skating. So he turned professional and began creating new horizons for himself and his sport. In fact, says the outspoken promoter/commentator/conscience of American skating, his best two skating efforts did not come in the competitive arena. Five days before the 1952 Olympics, Button "had the best skating day of my life in a practice session. I don't know what it was … your body just works right." And a couple of years after leaving the amateur ranks,

Button headlined a TV special for NBC's *Hallmark Hall of Fame* series in which he skated Hans Brinker and the Silver Skates with several movie and TV stars of the era.

"I was a better skater after I turned pro than before," says Button, who began studying with dance masters in New York City once his amateur days had concluded. "As an amateur, I didn't have the foggiest notion of what line was about. I wish I'd had when I was a young skater what I learned later."

Well, he had plenty when he was a young skater. Button himself finds it difficult to pick the best amateur skate of his career because there were so many: his farewell performance at the 1952 U.S. nationals; the 1952 Olympics, when he landed the world's first triple jump, although he says that skate had some flaws; and his first Worlds in 1947 at the age of seventeen, when he finished second to Arnold Gerschwiler of Switzerland. "But your first Olympics is always very special," says Button. And his Olympic victory on the outdoor ice of St. Moritz kicked off an American dominance in men's singles that lasted until the entire U.S. team was killed in a plane crash in 1961. It was the first Olympics since 1936, and with Canada's Barbara Ann Scott winning the women's gold, the postwar boom in North American figure skating was under way. "In those days, figure skating was a very glamorous and very different kind of sport," Button notes. "It was sort of adventurous to go off to places like Switzerland to go skiing or skating. This was not an average sport that you did … it was very avant-garde."

There were two full days of compulsory figures at that time, and the ice at St. Moritz "was fabulous" for those tracings, Button recalls. The ice surface, with weather and hockey eating it up, was less ideal for the free skate, but that did not stop the athletic eighteen-year-old from becoming the first skater to land a double Axel in competition. Button, as much as he espouses the virtues of body line and artistry, was first and foremost an athletic skater.

"I just started working on that Axel, and landed the first one in practice just two days before the competition," Button says. "In those days our jumps were bigger and we'd get as high as we could. We would emphasize delayed Axels, holding the position in the air as long as you could."

Gerschwiler, trying desperately to catch Button, fell in his program and Button won by what the Associated Press called "the most one-sided margin ever."

The victory at St. Moritz established the U.S. in a position of power that it has never really relinquished. "We had just been going along, doing our own thing, without any interaction with the Europeans or any other skaters," Button says. "That year, we knew that we were at the top of the heap."

8. EKATERINA GORDEEVA AND SERGEI GRINKOV, SOVIET UNION: WINTER OLYMPICS, CALGARY, FEBRUARY 18, 1988

The incomparable G and G may have been more complete skaters by the time they returned to win the 1994 Olympics after a couple of years as professionals, but their performance at Lillehammer was flawed.

In 1988, despite the wispy Gordeeva being only sixteen and her future husband just twenty-one, they had begun the maturing process that would separate them from the other power-oriented pairs teams of their era.

But Gordeeva and Grinkov had still not fully escaped their Mutt-and-Jeff moniker. She was still a featherweight at just over eighty pounds (36 kg) and, although she was growing, did not stand much taller than five feet (150 cm). They were still better known for their quadruple twist than for their artistry, but that changed in 1988. "They demonstrate the mature art of the duet," their coach, Stanislav Leonovich, said at the time.

Working hard with choreographer Marina Zueva on a more balletic look, the couple developed expressiveness in their faces, hands, and body language, to go with their technical superiority. Zueva encouraged the pair to act out bit parts in dance vignettes, rather than simply practice element after element. "We impersonated musketeers and musicians and imitated animals," Gordeeva said.

In their own country – where pairs skating was a revered pursuit – G and G had already come to be known as one of the best pairs of all time. The daughter of a teletype operator and a dancer and the son of army officers had long surpassed in popularity their older Russian rivals, Elena Valova and Oleg Vasiliev and Larisa Selezneva and Oleg Makarov. And in those years, winning favor in the Soviet Union usually meant winning the world or Olympic title.

Their energetic short program was set to Spanish music; their long program was skated elegantly and powerfully to classical music – something that would become their artistic forte. Many insiders say Gordeeva and Grinkov were the best pairs team of all time. In Calgary, they certainly showed that they were the best of their era. Grinkov's sudden death in late 1995 came when the couple was still skating brilliantly, and deprived audiences of at least 10 more years of the unforgettable G and G.

9. Tracy Wilson and Rob McCall, Canada: Winter Olympics, Calgary, February 23, 1988

There is nothing in sport so rigid as the hierarchy of ice dancing, and that was particularly true in the 1980s. Win a title, and it was yours as long as you wanted it. Jayne Torvill and Christopher Dean won the Worlds four times, turned pro, and made room for Natalia Bestemianova and Andrei Bukin, who took their quartet of gold medals, retired, and passed off to Marina Klimova and Sergei Ponomarenko.

Little changed in the other podium places, either. Judy Blumberg and Michael Seibert, a classically elegant couple from the U.S., were third three straight years, although Klimova and Ponomarenko jumped ahead of them to second when Torvill and Dean retired. Bestemianova and Bukin were second three times to Torvill and Dean, then moved up to the gold medal for four Worlds and the 1988 Olympics.

Bestemianova and Bukin were the logical heirs to Torvill and Dean, dramatic,

TRACY WILSON AND THE LATE ROB MCCALL WERE AT THE PEAK OF THEIR CREATIVE AND ATHLETIC POWERS IN 1988 WHEN THEY WON BRONZE MEDALS AT BOTH THE OLYMPICS AND THE WORLDS. THE ENERGETIC, SAUCY PAIR WERE CONSIDERED BY MANY TO BE THE BEST DANCE TEAM IN THE WORLD IN THAT 1988 SEASON. IN THEIR SEVEN-YEAR AMATEUR CAREER, THEY TACKLED A RANGE OF PROGRAMS UNEQUALLED BY THEIR PEERS.

creative, and synchronized in a way that only a veteran team can be. But they were not the top couple the night of the free-dance final at the Calgary Games, the best-skated Winter Olympics ever.

Tracy Wilson and Rob McCall were easily the best ice dancers on that final night, even though the judges placed them third, just as everyone knew they would before the night started.

A year later, several ISU members privately admitted that McCall and Wilson perhaps should have won that free skate, and they pointed to the Canadians' performance "as exactly what we think ice dancing should be," according to one inside source.

"Winning had kind of been secondary in our minds," says Wilson, who teamed with McCall in the summer of 1981 and went on to win Olympic bronze and two World Championship bronzes. "Given the system, we didn't think we could win. We wanted to make a statement, though, that there was a side of dance that uses footwork to music. That there is a real athletic/technical side to ice dance."

It was McCall and Wilson's best performance in a career filled with superb ones. They ignited the admittedly pro-Canadian crowd at the Olympic Saddledome with their lightning footwork to a ragtime medley that opened, appropriately, with the "Maple Leaf Rag." The idea came from a National Ballet of Canada production of "Elite Syncopations," which the couple had seen the year before. Two of the four pieces of music were from that ballet. Humor had long been McCall and Wilson's strong suit and had found its way into many of the programs in their incredibly varied repertoire.

"We wanted to be creative with the footwork and choreography," says Wilson. "I think our favorite part – and it was the audience's favorite too – was the final footwork sequence, where we ran quickly on our toes, squaring up to the audience."

McCall and Wilson expanded on the ragtime theme in winning the World Professional Championship two years later, but soon after, McCall became sick with the AIDS virus that would kill him, and the theme was never developed as fully as they had hoped. Wilson never considered finding another partner.

"My relationship with Rob was the biggest part of my love for skating," she said. "We had fought, and almost broke up the team in 1985, but we put the team ahead of ourselves. When I skate on my own now … it's kind of empty."

10. JOHN CURRY, GREAT BRITAIN: WINTER OLYMPICS, INNSBRUCK, AUSTRIA, FEBRUARY 11, 1976

Like Dick Button, Britain's John Curry had never won a World Championship when he arrived in Innsbruck hoping to take the Olympic gold. Curry's artistic flair had usually found disfavor among European judges, and he'd spoken aloud several times that those judges clearly favored the more "masculine" style of Russians Sergei Volkov and Vladimir Kovalev. But Curry also acknowledged that his technical aspects needed strengthening, and to that end was training with world-renowned coach Carlo Fassi in Colorado.

The men's field at Innsbruck – the first Olympics to include the short program

– was deep. Volkov was the reigning world champion, and Kovalev would win in 1979; East German Jan Hoffmann had won in 1974, and would win again in 1980. Canadian Toller Cranston was always a threat, with his lyrical interpretations, and together Cranston and Curry represented an identifiable artistic alternative to the Russians; the athletic alternative was presented by Canadian Ronnie Shaver and American Terry Kubicka, known for the banned back flip.

Curry was the leader after the figures and short program, skating the "short program of my life" to finish second to the mesmerizing Cranston in that segment. The compulsory figures had buried Cranston, but the Canadian rose to third after the short program.

Curry had rarely put back-to-back solid short and long programs together and there was some expectation that this inconsistency would continue in the free skate. But on Fassi's advice, he had been taking the then-popular EST seminars to help control his nervousness, and was prepared for this event. When he skated out first in the final flight – it was supposed to be Shaver, but he was forced to withdraw with a groin injury – Curry showed no sign of nerves and was simply magnificent. It was a magical performance that Scott Hamilton would call "the greatest I had ever seen until Brian Boitano at Calgary. Those are the two best." Cranston, who would finish third, was down the hall preparing for his free skate, and knew that the winner had already been decided. "I heard the entire British delegation whooping and hollering all the way down the corridor," he said. "Officials, coaches, press, photographers, all screaming and carrying on."

Seven judges gave the gold to Curry, the other two opting for home-country skaters: the Canadian for Cranston and the Russian for Kovalev, but this was clearly Curry's crown. It was Britain's first Winter Olympic medal in any sport in twelve years, but most important, it was a stunningly elegant performance for the ages.

Curry's marks were 5.8s and 5.9s, but it must be remembered that there were still talented skaters to come. "If he had skated last," one journalist wrote, "there would have been 6.0s nearly all the way."

HONORABLE MENTIONS (ALL OF WHICH COULD HAVE BEEN IN THE TOP TEN)

Elizabeth Manley of Canada had always been known as a strong skater and an energetic on-ice presence, but she suffered from competitive inconsistency. She had rarely strung together back-to-back excellent programs, unraveling in either the short or (more often) the long program. Still, she could skate, and she could jump. And she did both at the 1988 Calgary Olympics before a wildly enthusiastic home-country audience to win a silver medal in a wildly energizing performance.

If John Curry was the quintessential artist, Elvis Stojko is the prototypical competitive athlete. He had never required his competitive spirit more than at the 1995 World Championships at Birmingham, England. Sidelined with a bad ankle injury during the Canadian Championships a few weeks earlier, Stojko was still in doubt about participating at Birmingham a couple of weeks before the event. "He was skat-

ing in handcuffs," his coach, Doug Leigh, said of the injury. "It was mental torture for him. And then to see a guy do that in competition." Todd Eldredge, who had revived his career, skated before Stojko and skated strongly. Despite his injury, Stojko still attempted to become the first skater to do a quadruple–triple combination. When he missed the quad, he had a triple toe loop he could add, provided he could find a spot – which was right at the very end of a demanding program. He upgraded the double toe loop on the end of a combination to a triple jump, bad ankle and all. As Elvis skated off the ice, Leigh told him, "You are Superman."

Katarina Witt had lost the world title to American skaters three times: Elaine Zayak in 1982, Rosalyn Sumners in 1983, and Debi Thomas in 1986. She was not going to let it happen again in 1987, despite the fact that the Worlds were in the U.S.A., at Cincinnati, and that Thomas and the balletic Caryn Kadavy were at their peak. She simply willed and charmed her way to the title, and became a favorite of the American skating public in the process. It was her third World Championship, and after adding a fourth and the Olympic title the following year, she turned professional. "There was a lot of pressure on her," said her choreographer, Sandra Bezic.

(*LEFT*) Victor Petrenko skated under the patchwork banner of the Unified Team at the 1992 Olympics and won the gold medal over a generally uninspired field. He won his only world title a month later, beating career-long nemesis Kurt Browning. When he returned from the professional ranks to skate for Ukraine at the 1994 Games, he finished out of the medals.

(*OPPOSITE*) Marina Klimova and Sergei Ponomarenko are the only skaters to possess all three colors of Olympic medals. But they had to wait their turn to win the gold, superseded, first, by Jayne Torvill and Christopher Dean, and then by Natalia Bestemianova and Andrei Bukin. Klimova and Ponomarenko are still skating professionally and, in 1994–95, coached contenders Shae-Lynn Bourne and Victor Kraatz before the Canadian couple switched coaches again.

"Debi came out and skated well, and Caryn came out and was great, then Katarina had to skate … and she was fabulous."

Kurt Browning's Casablanca is one of the best, if not *the* best, singles free-skating programs ever designed. It is stuffed with difficult edges, dramatic artistic pauses, and jumps approached from unusual angles. Although he won the 1993 World Championships with it, he skated it better and with more energy at the 1993 Canadian nationals before a sold-out crowd of 17,000 screaming fans in Hamilton, Ontario. Browning lost his edge on one jump and crashed to the ice, but his showmanship was so keenly developed that he acted almost as if it had been part of the plan in the first place. That Browning was blazing a new artistic trail and doing it while Elvis Stojko was obviously nipping at his heels only added to the luster of the performance.

When Marina Klimova and Sergei Ponomarenko took to the ice for the free dance at the 1992 Olympics, they were facing 6,002 opponents: the defending world champions, Isabelle and Paul Duchesnay, who represented France, and 6,000 vocal French fans in the stands, who were acting almost like a hockey crowd. Because of their lead in the compulsory dances and Original Set Pattern (OSP), the Russian couple had the gold medal wrapped up unless they made a huge mistake. Their program, like the Duchesnays', had potential for mistakes because of the numerous difficult sections, but they presented a sensual, flawless performance. "It was incredible pressure with all they'd been through," said their agent, Michael Rosenberg. "They had the false-positive doping test at Europeans the year before, they had changed coaches from Natalia Doubova to Tatiana Tarasova, and there was the screaming French crowd. It was the most hostile, unbelievable crowd I'd ever seen. Marina and Sergei are both very tough people, but at the end, they both just collapsed."

SKATERS WHO WON AN OLYMPIC CHAMPIONSHIP BEFORE A WORLD CHAMPIONSHIP

MEN: Gillis Grafström, Sweden, 1920 (no World Championships were held from 1915–21)
Dick Button, U.S.A., 1948 (won 1948 world title)
Manfred Schnelldorfer, Germany, 1964 (won world title the next month)
Wolfgang Schwarz, Austria, 1968 (never won a world title)
John Curry, Great Britain, 1976 (won world title the next month)
Robin Cousins, Great Britain, 1980 (never won a world title)
Victor Petrenko, Ukraine, 1992 (won world title the next month)
Alexei Urmanov, Russia, 1994 (has not won a world title)

WOMEN: Magda Julin-Mauroy, Sweden, 1920 (never won a world title)
Dorothy Hamill, U.S.A., 1976 (won world title the next month)
Katarina Witt, East Germany, 1984 (won first world title the next month)

PAIRS: Maxi Herber and Ernst Baier, Germany, 1936 (won world title the next month)
Elisabeth Schwarz and Kurt Oppelt, Austria, 1956 (won world title the next month)
Ludmila Belousova and Oleg Protopopov, Soviet Union, 1964 (won 1965 world title)

DANCE: Oksana Gritschuk and Evgeny Platov, Russia, 1994 (won world title the next month)

MEDAL SWEEPS BY ONE COUNTRY AT THE WORLD CHAMPIONSHIPS

MEN:
Austria 1925: Willy Boeckl; Fritz Kachler; Otto Preissecker
Austria 1927: Boeckl; Preissecker; Karl Schafer
Austria 1928: Boeckl; Schafer; Hugo Distler
U.S.A. 1952: Dick Button; James Grogan; Hayes Jenkins
U.S.A. 1955: Hayes Jenkins; Ronnie Robertson; David Jenkins
U.S.A. 1956: Hayes Jenkins; Ronnie Robertson; David Jenkins

WOMEN:
U.S.A. 1991: Kristi Yamaguchi; Tonya Harding; Nancy Kerrigan

PAIRS:
Soviet Union 1969: Ulanov–Rodnina; Mishin–Moskvina; Protopopov–Belousova
Soviet Union 1988: Valova–Vasiliev; Gordeeva–Grinkov; Selezneva–Makarov

DANCE:
Britain 1955: Demmy–Westwood; Thomas–Weight; Lockwood–Radford
Britain 1956: Thomas–Weight; Jones–Markham; Rigby–Thompson
Commonwealth of Independent States 1992: Klimova–Ponomarenko; Usova–Zhulin; Gritschuk–Platov

MAXI HERBER AND ERNST BAIER OF GERMANY WERE PAIRS CHAMPIONS AT THE 1936 WINTER OLYMPICS IN GARMISCH, GERMANY, AND WON THE LAST FOUR WORLD CHAMPIONSHIPS BEFORE WORLD WAR II.

EIGHT

The Money Era: Professionals on the Rise

To many generations it was almost a dirty word. Now it has become a word almost without meaning.

Professional.

If professionalism is defined as accepting money for services rendered, then there is little difference between pro skaters and the top amateurs. Kurt Browning made a seven-figure income while still classified as an amateur. Elvis Stojko is rewarded handsomely, and justifiably, for the huge audiences he is able to attract to exhibitions at major arenas, at Major League ticket prices. So are Surya Bonaly and Philippe Candeloro and any other "amateur" skater whose mere presence on the marquee will guarantee a larger gate.

If professionalism is defined as demonstrating skill and dedication in pursuing specific work full-time, again the line between amateurs and pros became blurred some time ago. In fact, the pros are the ones who have made up ground in that area. Top amateur skaters have always put in a full day practicing their techniques; now the pros have upped their collective skill level, too. Amateur skaters, though, are still able to attend school or hold a part-time job, which would be impossible for a touring professional.

With the emergence of trust funds, amateur skaters, beginning in Canada with Brian Orser in the early 1980s, were able to cash in on their popularity and not lose their amateur status. Most of the income from exhibitions and TV commercials was deposited in trust with the governing body for skating in their country, and released to the athlete at the end of his or her amateur career. Led by Browning, the next generation of skaters was able to more freely use that trust-fund money when it was earned.

So the word "professional" has become less and less applicable, and skaters are officially designated as "eligible" or "ineligible" athletes. Eligible ones are permitted to compete in ISU events such as the World Championships, fall internationals, and Olympics, and ineligible ones may not. Where less than two decades

SHOW-STOPPERS: AS AN AMATEUR, GARY BEACOM EXCELLED IN SCHOOL FIGURES AND INNOVATIVE FREE-SKATING MOVES, BUT COMPETED IN THE SHADOWS OF BRIAN ORSER AND BRIAN POCKAR. AS A PROFESSIONAL SKATER, HE EXPANDED HIS CREATIVITY. IN THIS OFF-BEAT ROUTINE WITH PARTNER GIA GAUDAT, THEY PERFORM WITH SKATES ON THEIR HANDS IN A NUMBER CALLED "I THINK I'M LOSING MY MARBLES."

ago accepting money (more than $50) for a performance, or skating in the same show with professionals, or even being professional in a sport other than skating was enough to remove a skater's amateur status, practically the only way a skater becomes ineligible now is by participating in a competition that is not sanctioned by the ISU or its member associations.

What "turning pro" indicates now is simply the time when a skater determines that competing in the World Championships and Olympics is no longer his or her primary objective.

LIFE AFTER THE WORLDS

"There is more of a life after amateur skating than there was before," says world-renowned pairs coach Kerry Leitch of Cambridge, Ontario, who was forced to abandon his skating career in the early 1960s and become a teaching pro because he had signed a professional baseball contract, rendering him ineligible for amateur skating competitions.

"Up to ten or twelve years ago, when you reached the end of your amateur career, you either began teaching, or you joined Ice Capades or Ice Follies. You didn't need to do anything technically difficult … the crowd for those shows wanted entertainment.

"There are still those two avenues. But there are so many pro competitions, and tours like Stars on Ice provide a completely different kind of show. Stars on Ice draws a different audience than the production shows. Because of TV and the overall popularity of the sport, there is a much bigger market out there now for professional skating."

Skating fans – lifelong devotees or new converts – who tracked the careers of Kristi Yamaguchi or Kurt Browning on television do not suddenly become uninterested in their favorite skaters just because they have turned pro. Networks, facing splintering consumer markets and fierce competition, have taken note and found ways to keep these skaters, and the audience they bring with them, on the air.

Most of skating's biggest names have already had their own TV specials or have been the primary guest on somebody else's show. That's a trend that started with Peggy Fleming, but that has mushroomed in the 1990s. Sometimes a performance of a touring show will be taped for future television consumption. A version of Stars on Ice has appeared on North American TV the past few years, and in 1995, for the first time, the show was sold to networks in both Germany and France. Elvis Stojko's autumn cross-country tour has been packaged for both Canadian TV and Turner Broadcasting in the U.S.

Television is the driving force behind the explosion of professional competitions. At least a dozen pro events were held in the 1994–95 season, and the prevailing opinion at the time was that the number would soon thin out, because that season saw an unusual combination of circumstances: two Winter Olympics within three years and the Harding–Kerrigan incident.

But every single professional competition broadcast in prime time had ratings higher or equal to those of the 1995 World Championships in Birmingham, and so instead of declining, the number of major pro events actually climbed to fourteen for the 1995–96 season. That includes the open events – some new, some restructured pro events – in which ineligible and eligible skaters compete together for the same prize money. "The networks ordered even more figure skating. It makes sense for them for the numbers they draw compared to how much it costs to stage a pro event," said Kevin Albrecht of IMG, which owns Stars on Ice and helps administer several professional competitions, including the Canadian Pro Championships, open events, and the Olympic-winners-only Gold Championship.

Kristi Yamaguchi and Scott Hamilton each harvested $260,000 for winning their portion of the 1994 Gold Championship, and Hamilton gathered another $50,000 a couple of weeks later when he won the Canadian Pro Championships in, appropriately, Hamilton. Even to skaters accustomed to big money, that is not chump change.

The Canadian Pro, voted in a Professional Skaters' Guild survey as the best-run pro competition, proved so popular with live and television audiences that it immediately decided to return to Copps Coliseum for 1995, while other cities were pestering IMG to land the event for future years.

Among the other new pro events that bloomed after the 1994 Olympics were Ice Wars and the Fox Rock 'n' Roll Championships. Ice Wars is a transparent fabrication that pits U.S. skaters against skaters from the rest of the world in a team competition over two nights in two different cities. It offended purists with its almost hucksterish showmanship, even though the skaters – among them, Yamaguchi, Browning, Brian Boitano, Nancy Kerrigan, Oksana Baiul – were bona fide stars. "While we insiders say, 'Hey, that's pretty hokey,' the TV people are thrilled," counters Albrecht. "And remember that U.S. fans aren't quite as sophisticated as Canadians are."

Most revealing was the May 1995 release of the influential Q-ratings in the States, which measure celebrities on two components: the public's awareness of the celebrity, and the likability factor. In the athletes section, ten skaters had scores high enough to register … every single one of them was a professional. That's an indication that, rather than forgetting professionals, the general public recognizes them more than they did as amateurs. It takes a number of years of widespread exposure for a skater to push into the limelight that extends beyond skating audiences, unless, of course, the skater is Nancy Kerrigan or Tonya Harding.

RIGHT ON THE BUTTON

The granddaddy of pro skating events is Dick Button's World Pro Championship in Landover, Maryland. Button, who for several years owned the American TV rights to the amateur World Championships, originally tried to convince the ISU in 1973 that a professional competition would be viable. He promoted a competition in Japan that year with the likes of Janet Lynn, John Misha Petkevich, Donald Jackson, and the Protopopovs, but the ISU turned up its collective nose at the idea. Pros, the amateur governing body felt, were over the hill. In 1980, Button established the World Pro at Landover, and it has become one of America's most successful events. In the 1994–95 season, NBC earned a 12.9 audience share with Landover, while its highest rating from the World Championships in Birmingham was 9.3. Hamilton says that the biggest need in pro skating is for the events to have staying power and cites Landover as the example: it has developed a following and a history, and a devoted audience who can recite details of the competition that stretch back several years.

With the proliferation of pro events in the mid-nineties, Button has had his vision vindicated. His company, Candid Productions, is involved in several other competitions, including the Championship of Champions, the Gold Championship, and the World Team Championship. A trademark of a Button production is that it's a skater's event: sometimes the rosters are huge, because Button usually insists that all four disciplines be included, a practice not all promoters stick to or can afford. But then, Button was a skater – *the* skater of his time – and still has an athlete's sensibilities.

Although the World Pro always attracted a big crowd and found a reliable television audience, many critics inside the sport suspected, fairly or unfairly, that pro competitions were popularity contests, based on whoever was the biggest gate attraction at the time. It didn't help that the pros chose to differentiate themselves from amateurs by marking scores out of ten, and that so many of the scores were in fact perfect 10s.

"But Dick Button took a gigantic step for pro skating when he excused himself from selecting the judges," said Kerry Leitch, who is also president of the International Professional Skating Union, a coaches organization formed at the 1963 World Championships. "That gave a lot more credibility to professional competitions. A lot of thought went into who the judges would be. They had to have a high profile, and also a high level of skating knowledge."

The results are less predictable now – a good example is the unexpected trio of victories in the watershed 1994–95 fall season by Switzerland's Denise Biellmann, whose name does not help sell many tickets in North America. Although most pro competitions still use total points rather than ordinals to determine winners, several of the newer competitions have adopted the six-point scoring system of amateurs because it is more familiar to the huge audiences reared on amateur skating. Rules also differ from event to event, which may provide variety, but drives the skaters and judges crazy.

Leitch recalls that when he started judging professional events, the showmanship was high but the technical level low. Brilliant skaters like Dorothy Hamill would compete without doing a triple jump, but "now pros are skating up to the standards that amateurs were. It's a high priority now to even be selected to

BRIAN BOITANO SPEARHEADED THE DRIVE TO ALLOW PROFESSIONAL SKATERS TO BE REINSTATED TO THE AMATEUR RANKS, A CAMPAIGN THAT WAS WON IN TIME FOR THE 1994 OLYMPICS. BOITANO, WHOSE TECHNICAL FORM IS STILL ARGUABLY THE BEST IN THE WORLD, WON THE LEGENDARY BATTLE OF THE BRIANS AT THE 1988 OLYMPICS, THE EVENT THAT LAUNCHED SKATING ON ITS CLIMB IN POPULARITY.

compete. I think, especially in Canada, there's a more knowledgeable audience overall. There's been more television. Before, people watched it just because they enjoyed it. Now they also know it."

It remains to be seen if professional events will erode the status of amateur competitions, which was the course that tennis followed in the 1970s. In one sense, anything that broadens skating's base is good for everyone in the sport. In another, the flood of pro events means a smaller percentage of the pie for the amateurs, although the pie itself is much bigger. "I don't think you can be happy or sad. It's just happening" is the pragmatic approach of David Dore, director-general of the Canadian Figure Skating Association, and one of the most powerful men in skating circles. "I don't have a question about its legitimacy." Dore has been closely watching the emergence of pro skating for several years and at one time felt Canada should be the first nation to stage an international pro–am event. He and other Canadian executives backed off as the USFSA staged the first pro–ams, while the Canadians preferred to "do what we do best. We teach people to skate. We develop and create champions." But Dore continues to monitor the situation closely.

The prominent promoters and agents, such as IMG, Michael Rosenberg, Mike Berg, and Tom Collins, maintain a communicative relationship with the amateur governing bodies because it's mutually beneficial. "Without the skaters there would be no stars," says Collins, whose rights fees for his yearly spring tour have contributed as much as one-fifth of the USFSA's annual budget.

FASTER AND LONGER

A pro event still has less speed and intensity than a top amateur competition, because competition is not the main focus of pro skaters. But the gap is closing. Being a pro is more technically demanding now, both on tour and in competition, than it was a decade ago. The two pioneers of the new professionalism have been a pair of American Olympic champions, Brian Boitano and Scott Hamilton. Boitano established a new technical standard, still landing triple Axels in his show programs many years after his contemporaries had abandoned them. His dedication to training and his love of competition enabled him to return to the amateur ranks six years after his Olympic victory, with a reasonable expectation of doing well. Other pros had to keep up, or at least try to.

Hamilton provides the template for the contemporary professional skater. Olympic and four-time world champion, he was a beacon of artistry when athleticism, led by Brian Orser, Alexander Fadeev, Josef Sabovcik, and Boitano, was on the rise at the world level. The professional scene has changed radically since he appeared in 1984, but he has managed to stay one step ahead of the game. More than a decade later, against far younger skaters, he was able to win major championships, with major earnings. He has had dozens of disciples – Kurt Browning and Kristi Yamaguchi, among them – who study the way he controls a crowd, projects himself with humor, humility, and more than a little outrageousness, and night after night gives the audience at least what they came to see, if not more. He began his pro career with Ice Capades, but IMG, his management company, built their own tour, Stars on Ice, around him. Stars, as the name implies, plays on the celebrity status of its members. Other tours have followed suit. They are to skating what rockers are to music.

Until Hamilton rewrote the script, skaters faded into the background after they turned professional – a logical development, since their work was rarely seen on TV and the newspapers no longer covered them once they stopped seeking world titles. Ron Shaver, a brilliant free skater who had the misfortune of being Canadian in the same era as Toller Cranston, rose as high as fifth in the world and was well-known by the North American skating public. He joined Ice Capades as a headliner and eventually became the show's performance director. But when a series of professional World Cup-style championships was tried in Canada in the early 1980s it failed in large part, Shaver says, because the competitors, himself included, had disappeared from the public consciousness.

Only the very few who had been mythologized – Cranston, Fleming, Robin Cousins, and Dorothy Hamill – were untouched by time. As each new wave of Olympians flooded the professional ranks, they would wash those before them down the marquee, in turn to have themselves pushed to second billing four years later.

"My whole strategy when I turned pro was that whatever I did as an amateur was behind me now," Hamilton said. "It would open doors for me, but I wanted the long term. It was important to create things for myself in the pros. The idea is to dictate the direction of your career and create your own following. Let people know what they can expect, and that it will be good. Try to change just enough that you're unpredictable.

"So Brian Boitano comes along and it doesn't change what I'm doing at all. Skaters come along with more marquee value, but you're okay if you've planned it right. I'll have withstood three Olympic champions, plus Brian Orser and Kurt Browning, who are fabulous."

Many of the newcomers are fabulous. They hooked onto an artistic style while they were still amateurs and most of them have absorbed even more showmanship by skating in shows with professionals. Tom Collins runs the ISU-related Campbell's Soups World Tour of Figure Skating Champions, which traverses the U.S. directly after the Worlds with a roster of the top skaters from that competition. To suit a changing marketplace, in recent years the bill has also included a sprinkling of professionals. The amateurs use the pros as role models; the pros are invigorated by the energetic amateurs. And there's not that much difference between the two groups. "Years ago we'd get a kid skating with his head down on tour," Collins said. "Now they *work* the audience. They never used to do that."

Collins also points out that talented show skaters aren't always the most recognizable names. Canadian pairs team Christine Hough and Doug Ladret are

FROM THE MOMENT SHE BURST
ONTO THE WORLD SCENE IN 1993,
OKSANA BAIUL SHOWED A
MATURITY AND ARTISTRY FAR
BEYOND HER YEARS. HERE, ON THE
1995 TOM COLLINS TOUR STOP AT
NEW YORK CITY, SHE THROWS
HERSELF INTO HER NUMBER.

good examples. As an amateur, Canadian Gary Beacom always skated in the shadow of Brian Orser and never won a national senior title, but always unveiled remarkably creative programs that were ahead of their time. "He's on tour with us," said Collins, "and does a variety number where he and Gia Gaudat skate on all fours. It's a great act that gets away from traditional skating."

THE PRODUCTION SHOWS

Tom Collins's tour presents one skater's (or pair's or dance team's) program after another, because little time is available to rehearse integrated routines. Stars on Ice, Skate the Nation, the Boitano–Witt shows, Elvis Stojko's cross-country caravan, and other star-driven shows are of a similar genre, even though they have company numbers that are worked up and polished through heavy practice. The

A CHORUS LINE: BARBARA UNDERHILL, MICHELLE MENZIES, CHRISTINE HOUGH, SUSAN HUMPHREYS, AND JOSÉE CHOUINARD IN THE ROLLING STONES PRODUCTION NUMBER ON THE 1995 SKATE THE NATION TOUR.

WILL YOU MARRY ME? IN FRONT OF A PACKED HOUSE AT MAPLE LEAF GARDENS DURING THE 1995 STARS ON ICE TOUR, KURT BROWNING GRABBED A MICROPHONE AND PROPOSED TO HIS GIRLFRIEND, SONIA RODRIGUEZ.

YES, I WILL. BROWNING AND RODRIGUEZ EMBRACE AT ICE LEVEL AFTER SHE SAID YES.

guiding principle is that people pay to be entertained by skaters they've seen on television. The shows are living, changing organisms that depend on a rapport with the crowd. The most extreme, and touching, example may have occurred on April 21, 1995, at Maple Leaf Gardens in Toronto. During a pause in the action of Stars on Ice, Kurt Browning spontaneously proposed to his girlfriend, Sonia Rodriguez, in front of 16,000 onlookers, who were stunned into silence, then roared with approval when Rodriguez came out of the audience and accepted. Browning then carried her around the ice.

One of the most compelling attractions of the new tours is that they are profoundly human, driven by the personalities of the skaters, who are expected to interact with the crowd. Costumes may be elaborate, but they will never eclipse the identity of the skaters who wear them. The entire cast is well-known, and this is a fundamental departure from the traditional ice-show format that has endured through most of the twentieth century, where chorus lines and in-character production numbers are the main fare, spiced by a solo or two from the principal skaters.

The convenient myth is that the lavish production show originated with Sonja Henie, but she did not invent it. Rather, she revived it and elevated it to an art form. Production shows actually find their roots in the skating carnivals that date back to the 1700s but at the turn of the century began appearing regularly at local clubs, particularly the Toronto Skating Club, beginning its long history of elaborate carnivals. In the same period, Russian clubs had ice shows choreographed by ballet masters. They were extravagant, even if the skating might have been below par, and established the connection between Russian skaters and their heritage of classical dance.

Most top performers got their first exposure to an audience through a club carnival: Kurt Browning played a skunk in Caroline, Alberta; broadcaster Debbi Wilkes, a world pairs silver medalist, played Tinker Bell in Unionville, Ontario; others have been daffodils or puppets.

The first full-scale professional show in North America was imported to New York's Hippodrome in 1915 from the Admiral Palast in Berlin, where it had originated seven years earlier. It starred a young skating sensation who predated Cher and Madonna in the use of a single name: Charlotte. Her family name was Oelschlagel, but it was never used. *Flirting in St. Moritz* was originally slotted for a six-week stand, but it played to capacity crowds for 300 consecutive days, a Broadway record at the time. The next year, 400,000 pairs of skates were reportedly sold in the U.S. In response, some hotels, including the Sherman in Chicago and the Biltmore and Waldorf-Astoria in New York, installed small indoor rinks, called tank ice, so that entertainers could skate during their acts.

During the 1920s, the ice show lay dormant. But immediately after the 1936 Olympics, Henie stormed back into the U.S., where she had won the 1930 World Championship and 1932 Olympics, to tour nine American cities, her first venture as a pro. She formed a brilliantly successful partnership – Hollywood Ice Revues drew capacity crowds everywhere – with promoter Arthur Wirtz, although they eventually went their separate ways in the late 1940s. Henie's fame and success empowered female athletes: with her live shows and movies she became the first female athlete to earn $1 million. But she also crystallized the American perception that the most worthwhile champion is the Snow White, snow queen, stereotype.

In 1936, the same winter that Henie began her barnstorming pro career, Shipstad and Johnson's Ice Follies was born in Tulsa, Oklahoma. With the Depression, there were only twenty-three skaters in the original troupe, but the show quickly caught on and became a mainstay on the international skating scene. Roy Shipstad was famous for his 30 mph (50 km/h) spread-eagle exit from the ice. He and his brother Eddie have both been elected to the U.S. Figure Skating Hall of Fame.

In 1940, John Harris formed Ice Capades in California, bringing operettas and musicals to the ice-show format. From the start, ice dancing was a big part of Capades. Dancers Robert Dench and Rosemarie Stewart were among the inaugural headliners, and Rona and Cliff Thaell, as Ice Capades principals, helped popularize ice dancing.

In 1944, the triumvirate of ice shows was completed by the formation of Holiday on Ice, the first show to have its own portable ice-rink equipment, enabling Holiday to visit cities and towns that had never before experienced skating.

THE SHOW IS THE THING

Follies, Capades, and Holiday were the foundation of professional skating for decades. Each had its own style, but each depended on stunning production numbers, a large, low-paid chorus line, and a few individual stars. In North America, the rivalry eventually boiled down to two troupes – Capades and Follies.

"They were extremely competitive," said Ron Shaver, who started a ten-year Ice Capades career in June 1977, after winning his only Canadian Championship that spring. "We rushed to get bookings ahead of them, and it was a big thing to outdraw them. The Follies in my time was known as the ensemble group that didn't pay the money, while the Capades tended to hire the amateurs as they turned pro.

"Capades sent a representative to nationals every year. George Ebby, who ran the show, came to me after my first senior nationals in 1973 and said, 'I know you're not ready to turn pro now, but give us a call when you are.'

"It was a total jump to pro, but it was very easy for me. You talk about the star system they have now … it was already in place when I joined. Not to the same extent as with Dorothy Hamill, who got a limousine from door to door, but [four-time Canadian champion] Lynn Nightingale and I would have our own private or semiprivate dressing rooms. You'd do two numbers in the show and bow a bit at the end.

"We had all kinds of costuming. I did gangster things, I did space things, I did pirate things, whatever the production called for. Generally the names of the shows were pretty broad, like 'Hallelujah Hollywood,' whatever that meant, or 'Bravo America,' which you can imagine went over pretty well in Canada.

"Kids in the chorus line made good money to live on, but nothing to save. You could leave after five years and have saved nothing, but the purpose of a show for them in those days was to travel for three or four years and have a good time. You worked very, very hard, averaging nine shows a week and a rehearsal every day."

Shelley Barnett is a Canadian precision-skating coach who spent a year with Follies heir Disney on Ice as an ensemble member and later as understudy to world champion Dianne de Leeuw. She considers show skating a valuable experience and she encourages her better skaters to give it a try, but not if they have any kind of weight problem. "They set unrealistic weight demands and it's especially tough to maintain a diet if you're on the road," Barnett said. "Every Saturday morning they'd weigh you. I made the weight they set for me, then they lowered my requirement." Barnett said she learned how to eat properly under less than ideal conditions but pointed to the potential for anorexia nervosa and bulimia, two eating disorders that have afflicted young women in skating and gymnastics.

Capades and Follies were good business, playing major arenas in New York and Montreal, but also packing smaller rinks in Des Moines, Iowa, or London, Ontario. Shaver signed for "$100,000 a year, which was pretty good at the time,

German skating star Charlotte, who never used her last name (Oelschlagel), had a three-year run at New York's Hippodrome beginning in 1915, and was featured in several advertisements, including this one from 1916.

EVERYBODY LOVES PAIRS. TWO OF THE GREATEST SINGLES SKATERS IN THE LAST HALF-CENTURY, 1968 OLYMPIC CHAMPION PEGGY FLEMING AND 1980 OLYMPIC CHAMPION ROBIN COUSINS, TEAM UP FOR A PAIRS CARRY, ON TOUR DURING THE EARLY 1980S.

but even if you translated it into today's dollars, you couldn't touch an Elvis or a Kurt for that."

Ice Capades has survived, but not without some pain. The show went through enormous financial difficulties, was bought by Dorothy Hamill, who breathed life into it by designing and skating in its Cinderella tour. It was purchased again, this time by International Family Entertainment, evangelist Pat Robertson's company.

There were two touring companies, Cinderella and Hansel and Gretel, but the latter was canceled in mid-season, the first time in Capades history a show was terminated. In the 1996 season an all-new production is to hit the road.

Ice Follies, meanwhile, was bought by the Disney Corporation, which remodeled it into Walt Disney's World on Ice and quickly identified its primary market: young children. The children are accompanied to the arena by parents with their wallets. Disney has three different productions in operation in any one year, dropping one theme and adding another each season. Since the themes are Disney movies – *Aladdin, Beauty and the Beast, Snow White, The Lion King* – it is an enormous cross-marketing venture. The movies sell the skating show and vice versa, and both sell merchandise, readily available at concession stands. Gauging its audience acutely, Disney is crammed with larger-than-life skaters in familiar movie-role costumes, which grabs and holds a young fan's attention. The skating may be secondary, but the experience is a memorable one for the children.

Disney, however, may have a competitor in the cross-marketing game. Warner Brothers on Ice, another movie-studio project, booked some sites across North America for a 1994–95 tour, but it didn't get off the ground.

As well as the annual tours, there are ad hoc ones centered on certain stars. Jayne Torvill and Christopher Dean have had several; some wildly successful, some that had trouble cracking the market. Among the many things that make Torvill and Dean unique is the fact that they are the only dancers around whom an ice show could have been built in this half of the century.

In recent years, theater shows have become popular again. In 1995 Nutcracker on Ice offered two versions of the ballet: an arena tour that had Oksana Baiul, Brian Boitano, and Victor Petrenko in leading roles; and a scaled-down rendition starring Brian Orser. Often skated on tank ice, the largest of which measured sixty feet by forty feet (18 m by 12 m), the tour "played town theaters and concert halls from Owen Sound to Honolulu," said Orser. "You adjust when you go on the tank ice – you just have to make everything smaller." The biggest shock for Orser came when he was a late addition to the inaugural Canadian Pro Championships and stepped onto the huge ice surface at Copps Coliseum in Hamilton after weeks on the tank ice. In 1995–96 Orser joined Peggy Fleming in the larger production.

There are often stationary skating shows at warm-weather attractions like Knott's Berry Farm, Cyprus Gardens, Busch Gardens, Sea World, and Canada's Wonderland, even at gambling resorts. Caryn Kadavy headlined a five-week show at Harrah's in Lake Tahoe, Nevada, which featured Josef Sabovcik, Anita Hartshorn, and Frank Sweiding. Plastic or "slick" ice has meant that smaller productions can be staged virtually anywhere. Skaters aren't thrilled by the oily surface, but the use of plastic ice provides more jobs for pros.

PERFORM, NO MATTER WHAT

If there is a guiding principle in a professional skater's mentality, it is the old circus maxim that the show must go on. "There are no excuses as a pro," says Brian Orser. "People don't want to hear that you're not feeling well, or they should have seen you last night in another city. They paid to see you ... now. You adjust, and do it."

Top amateurs first learn this on Tom Collins's tour. Collins treats the skaters well, pays them handsomely, boards them in first-class hotels, and takes them to basketball or baseball games on their nights off. But the tour is still a grind, an accurate introduction to the rigors of professional touring. Tour rookies face daily performance expectations for the first time. And while the atmosphere is much looser than it is for amateur competition, there are still competitive benchmarks. The ultimate compliment for a skater is that other tour members are enticed to watch you perform. Janet Lynn, the best skater who never won, accomplished this many nights, even late in the tour. And since triple jumps became the norm at the upper levels, performers have paid close attention to who is doing what jump. A silent competition exists to see who can do the most. Debi Thomas and Katarina Witt, who staged three years of marvelous duels at the top of the women's standings, were also into jumping one-upmanship on the 1988 Tom Collins tour.

Although the pro life is more difficult in some aspects – the travel, the baseball-like daily performances, the lack of training time – than the amateur, it is easier in others. A triple turned into a double or a double singled isn't the end of the world, unless it happens every night. And the income level is much higher. Nancy Kerrigan's $10-million deal with Disney has been well publicized, but it's also estimated that the top-five draws on the Tour of World Figure Skating Champions gross nearly $1 million apiece for that tour alone. Elsewhere the biggest names can command $50,000 for a single performance, $15,000 per for a steady string of them. While winning pro championships is good for the ego and the pocketbook, it may eventually become necessary. If professional skating continues to expand, in order to command the big tour fees it might become essential to have the boost of a world or national pro title.

The most famous pros have the greatest financial and professional freedom, but a variety of career paths are open to those who come to the end of their amateur days: pro competitions; production tours; small stationary shows; and there's still the teaching-pro route, the backbone of all skating. Plus there is an expanding market for star-based tours. Stars on Ice has toured South America and in 1996 is scheduled to tour the Far East.

"Some people are better competitors, some people are better at just performing in the show," said Hamilton. "I'm happy that there are so many opportunities for skaters in pro now. You can pick the lifestyle that suits you."

(*OPPOSITE*) NO ONE WHO WAS THERE WILL EVER FORGET THE ONCE-IN-A-LIFETIME FREE SKATE THAT GAVE ELIZABETH MANLEY THE SILVER MEDAL AT THE 1988 OLYMPICS. WHEN SHE APPEARED ON ELVIS STOJKO'S TOUR, DURING WHICH THIS COQUETTISH PICTURE WAS TAKEN, MANLEY WAS IN THE BEST SKATING CONDITION SHE'D BEEN IN SINCE THE "NIGHT TO REMEMBER." MANLEY'S CAREER HAS BEEN FILLED WITH PEAKS AND VALLEYS, BOTH BEFORE AND AFTER THE CALGARY GAMES.

ELVIS STOJKO'S WORLD MEDALS.

NINE

The Emergence of
Precision Skating

I f figure skating is enjoying unprecedented popularity with one or two skaters on the ice at a time, how about with a couple of dozen? Apparently there is strength in numbers, because precision skating is the popular new kid on the block. It's expanding rapidly in Canada and it's the fastest-growing division of the United States Figure Skating Association.

Nearly 600 precision teams exist in Canada, and the 1995 national championships at Calgary drew a record ninety-seven entrants. The 1996 nationals at Copps Coliseum were expected to do at least as well.

In the U.S. there are 294 teams, and precision has blossomed to the point where the 1995 nationals in San Diego attracted a title sponsor, the U.S. Postal Service, and got an hour's exposure on ABC-TV. The precision team at the University of Miami of Ohio became the first collegiate figure-skating team in the country to have precision skating recognized as a varsity sport.

Precision is a relatively new phenomenon, but it helps plug a huge gap in competitive skating. Skaters who discover that their talent or commitment is not up to the demands of the regular competitive stream still have an opportunity to qualify for a national, even international, championship by joining a precision group. Some skaters who aren't suited to the inherent pressure and loneliness of singles events thrive in the team atmosphere of precision.

TEAM SURPRISE OF SWEDEN IS CONSIDERED THE TOP PRECISION SKATING TEAM IN THE WORLD, A RANKING THAT WAS RICHLY DESERVED AFTER THEY WON THE TWO PREMIER NORTH AMERICAN INVITATIONAL EVENTS IN TORONTO AND DETROIT DURING THE 1994–95 SEASON. SOME OBSERVERS SAY THAT THE SWEDISH STRENGTH IN PRECISION COMES BECAUSE SO LITTLE ATTENTION IS PAID TO DEVELOPING A SUCCESSION OF SINGLES SKATERS AT THE NATIONAL LEVEL THAT GOOD, BUT FRUSTRATED, SINGLES SKATERS TURN TO THE TEAM EVENT.

"We've got girls on the team who would never have had a chance to even get to a sectional in singles skating, and now they get to go to nationals," says Shelley Barnett, a former singles skater and one of the most successful precision coaches in Canada. Her Ice Image squads from Burlington, Ontario, won two successive Canadian novice championships and were bronze medalists at the junior level.

Precision teams comprise anywhere from twelve to twenty-four athletes, who skate in unison to create intricate, high-speed patterns that have a stunning visual impact.

"The ultimate is to take twenty-four bodies and clone them so they look like one person on the ice," explains Doug Steele, a former Canadian Figure Skating Association president. "In a line, if the girl on the end is not doing the same as everyone else, then the team is penalized. It is definitely not an individual sport and it never will be. It's the whole team-spirit thing that is important."

GOING INTERNATIONAL

Despite its late entry into the skating public's consciousness, precision has quickly gathered momentum. In 1992 the International Skating Union formed its first standing committee on precision. Patricia French of Buffalo, New York, is the chair. Other members include Steele and representatives from Finland, France, and Switzerland. Their mandate is to develop rules, train judges, and establish competition schedules. They are also working toward having the ISU approve an official world championship for precision in 1998. As part of the preparations, a World Challenge Cup will probably be held in Boston during April, 1996. A second World Challenge Cup is tentatively planned for Turku, Finland, in 1997. If precision advocates are successful, the 1997 event will act as a qualifying round for the first world championship the following year. And could the Olympics be far behind?

"I suppose we have that in mind, but it's a long, slow process," says Steele. "We couldn't have it in as a demonstration sport until at least 2002, which means it would be at least 2006 before it could be in the Olympics."

And that's if the International Olympic Committee consents to yet another judged sport joining the Olympic family. For now, precision organizers are content and busy, broadening their grassroots programs and spreading the sport into the international arena.

The major attractions each year are invitationals, which are paired for the sake of travel economy. One year the events are in Europe, the next in North America. Successful international invitationals were held in Laval, Quebec, but they did not have official ISU status. The first sanctioned international event in Canada was Precision Canada, at Varsity Arena in central Toronto, in December, 1994. Precision Canada was paired with the primary American competition, the Snowflake, at Detroit in January, so that European teams could attend both competitions. A similar twinning of events in Finland and Sweden in alternate years makes it more affordable for Canadian and American teams to participate. There are also competitions in Lee Valley, Great Britain; Milan, Italy; and Rouen, France.

The most highly regarded precision team in the world is Team Surprise, representing Uddevalla Konstaknings Forening, a club in Vodevalla, Sweden. Team Surprise won both Precision Canada and the Snowflake. Five of the twenty-four Swedes were men, fueling the continuing controversy over whether men actually strengthen a precision team. Some argue that the Swedes' triumphs prove that they do. Others say that if the five men were removed, the Swedes would still have nineteen superb precision skaters good enough to win.

Some teams in Canada have male members, but generally precision is still the domain of female skaters. At the adult level, what men offer in any added strength to a precision line can often be negated by the physical imbalances. Precision skating works in lines, with athletes of similar sizes and abilities linked for a cohesive look. If the size difference is too dramatic, problems occur when a skater tries to drape his or her arms over the shoulders of the adjacent skaters, and holding the line straight becomes difficult.

INCREASING SKILL LEVEL

As the sport evolves, coaches and judges are starting to demand more intricate and creative moves, and the use of edges is becoming as important as it is to singles skating and ice dancing. "We're not walking on skates anymore," says Margaret Faulkner, chair of the precision committee of the USFSA.

At the junior and senior level, competitions involve both a short (two minutes forty seconds) and long (no more than four minutes thirty seconds) program. As in singles or pairs, there are required elements in the short program.

Lifts are not allowed, and some sequences – such as a line moving backward in a spiral with another line passing through it in a forward lunge – are about to be banned because they are too dangerous, but overall, precision encourages creativity. A competition can send the audience to the exits in a hurry if every team performs variations on the same theme. At the same time, however, the basic principles of precision must be maintained, because the discipline's strength lies in its uniqueness. It is not a grouping together of singles skating elements, and it depends on mass movement to create a distinct effect.

"We don't want to see twenty-four skaters trying to do camel spins or sit spins," says Steele. "This is not show biz. It's not a dance routine. It's not dancing drills. It's an athletic endeavor. One of the teams was doing a Send in the Clowns routine, where the girls were wearing costumes half one color, half another, with red noses and clown hats. We said, 'Could you see Josée Chouinard skating to that, in those costumes? No? So then why are you?' If we want to be considered an Olympic kind of sport we have to act like it."

MIDWEST U.S.A.: BIRTHPLACE OF PRECISION

To arrive at the point where its leaders can even fantasize about the Olympics, precision skating has traveled a long road in a short time. In the early part of the century a form of hand-to-hand group skating existed in both Ottawa and New York, involving eight to sixteen skaters, usually coupled. These groups, called Lancers, formed lines facing each other and executed moves to a caller, like square dancing. This may have been a rudimentary form of precision skating, but the real birth of the sport took place in Ann Arbor, Michigan, in the early 1960s.

The grandfather of precision skating is Dr. Richard Porter of the Ann Arbor

ONE OF AMERICA'S BEST TEAMS, THE STARLETTES OF BARRINGTON, ILLINOIS, SHOW GOOD INA BAUER FORM IN THEIR THREE-LINE BLOCK FORMATION AT THE U.S. NATIONAL CHAMPIONSHIPS.

Skating Club. Dr. Porter recognized that skating was losing teenage athletes, mostly women, because they were no longer willing or able to keep up with the competitive or test streams of "regular" figure skating. Searching for an attraction to hold those skaters in the sport a little longer – a motivation that still exists today as more and more community clubs form precision teams – he founded the world's first formal precision team and called them the Hockettes. The name was chosen as a parody on the famous chorus line of the Radio City Rockettes of New York, but it had a secondary pun, as well. The group got its initial public exposure performing during the intermissions of hockey games at the University of Michigan.

In the early years, precision was more closely aligned to drum and bugle corps or marching bands. It was basically a kick line. But Dr. Porter and his skaters began to improvise, adding configurations and steps.

The Ann Arbor team was the Johnny Appleseed of precision skating, performing a lot of exhibitions throughout the Midwest and planting the idea of precision skating everywhere it appeared.

Meanwhile, on the West Coast, a drill-team-on-ice competition began at Lake Arrowhead, California, in 1968, but the Midwest version involved more figure-skating moves and became the template for precision skating.

By 1972 there were enough teams in Michigan, Indiana, and Ohio to add precision skating to the Tri-State Championships, the first official precision competition.

The small town of Ilderton, outside of London, Ontario, was the site of the first competition in Canada, in 1979. The Hockettes, well advanced in the sport, attended and won easily. "But from there, the Canadians took the ball and ran with it," says Faulkner, a Toronto-born American who is a world judge in ice dancing and ISU-accredited judge in singles and pairs. "We had the organization in the States, but they had the skaters."

When David Dore, then president of the CFSA, asked Doug Steele to take over the precision-skating portfolio in 1982, Steele reported the appointment to his wife, Patricia, who asked, "What's precision skating?" Steele replied, "I don't really know." He soon found out. In 1983, the year before the Americans had their first formal national championship at Bowling Green, the Canadians tacked a loosely knit national championship onto the back of the Ilderton international. There had been 168 teams in the international event and sixty-nine entered the one-day Canadian Championships.

Now, as well as the Americans and Canadians, host cities of international events can expect to see teams from Finland, Sweden, Japan, Italy, Great Britain, Russia, South Africa, and Switzerland. Canada and Australia have had exchange visits of precision teams.

RECREATIONAL AND ELITE LEVELS

In the U.S., the largest number of, and strongest, teams come from the Midwest, where the sport was born and where clubs cater more to skaters who don't enter the singles competitive stream. In Canada, good young teams are emerging from Burlington, Unionville, and Brampton, all in Ontario. The most highly regarded senior programs are Black Ice from Toronto and Les Pirouettes of Laval. Les Pirouettes exemplify Quebec's spectacular improvement at all levels of skating since the nationals were held in Montreal in 1983. "They have a lot of skaters to draw upon. They have a lot of money in corporate sponsors to back them," said Steele. "And they have an incredibly creative coach in Lynn Forget, who has choreographic brilliance. They also strive for excellence. Not just in precision but in all skating, Quebec has this motivation. Their skaters are all well trained, well groomed, and well polished."

As precision broadens its scope and skill level, a greater commitment is required from skaters and coaches who want to compete at the highest level. Barnett says that precision is becoming so strong that in the future it will be an elite sport, like the upper reaches of "regular" figure skating.

Steele concurs. "There are two different tiers. There's a very definite recreational base and a very definite elite section that does not want to think of itself as recreational."

"It's much more difficult than people think," says Faulkner. "One of the hardest things in ice dancing and pairs is the difficulty of achieving the unison. For precision, take that difficulty and multiply it by eight." The sheer number of athletes also creates another problem for coaches: the psychological component of competition. "The hardest part is trying to motivate twenty-four girls and keep control of twenty-four girls and their emotions at a competition," says Shelley Barnett. "With a singles skater it's easier to get a sense of how they're feeling, and then you deal with it."

While coaching is one of the most important ingredients in any branch of figure skating, it may mean even more to precision. Every performance has the unmistakable stamp of coach and/or choreographer (they're often the same person) all over it. A team is only as strong as its weakest link and it's up to the choreographer to both hide that weakest link and implement programs that are not beyond that skater's reach.

A GROWTH INDUSTRY

Because precision is attracting increasing numbers of skaters, to the point where they are the majority of members in some clubs, the sport is developing a strong power base, particularly in Canada. Within skating organizations, they will be a political force to be reckoned with.

More and more clubs are discovering that precision teams provide an outlet for many skaters well into adulthood. In fact, the USFSA has a masters division – twenty-five years of age and older, with 75 percent of the team being thirty-five or older – at its national championships. And precision teams provide ready-made acts for the hundreds of clubs that stage an annual skating carnival. It may appear that precision is nothing more than an outgrowth of carnival skating, but the quickest way to incur the wrath of a precision supporter is to suggest that it's really just Ice Follies for locals. The edges, stroking power, and rhythms sought by choreographers and judges are becoming more demanding each year. What started out as a just-for-fun sport is now a highly competitive one. Members of the international committee, which developed a unified rules package out of the once-disparate Canadian and American regulations, are in constant contact with each other by fax, reporting new developments from various competitions. Those innovations establish new standards for the sport.

The name "precision" itself may not remain in vogue much longer. The ISU defines the disciplines of figure skating as singles, pairs, ice dance, and team skating. Team skating usually meant "fours," which is two pairs on the ice at a time. Since

only Canada – and sometimes the U.S. – has enough pairs depth for fours competitions, precision officials are hoping team skating will come to be synonymous with precision. In fact, they're emphasizing "team" rather than "precision" whenever they can. It's a better marketing tool, and it focuses on what supporters say is precision's number-one draw for athletes: being part of a team with common goals.

Because precision skating has such a brief history, its identity is still evolving. And as more athletes grow up with precision, rather than switching to it from another discipline, it will evolve even further.

Shelley Barnett skated with Disney on Ice for one season, in 1979. When she returned to coach amateur skaters in Windsor, Ontario, she and Lee Armstrong, a former Canadian novice and junior singles champion, were asked by club officials to handle the new precision division.

"They figured anyone who had skated in a line might have some clue about it," Barnett says with a laugh. "That wasn't true at all. It's nothing like a line show, but it's similar to ice dance."

HIGHLY RANKED BLACK ICE FROM TORONTO. AT THE UPPER LEVELS, PRECISION TEAMS ARE DEMANDING MORE SKILL AND DEDICATION. "FOR THE BEST TEAMS, IT WILL BECOME AN ELITE SPORT," SAYS BURLINGTON COACH SHELLEY BARNETT.

Silver Blades, Silver Screen: Skating and the Movies

Movie makers have always been quick to jump on whatever is in vogue and give it a good hard ride, so it's no surprise that the 1990s have seen an increase in skating films.

Almost all of them have been made-for-TV movies, a genre that latches onto what's current and hot and gets it to the marketplace quickly. Thus it took less than four months for *Tonya and Nancy: The Inside Story* to be written, cast, taped, and brought to television as a full-length movie.

And it was just a year, almost to the day, after Oksana Baiul won the 1994 Olympics that her emotional life story was dramatized in a CBS movie called *A Promise Kept*. Baiul was played by fifteen-year-old actress Monica Kenna, but the double for on-ice scenes was an actual competitive skater. Bridget McErlane of Meadville, Pennsylvania, skates for the Figure Skating Club of Erie and was eighth in the novice ladies event at the 1995 North Atlantic regionals.

In the Nancy–Tonya story, Kerrigan was played by Heather Lagencamp and Harding by Alexandra Powers, who was best known for her role as socially reserved Christian lawyer Jane Halliday on the popular prime-time series *L.A. Law*. As Harding, she was doing a 180-degree turn in character. "There must be some white trash in me somewhere, because I like the clothes," Powers told *TV Guide*. Producer Brian Pike, perhaps looking for extra viewers, said, "She smokes, she wheezes, she uses her inhaler, just like Tonya. Alex is having a hoot of a time." Former singles and pairs competitor Tracy Damigella performed the skating scenes for Lagencamp, and Powers's skating double was Tisha Walker, who rose as high as fifth in the U.S. nationals (1991).

SINGIN' IN THE RAIN: KURT BROWNING IN ONE OF THE BEST TV SPECIALS EVER.

The Baiul and Kerrigan–Harding movies were naturals: dramatic, current, and they had already received millions of dollars in free advertising because of the massive newspaper and network coverage of the Lillehammer Olympics. Another TV movie, *Fire and Ice*, chronicled the careers of Isabelle and Paul Duchesnay, the ice dancers from Aylmer, Quebec, who left Canada in frustration and skated for France, eventually winning the World Championship. Geneviève Rioux and Michel Berubé starred.

Yet another nineties TV movie was the minimusical *You Must Remember This*, starring Kurt Browning, which expanded on the Casablanca theme of his milestone Olympic long program. Browning acted out a Bogey-style murder mystery with co-stars Kristi Yamaguchi, Josée Chouinard, Christine Hough, Doug Ladret, and Michael Slipchuk. The highlight was a "**Singin' in the Rain**" salute to dancer/actor Gene Kelly, probably the best skating scene ever created on-screen. The Duchesnays and Brian Orser starred in *Planets*, skated on black ice to the music of Gustav Holst. Set high in the mountains of ancient Greece, it was a lyric, metaphorical look at beauty and death. It was also typical of many of the few dozen TV skating specials – even Browning's classic Bogey characterization – that appeared from the Calgary Olympics to the mid-nineties, in that it was difficult to label as either a movie or a skating show.

The first skaters to win Emmys, American TV's version of an Oscar, for their work were Katarina Witt, Brian Boitano, and Orser for their *Carmen on Ice*. While the movie musical appeared on both HBO in the U.S. and CBC in Canada, it was originally released in theaters in Europe in the late 1980s. Like Browning with *You Must Remember This*, the movie expanded on a signature Olympic number, Witt's 1988 Carmen free skate.

THE EARLY FLICKS: CHARLOTTE AND SONJA

When filmmaking was little more than an infant industry capitalizing on new technology, the first skater to make her way onto the screen was Broadway sensation Charlotte. *The Frozen Warning* was made in 1915, the same year as her American ice-show debut, and played on the paranoia surrounding World War I – a dominant dramatic theme in those years when the U.S. was trying to decide whether to involve itself in the Great European Conflict. The centerpiece skating scene was also the film's climax, as Charlotte, attending a skating party of espionage agents, helps save her country by etching the word S-P-I-E-S in huge letters on a frozen pond.

While Charlotte may have been the first to portray figure skating for moviegoers, the real celluloid pioneer was the dimpled, blonde Norwegian who won her first World Championship at Oslo in 1927 when she was fourteen. In America, movie moguls took notice of the Sonja Henie phenomenon when she captured New York at the 1930 World Championships. Strict rules governing amateurism prohibited Henie's involvement in any obvious skate-for-profit ventures like movies, but she would later more than make up for the wait. When her third and final Olympic gold-medal performance, at Garmisch in 1936, was filmed in its entirety for filmmaker Pete Smith's short *Sports on Ice*, Hollywood went into a swoon. Twentieth Century–Fox and Darryl Zanuck won the sweepstakes, but not before discovering that while Henie's public persona may have been blonde Scandinavian innocence, behind corporate doors she was a shrewd, calculating businesswoman. She could speak Norwegian, French, English, and German, but her most fluent language was

Bottom Line. "When the subject was business, the first question she asked was 'How much money is there in this for me?'" wrote one historian. She asked for – demanded, actually – and got a staggering $75,000 for her first movie, *One in a Million* in 1936, and successfully upped the stakes to $100,000 for her second film, *Thin Ice*. As one reviewer put it, she worked her "perky, pouty way" into the hearts of the American movie-going public and, reaching the box office top-ten in 1937, 1938, and 1939, quickly established a movie income of half-a-million dollars annually.

As skating gained a foothold in North America, so did an increasing number of traveling professional ice shows. They helped whet the appetite for the Henie-formula flicks: lighthearted musicals that featured the leading dance orchestras of the day – Woody Herman, Glenn Miller, Sammy Kaye – backed by intricate sets and fancy skating. Henie's blades and beaming smile, real or affected, were the centerpoints of the predictable scripts. Henie, though, had to battle to include more skating in the films. As a later generation of television producers would discover, skating scenes are expensive and difficult to film. In Henie's day, 1990's camera techniques and technologies were not available, and capturing the sport's inherent speed was a challenge. In some of her pictures, the production numbers were pared to two from Henie's preferred three, but that was still enough to spread the skating gospel worldwide. Her best film was probably her debut effort, *One in a Million*, in which she is a Swiss skater whose father is preparing her for the Olympics. Don Ameche plays the smitten suitor, Adolphe Menjou the evil promoter.

Thin Ice found Henie as a properly respectful skating instructor who believes that the prince she loves is of too high a station for her. It comes as absolutely no surprise when her humility is rewarded in the end. A memorable moment in the film is singer Joan Davis's rendition of "I'm Olga from the Volga."

In real life, Henie seemed to choose her husbands the way she chose her movies – with a balance sheet. Each of her three spouses was a millionaire. Henie went on to star with some of the most famous actors of the day: Richard Greene, Cesar Romero, Tyrone Power, Rudy Vallee, Ray Milland, Bob Cummings, John Payne, and Milton Berle. Twentieth Century–Fox released *One in a Million, Thin Ice, Second Fiddle, Everything Happens at Night, Sun Valley Serenade, Iceland,* and *Wintertime* from 1937 to 1943 and generated millions in box-office receipts. To stimulate interest in Henie's early movies, the studio fabricated a romance between her and dashing heartthrob Tyrone Power, and fed tidbits about the phony love affair to the Hollywood rumor mill. "We had to consult the gossip columns every day to see if we were still in love or not," Henie joked.

A collection of Henie films is now available on videocassette.

GETTING IN ON THE ACT

Skating became such a hot commodity that MGM plunked its studio star Joan Crawford into *Ice Follies of 1939* even though she was unable to skate. Lew Ayres and the legendary Jimmy Stewart are a skating pair, but Stewart's marriage to Crawford

A UNIVERSAL PICTURE

threatens the act. Crawford can't stand the prospect of breaking up the pair and heads off to become a movie star. The film was described, as so many skating movies are, as "boring" despite a then-new Technicolor ending. The movie was little more than a vehicle for the marquee actors and for the Follies tour itself, whose owners, Roy and Eddie Shipstad and Oscar Johnson, were in the film.

Other studios got into the act, and so did other ice shows. In 1942, Republic Pictures released *Ice Capades*, starring James Ellison, Jerry Colona, and Dorothy Lewis, and featuring the popular ice dancing of Robert Dench and Rosemarie Stewart Dench. They were backed by music, comedians, and the Ice Capades

EVEN UNIVERSAL'S COMEDY DUO OF BUD ABBOTT AND LOU COSTELLO SCORED A HIT IN 1943's *HIT THE ICE*. CO-STAR AND BIG BAND SINGER GINNY SIMMS IS SHOWN HERE.

155

company. The movie is still shown on U.S. cable TV. Another single-named performer, Belita, was a legendary show skater in the early 1940s and tried a skating picture in 1943. *Silver Skates* found Belita attempting to save a skating show from bankruptcy. Belita also appeared in the 1945 *Suspense*, a none-too-successful effort that has an "ambitious heel" (Barry Sullivan) hitting on a married ice star (guess who?) and features the questionable musical highlight called "Ice Cuba." But only one actress could play Sonja Henie–type roles and that was Sonja Henie, so Belita's pictures, including *The Hunted* (1947), were often more serious than Henie films and skating scenes were tangential to the plot.

RKO Pictures released Henie's *It's a Pleasure* in 1945, but her momentum was obviously slowing. It took another three years for Universal–International to bring out *The Countess of Monte Cristo*. The bloom was off the Norwegian rose, and skating pictures in general, and when Henie tried to make a motion-picture comeback with *Hello London* in 1958, she and her third husband, Neils Onstad, had to produce it. *Hello London* was a travelogue that featured Henie's skating prowess, but after final editing was completed a full year after production was done, the film received some interest in European theaters, was never released in North America, and the curtain was drawn on Henie's reign as queen of the ice and of the screen. Times, and films, had changed direction, and without Henie's personality to carry them, skating films as a separate genre faded from the scene until TV revived and changed the art form with the discovery of Peggy Fleming in the late 1960s.

ICE CASTLES

There were some isolated skating scenes in movies before the advent of TV specials, but skating movies or films starring skaters were few and far between. It had, in short, already been done. American, Olympic, and five-time world champion Carol Heiss showed that she wasn't stuffy in her brief sortie onto the silver screen in *Snow White and the Three Stooges* a year after she retired from amateur competition in 1960. One critic gave the movie a "bomb" rating. The same year, German champion Ina Bauer, after whom a gorgeous skating move is named, starred in *On Thin Ice*, about a woman who falls in love at the arena. Then began a long, and probably deserved, drought for skating in the movies.

In the 1970s, however, sports again became a hot ticket, with films like *Brian's Song* and *Bang the Drum Slowly*. The most successful of these were the *Rocky* movies, about a working-class Philadelphian who reaches the top of boxing's seedy world. In the initial installment, Rocky (Sylvester Stallone) takes his future wife (Talia Shire) to a skating rink for their first date.

Finally, in 1978, Columbia Pictures decided to take a chance on a skating film. *Ice Castles* had a strong hockey presence – *Slap Shot*, a fanciful look at a minor pro-hockey team had done well at the box office for Universal Pictures the previous year – in the form of male lead Robbie Benson, who played a Minnesota hockey player trying to make it as a pro. But it also had a massive dose of figure skating in the char-

It's Got RHYTHM!
It's Got ROMANCE!
It's Got REVELRY!

SONJA HENIE
WINTERTIME

DIRECTED BY JOHN BRAHM
PRODUCED BY WILLIAM LeBARON
SCREEN PLAY BY ARTHUR KOBER JOHN STERLING
AND LILLIE HAYWARD

CK | CESAR | CAROLE | AND S.Z. | CORNEL | WOODY | AND HIS
KIE ROMERO LANDIS SAKALL WILDE HERMAN ORCHESTRA

SONJA HENIE PARLAYED HER BROAD SMILE, RAPID SKATING, AND WORLDWIDE FAME INTO A HOLLYWOOD CAREER. SHE HAD ACTED IN ELEVEN MOVIES AND AMASSED A FORTUNE SAID TO HAVE REACHED $47 MILLION BY THE TIME SHE DIED OF LEUKEMIA IN 1969.

acter of Lexie, a figure skater being coached toward the Olympics by her father.

An accident leaves Lexie virtually blind and her world collapses around her, until she finds strength and inspiration in Nick Peterson, Benson's character. Leading film critic Leonard Maltin gave the film a decent rating for its photography and acting and said, "It's tops for the disease/affliction genre." The story line is somewhat maudlin, and Benson, despite training with two NHL teams, is somewhat unconvincing as a hockey player. But Lexie's figure-skating scenes, of which there are many, are attractive and more realistic than any previous effort. And they should be. The female lead was Lynn-Holly Johnson, nineteen at the time, who won the free skate and was overall runner-up in the novice division at the 1974 U.S. Championships.

"Scott Hamilton and I are from the same era," says Johnson, who lives in Los Angeles and, after a few years off, is trying to remount her show-business career as a producer and actor. "I was called 'Trixie' or 'Gabbie' at home [in Chicago] because, like Trixie Schuba or Gabbie Seyfert, I'd always win figures, then be third or fourth in freestyle and hang on for a medal. At the nationals I was fourth in figures, and I had never been that low before, so it got me motivated and I won the free skate." But a fracture to a bone at the top of her leg cost her a couple of years of training, and although she stayed in skating another two years, she had lost the competitive fire. She moved to California and was coached by John Nicks, but faced the reality that she would be better off skating professionally, and joined Ice Capades.

Johnson had a background in commercials and modeling, and Canadian-born coach Michael Kirby, now based in California, recommended her to the producers at Columbia. She had everything they were looking for, including a successful stint playing a blind girl – Helen Keller in a Chicago theater's version of *The Miracle Worker* – so she got the job.

She made a total of fourteen movies, mostly in the early-to-mid 1980s, and says she is most recognized for *Ice Castles*, along with *The Watcher in the Woods* and a part in the James Bond movie *For Your Eyes Only*.

THE CUTTING EDGE

Despite *Ice Castles*'s generally positive reviews and box-office success, more than a decade passed before another film was built around figure skating. *The Cutting Edge* stars Moira Kelly as a cantankerous, spoiled pairs skater who chews up and spits out partners. Yet another hockey player (actor D. B. Sweeney) discovers figure skating in this 1991 offering. It's a bit of a stretch – a huge stretch if the viewer is familiar with figure skating or hockey and their almost contradictory skating styles – but Sweeney overcomes his initial contempt for figure skating to become Kelly's partner, and they develop a revolutionary pairs throw for the Olympics.

"*The Cutting Edge* is not interested in discussing anything original about figure skating or the Olympics – it's all sports and romantic clichés – yet the skating scenes [photographed by Elliott Davis] are good to look at and the actors have character," wrote renowned critic Roger Ebert, one-half of the famous Siskel and Ebert team.

The mounting athletic and sexual tension between the skating partners is entirely believable and the skating segments exhibit just how far technology and film's familiarity with skating had developed since Henie's time.

Adding extra interest for skating fans was the appearance, in nonspeaking roles, of world-class pairs team Christine Hough and Doug Ladret. Most of the skating scenes were filmed at Copps Coliseum in Hamilton, Ontario, which the production company leased for thirty days. Robin Cousins, the 1980 Olympic champion, was organizing and choreographing the skating scenes for MGM, and knew that the Preston School of Skating, run by noted pairs coach Kerry Leitch, was only a half-hour from the arena. Cousins signed four or five Preston pairs for the movie, including Hough and Ladret, Michelle Menzies and Kevin Wheeler, the 1987 Canadian

MOIRA KELLY AND D.B. SWEENEY ARE AN IRRESISTIBLE PAIRS TEAM IN *THE CUTTING EDGE*, PARTLY FILMED AT COPPS COLISEUM IN HAMILTON, ONTARIO.

SONJA JOHN
HENIE ★ PAYNE
GLENN MILLER
AND HIS ORCHESTRA
MILTON BERLE · LYNN BARI
JOAN DAVIS · NICHOLAS Brothers
IN **SUN VALLEY SERENADE**

THE HENIE FORMULA: LAVISH SKATING SCENES, SOLID MALE CO-STAR, INOFFENSIVE PLOT, AND THE TOP ORCHESTRAS OF THE ERA. GLENN MILLER PROVIDED THE MUSIC FOR *SUN VALLEY SERENADE*.

junior champions, and Penny Papaioannou and Raoul LeBlanc, who would win the 1991 national junior title.

In the finished product, the audience saw mainly the skates and brief flashes of most of the Canadian pairs, but Hough and Ladret had more significant roles. They played the Russian skaters Shmilkov and Brushkin, the silent, proud Russian pair who were Olympic favorites. "No first names. I think I was supposed to be Shmilkov," recalls Hough. There is one effective scene in *The Cutting Edge*, where, from the background, they fix the American stars with cold, arrogant stares. "We were known just as 'The Team,' we were talked about during the whole movie … long before we were actually shown. We were chosen to play the Russians because our skating skills were more of a classical type. We could imitate them because we'd seen so many of their teams from going to Skate Moscow and skating against them so much at other internationals. All I did was think about what they'd look like in those days when they came into the arena. They didn't speak English and they were taught to be intimidating. It's a head game … there're lots of head games in skating.

"Even though I had blonde, short hair then and I don't now, kids still come up to me and say, 'You were the Russian team.'"

SKATES, SCREEN, AND TRIVIA

Although Disney is planning a movie with Nancy Kerrigan and there have been skating scenes in recent feature films such as *Little Women* (with the U.S. Figure

Skating Hall of Fame providing technical advice), *The Cutting Edge* was the last full-length theater release to revolve around skating.

Over the years, though, skating has landed bit parts in a variety of movies. Skating/movie trivia lovers might find the following quiz something of a challenge. (Reproduced by permission of Barb McCutcheon and *American Skating World*.)

THE QUESTIONS

1. Richard Dreyfuss dies in a wheelchair while holding his infant child as Holly Hunter does spins on a frozen lake in this 1991 film.

2. Kurt Browning played a small role as a club pro in this Canadian production about one man's hockey fantasies.

3. A doomed Ali McGraw loved to watch Ryan O'Neal skate in this classic tearjerker.

4. Cary Grant and Loretta Young take their cabdriver skating in this 1947 movie that is now a Christmas favorite (David Niven also stars).

5. Ricki Lake finds love with a figure-skating motorman in this made-for-TV movie.

6. Kiefer Sutherland's first starring role saw him not only playing hockey but "pleasure skating" with the girl next door.

7. Macaulay Culkin tries to escape through an outdoor rink, with toothbrush in hand in this blockbuster.

8. Clark Gable and Jean Harlow play crack-the-whip at the office skating party while Myrna Loy, as Gable's wife, looks on in this 1936 film.

9. Abbott and Costello visit the skating rink.

10. Loretta Young's character ran to keep in shape for skating and skated to keep in shape for running in this 1947 film with Joseph Cotten.

11. Frost sprites skate across a stream of ice to the strains of Tchaikovsky's "Waltz of the Flowers" in this Disney animated classic.

12. Sonja Henie, John Payne, and the Glenn Miller Orchestra visit a popular winter resort.

13. Sandra Bezic coached Marlon Brando to skate for this film, which co-starred Matthew Broderick.

14. Jill Clayburgh and her women friends go skating at Rockefeller Center in this Paul Mazursky film about separation and divorce.

15. This documentary film on the 1988 Winter Olympics chronicles the Battle of the Brians.

16. Lynn-Holly Johnson plays a teenage ice skater in this James Bond film.

17. Fred Astaire starred in this lesser 1952 musical, but Astaire does briefly wear ice skates in the part.

18. Kris Kringle sends a Macy's customer to Gimbel's for ice skates better suited to her tiny ankles.

19. June Allyson makes her entrance in this film carrying antique skates.

20. Lana Turner finds herself in white boots and blades in this 1940 MGM film.

VERA HRUBA SKATING AT THE 1936 OLYMPICS.

THE ANSWERS

1. *Once Around*
2. *Life After Hockey*
3. *Love Story*
4. *The Bishop's Wife*
5. *Baby Cakes*
6. *The Bay Boy*
7. *Home Alone*
8. *Wife Versus Secretary*
9. *Hit the Ice*
10. *The Farmer's Daughter*
11. *Fantasia*
12. *Sun Valley Serenade*
13. *The Freshman*
14. *An Unmarried Woman*
15. *16 Days of Glory*
16. *For Your Eyes Only*
17. *Belle of New York*
18. *Miracle on 34th Street*
19. *Little Women*
20. *Two Girls on Broadway*

The Future: Where Is Skating Headed?

Influential agent Kevin Albrecht of International Management Group – the management and promotion company that is one of skating's biggest power brokers – has the same short, definitive conversation over and over again with IMG employees. "I tell our staff that the key word in figure skating is *change*," Albrecht says. "Get used to it. Spell it out. And be prepared to deal with it."

The figure-skating landscape is changing so rapidly in the 1990s that it is impossible to freeze it long enough to take a snapshot, let alone make a full-length movie.

At the start of the decade, compulsory figures were still a factor in the sport, and professional competitions weren't. TV coverage was limited to a couple of single-week splurges for national and World Championships, and isolated broadcasts of one or two pro and amateur fall competitions.

By the end of the decade, big-time skating may not be recognizable to those who have spent a lifetime in it. The sport seems to be moving in the direction that tennis did in the 1970s, when the world amateur governing bodies did not see that they had to keep up with, or be ahead of, the burgeoning professional world. It took only a few years for those associations to lose their once-viselike grip on the sport.

"I think that by the year 2000, skating will be more like the ATP Tour in tennis and the PGA Tour in golf," Albrecht predicts. "Tennis players have their own coaches and strength coaches and come back to represent the country for the Davis Cup. I see the USFSA and CFSA being more involved with event sites. Skaters will come back and wear the Maple Leaf [or the Stars and Stripes] a couple of times a year."

That process already began with reinstatement of ineligible skaters for the 1994 Olympics and the do-it-now-absolutely-last-chance-and-we're-not-kidding April 1, 1995, deadline for professionals to reapply for amateur status. But there is a widespread belief that by 1998, the Olympic Games will be open to all skaters, pro or amateur, eligible or ineligible.

MICHELLE KWAN WAS FOURTH AT THE WORLD CHAMPIONSHIP IN 1995 AND HER COACH FELT THAT SHE WAS KEPT OFF THE PODIUM ONLY BECAUSE SHE LACKED MATURITY. SHE RETURNED WITH A NEW, MORE SOPHISTICATED LOOK FOR THE 1995–96 SEASON AND IT IMMEDIATELY PAID DIVIDENDS. SHE WON $60,000 IN SEVEN DAYS (DESPITE HER "AMATEUR STATUS") WHEN SHE FINISHED FIRST AT BOTH SKATE AMERICA AND SKATE CANADA, THE OPENING EVENTS OF THE NEW CHAMPIONS SERIES, BETTER KNOWN AS THE GRAND PRIX, AND ADDED THE NATIONS CUP CROWN BEFORE WINNING HER FIRST U.S. TITLE AT SAN JOSE. THEN SHE WON THE INAUGURAL CHAMPIONS SERIES FINAL (CHAMPIONSHIP TITLE), AND TO CAP A SENSATIONAL SEASON SHE TOOK THE 1996 WORLD CHAMPIONSHIP IN A BRILLIANT BATTLE OF ELEGANT FREE SKATES WITH THE DEFENDING CHAMPION, LU CHEN, WHO ALSO TRAINS AT LAKE ARROWHEAD, CALIFORNIA. WITH ALL HER PRIZE WINNINGS FROM THE ONCE "AMATEUR" EVENTS, PLUS WHAT SHE STANDS TO EARN ON THE POST–WORLDS TOUR OF CHAMPIONS, KWAN'S 1996 INCOME WILL BE WELL OVER $1 MILLION, WITHOUT ENDORSEMENTS.

VIACHESLAV ZAGORODNIUK OF UKRAINE JOINED THE RANKS OF RISING INTERNATIONAL STARS WHEN HE EDGED OUT OLYMPIC CHAMPION ALEXEI URMANOV FOR THE BRONZE MEDAL AT THE 1994 WORLD CHAMPIONSHIPS, BUT HE DROPPED TO SIXTH THE FOLLOWING YEAR.

"With the NHL in the Games, you *know* '98 will be a wide-open Olympics," says Michael Rosenberg, another of skating's most influential agents. "And all further Olympics will be the same. They have to be – they have to have the greatest names."

And names are the key. The star system, not national affiliation, is moving closer to the driver's seat as skating puts the pedal to the metal. The argument over Oksana Baiul's potential reinstatement to the pro ranks in 1995 was illuminating. When the ISU decided to offer prize money for the World Championships, it was in the hope of keeping its current major stars in the amateur game and luring back those who had "turned pro," such as Baiul.

"Oksana Baiul, Oksana Baiul, who is Oksana Baiul?" ISU president Ottavio Cinquanta of Italy was quoted as saying. "She is not God. We will not be blackmailed by Oksana Baiul. If we lose her, we will create other Oksana Baiuls."

The ISU could indeed create another Oksana Baiul, but how long could it keep her to itself? The talent pool has never been deeper in elite skating, but there is a huge difference between being good and being marketable.

While the amateurs continue to train and develop the skaters who feed the pro system, for the first time in skating history the amateurs need the professionals as much as the pros need them. Maybe more so. The ISU has been slow to grasp this, although both the CFSA and the USFSA have been worriedly pleading a case behind closed doors for years. If the professional promoters and skaters had been able to organize themselves into a cohesive body, it would have wrenched control of the sport – other than the Olympics, the ISU's big hammer – from the amateurs some time ago.

In the United States, skating faces stiff competition from a myriad of sports, both college and professional, and must have the marquee value of the biggest names. At first resistant to Brian Boitano's one-man crusade to have pros reinstated for the Olympics, the USFSA eventually championed it and the Boitano Rule was successfully shepherded through the ISU. The Americans were also the first to stage a pro–am competition when they became permissible, and the first to extend pro–am invitations to international skaters.

North of the border, the grassroots base is much stronger and deeper. "In Canada skating is big because skaters have been that good," theorizes Brian Orser, the first cavalry leader of Canada's resurgence as a world skating power. "They're putting out. It started out with Barb [Underhill] and Paul [Martini], Tracy [Wilson] and Rob [McCall], and Liz [Manley], and when that group pulled it off, the next group picked up the pieces and they pulled it off. That's why people are in love with it in Canada."

Canada hopes to proceed more slowly than the U.S. in connecting itself to professional skating, because it wants to preserve its broadly based pyramid of skating development. But Canadian officials have always had a friendly relationship with the pros. It was Canadian David Dore who first rang the warning bells to the ISU that it had to stage more competitions, promote and develop a bigger star system, and find a more cooperative and mutually beneficial way of working with professional promoters.

Dore may have a sometimes-abrasive personality, but for nearly twenty years he has been one of the sport's brightest visionaries. He was the driving force behind Canada's resurgence as a skating power in the 1980s, demanding competitive successes and getting them, enticing big business into backing figure skating, to the point that there was a lineup of willing sponsors.

First as elected president of the CFSA, and now as its director-general, Dore has made countless suggestions – many of them falling by the wayside in an ISU bureaucratic structure created for another, less-volatile, era – on how to strengthen the viability and power of amateur skating in a changing world scene. "We have a good open relationship in Canada with professionals," says Dore. "They're in a different kind of business than we are. It doesn't do any good to pretend they're not out there and doing things – just as it does them no good to pretend we're not there. We have an open dialogue. And we have to realize the roles that we all play."

It was Dore who first suggested, back in the late 1980s, that the top fall internationals be combined into some kind of Grand Prix circuit, to make sure that there would be quality fields. It is important that the fall internationals do well, because they help fund domestic programs in the countries that stage them. But it was only with the sudden arrival of a large number of pro events and the withering of many of the autumn amateur competitions that the ISU hurriedly adopted the Champions Series for the 1995–96 season.

Five formerly independent internationals – Skate Canada, Skate America, NHK in Japan, the Nations Cup in Germany, and the Trophée de France (formerly the Lalique Trophy) – were banded together to form a circuit formally called the Champions Series of Figure Skating. First-place winners receive $30,000 in each event. That amount doubles for the final, to be held January or February each year, with the site rotating. To qualify for the final, a skater must participate in at least two of the autumn Grand Prix events and accumulate enough standings points.

The Grand Prix is for eligible skaters, but even that has a rider to it. In order to stimulate domestic interest, the host country may invite ineligible skaters to participate. There is some concern that with the cream of the amateur crop competing in the Grand Prix and the Grand Prix final, some of the luster may be stripped off the World Championships. "That would be like the NFL holding another championship right before the Super Bowl," said one insider. But the system works well in soccer nations, which have several important tournament championships.

As well as the Grand Prix, the ISU has had a hand in designing special, standardized rules for a series of open championships in the autumn, for which both pros and amateurs are eligible. IMG, Dick Button's Candid Productions, and Jefferson

OKSANA BAIUL'S CONCENTRATION MOUNTS AS SHE PREPARES TO SKATE TO HER STARTING POSITION FOR HER BLACK SWAN SHORT PROGRAM AT THE 1994 WINTER OLYMPICS.

SHAE-LYNN BOURNE AND VICTOR KRAATZ HAVE MADE A METEORIC CLIMB THROUGH THE WORLD ICE-DANCING RANKS. CRITICS AT FIRST SCOFFED AT THEIR HYDROBLADING FORM, BUT A CLOSE LOOK AT THEIR BLADES AND LEG ANGLES SHOW THAT THEY HAVE INDEED MASTERED IT. THE ANGLE OF THEIR EDGES AND BODY LEAN ARE MORE SEVERE THAN THOSE OF ANY PREVIOUS SKATERS. BOURNE SUFFERED A 17-STITCH CUT IN HER LEFT KNEE JUST BEFORE 1995 SKATE CANADA WHEN KRAATZ'S SKATE SLICED HER DURING PRACTICE.

Pilot of Charleston, South Carolina, another large agency, have all been heavily involved in the production and promotion of those events.

In less than two years, then, the intense competitive skating season simply outgrew its former January-to-March boundaries. The competitive season is now October to March, with longer performance tours before and after the season.

SOME HAVE WORRIES

The proliferation of figure-skating events and tours, particularly in the fall season, does not come without a price. Some of the sport's biggest boosters wonder if figure skating hasn't come too far, too quickly.

"I don't know how long it will last," says promoter Tom Collins. "It could be a fad, or it could go on a long, long time. I get a little worried about it because of the TV exposure. Maybe after a while people get tired of seeing the same people time after time, doing the same things."

That is a concern of Lloyd Eisler's. Since the biggest names are the ones most in demand – one promoter says that TV network schedulers always ask for the same half-dozen skaters when events are pitched to them – they'll get the most exposure. Eisler says, "You can't prepare twenty different programs for twenty different events … and make them good. And if you don't make them good, you're cheating the audience and they'll begin to notice." He predicts an era of exclusivity contracts in which skaters competing in a pro competition will have to agree not to use that program in another competition.

Agents have always walked a thin line with those who organize amateur sports because their objectives sometimes conflict. Since the mid-1980s, skating officials have learned to work with those agents, but suddenly they are reporting an alarming increase in the number of second-tier, even third-tier, skaters who are signing on with agents – "kids who really haven't done anything internationally, yet are starting to ask money for everything you ask them to do," said one official.

And that could evolve into a larger problem. One of skating's long-held traditions is that its biggest stars are accessible to the up-and-comers. Brian Orser was inspired by seeing Donald Jackson at a club carnival in Midland, Ontario, and there are similar stories throughout the ranks of North American skaters. Orser, Eisler and partner Isabelle Brasseur, and Barbara Underhill and Paul Martini have all made a point of trying to skate as often as they can in smaller-city carnivals, seeding interest in the next generation of skaters. When carnivals could no longer afford the national champions, they would settle on the next tier. If they can no longer afford them, one of skating's best forms of advertising – word of mouth – will dry up.

While the highest-profile agents usually have the best interests of the sport in mind in the long run, more and more agents are arriving on the scene, attracted by the smell of big money. More and more promises are made, some not kept. Tennis ran into this problem in the early 1980s, and it nearly choked its golden goose. Baseball players finally had to develop a process to accredit agents, in an effort to keep the unscrupulous ones out of the game. Figure skating may have to take the same step.

Two of the major concerns that national officials have with the radical changes

THREE YEARS, THREE CHAMPIONS. ELVIS STOJKO (MIDDLE) CELEBRATES HIS FIRST CANADIAN CHAMPIONSHIP VICTORY IN 1994, FLANKED BY RUNNER-UP AND THEN REIGNING WORLD CHAMPION KURT BROWNING AND BRONZE MEDALIST SEBASTIEN BRITTEN. BROWNING HAD WON FOUR NATIONAL TITLES, AND IN STOJKO'S ABSENCE BECAUSE OF INJURY, BRITTEN WON IN 1995.

IRINA SLUTSKAYA OF RUSSIA FINISHED AN IMPRESSIVE SEVENTH AT THE 1995 WORLDS AND IS AMONG THE NEXT WAVE OF YOUNG SKATERS WHO SHOULD MATURE IN TIME TO MAKE THE 1998 OLYMPIC FIELD THE MOST FORMIDABLE EVER. SHE WON THE 1996 EUROPEAN CHAMPIONSHIP AND FOLLOWED UP WITH THE BRONZE MEDAL IN A TIGHTLY CONTESTED WOMEN'S EVENT AT THE WORLDS IN EDMONTON.

in skating are their impact on training and the bottleneck effect they create at the lower levels. The latter particularly affects Canada. With a large feeder system, Canada has had a fairly good track record at replacing retiring stars with promising newcomers. But if the reigning champion keeps returning from the pro ranks to skate only at nationals, and grabs one of his or her country's valuable berths at the Worlds and Olympics, what incentive is there for younger skaters to keep training at the amateur level? Already some younger skaters, who have started to level off but who may just be at one of the many periodic plateaus in a skating career, have talked of retirement because they see no future for themselves at the world level. Canadian officials consider that a very real danger, and always have.

A NEW TRAINING REGIMEN

With the Tour of World Figure Skating Champions stretching into July, and some tours, such as Elvis Stojko's, beginning in late September, the long-established training regimen of top-flight amateur skaters has been shattered.

At one time the routine rarely varied: finish the Worlds; go on tour for a few weeks; return to the home rink in May for spring skating school; get the music selected and the program blocked out; take a couple of weeks off in June; work hard five or six days a week all summer, perfecting elements and familiarizing yourself with the new programs; then spend the fall in rigorous training, with a couple of low-key international events thrown in as program testers with the judges.

That routine still exists for those on the way up, but for those close to the top, forget it.

"Everything is different now," says Stojko's coach, Doug Leigh, who has no trouble working with the new realities. "You have to adjust your schedule to the times. There is not one thing the same as it was ten years ago, or eight, seven, or four years ago. Or even last week. For two months in the spring, Elvis would have been working on his program and his music. Now he does it on the road, or he comes off the road briefly to do it. [Choreographer] Uschi Keszler goes on the road with him for a while. When he takes two weeks off, we do the music and get the programs roughed in. So by early May the programs are already planted.

"You just have to arrange your time. If you can't do it here, do it somewhere else. In a hotel room, or in another rink on the road.

"In the summer, they'll be here most of the time, but instead of having weekends off, they have things to do. A show here and there, a benefit golf tournament, because they're big names now.

"The training never quits. And don't forget you don't need that three hours a day you used to have to spend on figures. Elvis might be missing training at home with his tour in September, but he's doing his long program in the show every night. That's twelve run-throughs of his program in front of 15,000 people. Skating in front of people is not an issue for these kids anymore. He's getting training and making money doing it."

Not everyone has the organizational skills or pragmatic optimism of Leigh and his prize pupil, Stojko. Less-disciplined skaters may tend to train less intensely with the enormous travel loads and lack of regular practice hours. If landing a jump in competition is a function of doing it a thousand times in practice that year, surely the technical consistency has to suffer occasionally.

"You can make it simple on yourself, or you can make it tough," Leigh answers.

Some worry that, as baseball discovered, too much money can tear a sport apart. Paradoxically, it is somehow more difficult to carve up a fatted cow than a thin one. "If we keep overexposing the sport, then it's going to be bad for everyone," said one promoter.

WHEN THE WINTER OLYMPICS WERE HELD IN THEIR NATIVE FRANCE IN 1992, ERIC MILLOT WAS SELECTED FOR THE NATIONAL TEAM BUT PHILIPPE CANDELORO WAS NOT. SINCE THEN, MILLOT, WHOSE HIGHEST WORLD RANKING THROUGH 1995 WAS FIFTH, HAS LABORED IN THE SHADOW OF HIS MORE FLAMBOYANT COUNTRYMAN. NONETHELESS, HE CANNOT BE DISCOUNTED AS A MEDAL CONTENDER.

But others disagree.

"I'm not with the conventional wisdom of all the doomsayers and traditionalists," says Michael Rosenberg. "A lot of that is coming from old-time national-federation-type people who have lost their control and don't see that skating has gone through the roof.

"The rinks are filled to capacity for shows and competitions. Other sports would give their left arm for this kind of prosperity.

"Most U.S. coaches are so filled up with students that they're turning away skaters. It's like Little League fever, and that builds future champions and stars.

"To me the state of skating has never been better, and there is no end in sight. You look at Bonaly, Chen, Kwan, Stojko, Eldredge, and Candeloro, and that's not even counting the Steven Cousinses or an Ilya Kulik. The next class is potentially more exciting than the one preceding it."

SPREADING WORLDWIDE

Change has always been a part of figure skating, but it has usually been gradual, or influenced by outside factors such as a world war. But then, figure skating was always the province of a relatively small number of countries, so change wasn't as dramatic or as noticeable.

And there have always been power shifts. In the early part of the twentieth century, the sport was dominated by the Austrians and Scandinavians: until 1939, when debonair Briton Graham Sharpe took the title, all but one men's World Championship had been won by either Swedes or Austrians. After World War II destroyed most of Europe's rinks, American and Canadian men, women, and pairs dominated the standings, until the Soviets broke through in the 1960s and Europe rebounded. Canada, a nonthreat through the 1970s and early 1980s, returned with a vengeance in the mid-1980s and, outside of the women's event, has been a constant medal contender. In men's and women's singles, American skaters have had only rare and brief down troughs.

But as we approach the twenty-first century and competitive skating embarks on its second 100 years, its talent base is broadening. Two countries, Ukraine and China, have had their first women's world champions in the 1990s, and Japan celebrated only its second. France, with a war chest stuffed with TV money, has title contenders in three divisions and is enjoying its most successful skating era ever.

"And I think you have to watch the rise in the East, particularly China," says Albrecht. "The government is starting to throw the resources behind the sport and we know that when that happens, the sport takes off. Just by sheer numbers, China will be a factor in the future." Stars on Ice is touring China, Singapore, and Japan in the 1996 season, and the previous year it went to Brazil, Venezuela, and Mexico. Professional shows can be skating's evangelists, stimulating an interest that eventually translates into a domestic industry.

With the success of Lu Chen, China has begun a modest arena-construction program. The Canadian Figure Skating Association has sold several of its coaching and grassroots programs to China and has provided expertise in implementing them. But it will probably be well into the twenty-first century before China approaches real power in the sport. "Lu Chen is really an aberration of a system that does not yet exist," says one insider. "She is kind of an American product."

Chen, like many other international stars, has spent considerable time training at Ice Castles in Lake Arrowhead, California. With the globalization of the sport, more European, Asian, even Australian, skaters are training in North America.

There has always been a blurring of international borders when it comes to training sites: Donald Jackson spent time training in New York; dozens of international stars sought out coaches like Carlo Fassi in the U.S.; several Scandinavian champions have spent their winters in Canada with Doug Leigh; Obertsdorf, Germany, with its multifaceted training center, was the training base for Torvill and Dean, the Duchesnays, and many others.

But with the expanding appetite for figure skating in North America, athletes want to have ready access to that market, while still being able to train. That is particularly true of skaters from some of the former republics of the Soviet Union, where the economy has crashed and skating facilities have deteriorated or disappeared. During the 1990 Skate America in Buffalo, Jutta Muller, who coached Katarina Witt to two Olympic titles, was close to tears when she described the sudden changes in the former East Germany. "They are turning the rinks into car showrooms," she said.

Large training centers in Arrowhead; Detroit; Simsbury, Connecticut; and at Leigh's Mariposa School north of Toronto are attracting international stars who train at the rink, then hop on a plane for a short flight to an exhibition performance or money competition. The skaters return to their home countries only for holidays, national championships, and the occasional tour. The best of the sites offer one-stop shopping: Leigh's Mariposa School has both an Olympic-sized and an NHL-proportioned rink; a fully equipped weight-training room; an extensive music library; a dance and aerobic center; and a classroom for tutoring skaters individually. As well, there is a huge swimming pool in the building and a public high school just a stone's throw away.

The former Eastern bloc countries can no longer offer the same kind of facilities. Russian coaches at the 1994 Olympics complained of inadequate funding, difficulties in obtaining proper food, and unscrupulous arena managers charging exorbitant rates. One Russian coach estimates that there is one group left of young skaters – led by Ilya Kulik – who benefited from the former system. Then, he predicts, the world will see a serious decline in Russian singles skating.

Ice dancing may not suffer the same drop-off because several of the former Soviet republics are actively involved in ice dancing and are maintaining the Soviet tradition of developing dancers.

As an example of the financial hardships faced by the Russians, just before the 1995 World Championships the entire team flew to Mexico for a series of exhibitions, then flew all the way back to England for the Worlds. That trip was physically exhausting and in complete conflict with accepted preparation procedures, but the national federation needed the money the exhibitions would generate.

At the 1995 World Championships, seven countries that used to be represented solely by the Soviet Union were entered. Coupled with the expansion into the Pacific and South America, that raised the roster of competitors to forty-five in the men's division and forty-two in the women's.

That's far too many to judge fairly, so in recent years a qualifying round was introduced to pare the field to a manageable size. Anyone in the top ten the previous year does not have to qualify. In 1995, thirty-seven men and thirty-five women skated their long programs, with the roster reduced to thirty (including top-tens from the previous year) for the actual competition. After the short program, the field is sliced again to the top twenty-four.

Many skaters hate the qualifying round because it makes the week too long, and too many things can go wrong. Canadian champion Netty Kim, for example, did not survive the qualifying round in 1995. "It adds to the pressure for young skaters," said Doug Leigh. "But it gives them a chance to compete under some pressure, but less than in the actual competition. It gets them accustomed to the building and the crowd."

Said Canadian Marcus Christensen, "It's actually an excellent tune-up, unless, of course, you botch it up. It's a bit of a numbers game, and with the large field of skaters, the judges have a tough job. It would be easy to get caught in the numbers." Christensen's words proved to be prophetic, because he struggled in the qualifying round in 1995 and did not advance to the formal championships.

A Great Ride

No one has yet been able to accurately measure the economic spin-off of the figure-skating industry in North America, but it is over a half-billion dollars a year and has – at the performance, television, and cross-marketing level – at least tripled since the 1990s began.

Precision skating will continue to expand through the rest of the century because it offers skaters below elite status an opportunity to be part of national and international competitions. There is a ceiling on the potential of that expansion, however, because precision lacks the star quality that has driven the stock of "mainstream" figure skating sky-high. And there is some concern that as precision becomes the driving force at the club level, the internal politics of skating organizations could change. Precision does not generate the live-gate income that singles, pairs, and dance do, but if more and more of the grassroots skaters are involved in precision, there could be a demand for more and more income to be directed its way.

Professional touring shows will continue to do well in North America, playing off either the big-star system, as Stars on Ice and the Brian Boitano tours have, or off cross-marketing, which Disney on Ice has been so successful at.

At the ill-named "amateur" level, it remains to be seen if the International Skating Union and its national organizations can maintain control. The power to deter-

SURYA BONALY OF FRANCE WON
THREE STRAIGHT SILVER MEDALS
FROM 1993 TO 1995, AND
REMAINS A THREAT FOR THE 1998
OLYMPIC TITLE, DESPITE FINISHING
FIFTH WITH A DISAPPOINTING
PERFORMANCE AT THE 1996
WORLDS.

mine who takes part in the Olympics is their trump card, but public opinion (and the International Olympic Committee) could eventually override even that. The World Championships and Champions Series are marquee events, and they're in the right hands with IMG promoting them. By elevating the status of five fall internationals, the ISU is trying to make sure that they have a high profile in the five countries where skating generates the most money. It is no accident that in the past twenty years of World Championships, Canada has played host to five, the U.S. to four, and Japan and Germany to three each.

Skating continues to draw its primary audience from females. At touring shows, 70 percent of those attending are female. Television audiences have attracted more males than ever before – the split is now about 60–40 – but in merchandising, only about 30 percent of videos, books, commemorative T-shirts, and other apparel are

bought by men. And an insider says that almost all of those are for gifts, presumably to women. Figure skating has been found in several polls to be the favorite sport of women and their teenage daughters. In short, women have finally found a sport in which they are the power base. And the first print or electronic news media to establish a regular skating beat, on a par with baseball, football, basketball, and hockey beats, will find a huge, largely untapped, new market.

There can be no doubt that by the turn of the century, skaters will form their own organization, as golfers and tennis players did in decades past. The amateurs met briefly in this regard at the '95 Worlds. But likely the first major step will be a movement among professional skaters trying to gain some control over the dizzying array of opportunities presented to them by a dynamic, but helter-skelter, marketplace. "There are five or six skaters who control pro skating right now," says Albrecht. "If you can get three or four of them, you've got an event." A professional organization would try to broaden those opportunities and promote lesser stars, who could eventually carry events on their own.

A professional-skaters' association would help standardize rules for competitions, separate the wheat from the chaff among promoters and agents, and give the skaters some sense of control over the sport in which they've spent their lives. Coaches already have such an organization, and they've made an impact on the skating world, most recently in the judging at pro competitions.

As the nearly invisible lines between professional and amateur skating disappear, elite amateur skaters would likely become part of the professional organization. On the current scene, for example, it would be impractical to have a big-name group that did not include Elvis Stojko and Surya Bonaly. And if agents, marketers, business people, even national associations are wise, they'll affiliate themselves with the process.

Scott Hamilton would be the logical choice as leader for any new organization. He's been the best in the world at both the amateur and pro levels, has headlined both traditional and groundbreaking touring shows, and he's a broadcaster, intimate with the television politics and economics that drive the sport. And as a favorite of the North American skating public, he's an instant legitimizer. The time to gain control is when skating is hot, and it's never been hotter.

"No one is sure how long it will last – a lot of people thought it would only be for the one year after the Tonya–Nancy Olympics," says Albrecht. "But it didn't settle. It will probably last one more year, and then find its proper level. But it will be a level much higher than it was before."

Skating is to the sporting world what rock 'n' roll is to music, and the trick will be to extend its popularity to the next generations, as rock 'n' roll has. Figure skating is now like a thoroughbred, but without proper handling, the animal could turn into a bucking bronco.

"With each new group of young skaters, with what they bring to the sport, I get energized again," says Scott Hamilton, the man for all seasons.

"It has been a tremendous ride. I don't think I ever want to get off."

SCOTT HAMILTON IN HIS EARLY YEARS AS A PROFESSIONAL SKATER. FEW SKATERS HAVE BEEN ABLE TO STAY AT THE FOREFRONT OF THE SPORT AS LONG AS THE 1984 OLYMPIC CHAMPION.

APPENDIX 1

The World Figure Skating Hall of Fame

(COLORADO SPRINGS, COLORADO)

Established in 1976, the World Figure Skating Hall of Fame accepts nominations from the figure-skating community and the general public. There are eighteen members on the selection committee, comprising former champions, judges, and skating officials. For induction a nominee must be retired for at least five years and receive a two-thirds majority approval of the selection committee.

MEMBER	YEAR OF INDUCTION
Tenley Albright, U.S.A.	1976
Andrée Joly and Pierre Brunet, France	1976
Richard Button, U.S.A.	1976
Peggy Fleming, U.S.A.	1976
Gillis Grafström, Sweden	1976
Carol Heiss, U.S.A.	1976
Sonja Henie, Norway	1976
David Jenkins, U.S.A.	1976
T. D. Richardson, Great Britain	1976
Jacques Gerschwiler, Switzerland	1976
Jackson Haines, U.S.A.	1976
Gustave Lussi, Switzerland	1976
Hayes Alan Jenkins, U.S.A.	1976
Axel Paulsen, Norway	1976
Ulrich Salchow, Sweden	1976
Karl Schafer, Austria	1976
Reginald J. Wilkie, Great Britain	1976
Howard Nicholson, U.S.A.	1976
Edi Scholdan, Austria	1976
Montgomery Wilson, Canada	1976
Willy Boeckl, Austria	1977
Jean Westwood and Lawrence Demmy, Great Britain	1977
Donald Jackson, Canada	1977
Ludmila Belousova and Oleg Protopopov, Soviet Union	1978
Maxi Herber and Ernst Baier, Germany	1979
Barbara Ann Scott, Canada	1979
Cecilia Colledge, Great Britain	1980

MEMBER	YEAR OF INDUCTION
Barbara Wagner and Robert Paul, Canada	1980
Madge Syers, Great Britain	1981
Willie Frick, Germany	1981
William O. Hickok IV, U.S.A.	1981
Herma Szabo-Stark, Austria	1982
Louis Rubenstein, Canada	1984
Werner Groebli (Mr. Frick), Switzerland	1984
Frances Dafoe and Norris Bowden, Canada	1984
Charlotte Oelschlagel, Germany	1985
Arnold Gerschwiler, Switzerland	1985
F. Ritter Shumway, U.S.A.	1986
Courtney Jones, OBE, Great Britain	1986
Ludmila Pakhomova and Alexander Gorshkov, Soviet Union	1988
Irina Rodnina, Soviet Union	1989
Jayne Torvill and Christopher Dean, Great Britain	1989
Scott Hamilton, U.S.A.	1990
John Curry, Great Britain	1991
Jeannette Altwegg, Great Britain	1993
Richard Dwyer, U.S.A.	1993
Ria Baran Falk and Paul Falk, Germany	1993
Jacques Favart, France	1993
Georg Hasler, Switzerland	1993
Ronald Robertson, U.S.A.	1993
Dianne Fowler and Bernard Ford, Great Britain	1993
James Koch, Switzerland	1994

APPENDIX 1 (CONTINUED)

United States Figure Skating Hall of Fame

Established in 1976 to honor those who have made outstanding contributions to figure skating in the U.S.A.

MEMBER	YEAR OF INDUCTION
Sherwin C. Badger	1976
Theresa Weld Blanchard	1976
Irving Brokaw	1976
Maribel Vinson Owen	1976
A. Winsor Weld	1976
Eddie Shipstad and Oscar Johnson	1976
Beatrix Loughran	1977
Heaton R. Robertson	1977
Henry M. Beatty	1977
Nathaniel W. Niles	1978
Harold Hartshorne	1981
George H. Browne	1983
Eugene Turner	1983
Yvonne Sherman Tutt	1991
Dorothy Hamill	1991
Charles Tickner	1991
James Grogan	1991
Judy Schwomeyer and James Sladky	1991
Lois Waring and Michael McGean	1991
Karol Kennedy and Peter Kennedy	1991

MEMBER	YEAR OF INDUCTION
Tai Babilonia and Randy Gardner	1991
William Thayer Tutt	1991
Ardelle Sanderson	1991
Linda Fratianne	1993
Harry N. Keighley	1993
Nancy Luddington Graham and Ronald Luddington	1993
John Nicks	1993
Colleen O'Conner and Jim Milns	1993
Walter S. Powell	1993
Tim Wood	1993
Janet Lynn	1994
Roger F. Turner	1994
Carlo Fassi	1994
JoJo Starbuck and Kenneth Shelley	1994
Maribel Vinson Owen and George E. B. Hill	1994
Robin Lee	1995
Cynthia Kauffman and Ronald Kauffman	1995
Roy Shipstad	1995
Judy Blumberg and Michael Seibert	1996
Brian Boitano	1996
Frank Carroll	1996
Joseph L. Serafine	1996
Jane Vaughn Sullivan	1996

SHERWIN BADGER WAS NINETEEN YEARS OLD WHEN HE WON THE 1920 U.S. TITLE. THE JUNIOR CHAMPION THAT YEAR, OSCAR RICHARD, WAS SIXTY-FIVE.

APPENDIX 1   (CONTINUED)

Canadian Figure Skating Hall of Fame

Established in 1990 to honor contributions to Canadian skating by athletes, coaches, officials, and builders.

MEMBER	YEAR OF INDUCTION	MEMBER	YEAR OF INDUCTION
Montgomery Wilson	1990	Robert Paul	1993
Constance Wilson	1990	Barbara Wagner	1993
Louis Rubenstein	1990	Gus Lussi	1993
Melville Rogers	1990	Nigel Stephens	1993
Otto Gold	1990	Charles Cumming	1993
Barbara Ann Scott	1991	Norman Gregory	1994
Cecil Smith	1991	Bruce Hyland	1994
Sheldon Galbraith	1991	Margaret Hyland	1994
Donald Cruikshank	1991	Otto Jelinek	1994
George Blundun	1991	Maria Jelinek	1994
Donald Jackson	1992	Ralph McCreath	1994
Wallace Distelmeyer	1992	Peter Mumford	1994
Suzanne Morrow	1992	Osborne Colson	1995
Ellen Burka	1992	Isabelle Henderson	1995
Granville Mayall	1992	Donald McPherson	1995
Frances Dafoe	1993	Elizabeth Swan	1995
Norris Bowden	1993	Mary Rose Thacker	1995

MONTGOMERY WILSON HOLDS THE CANADIAN RECORD FOR MOST MEN'S NATIONAL TITLES (NINE) AND WAS THE FIRST CANADIAN MAN TO WIN A WORLD CHAMPIONSHIP MEDAL — SILVER IN 1932, WHEN HE ALSO WON OLYMPIC BRONZE.

APPENDIX 2

Leading Host Countries for the World Championships

Switzerland	15 times	Hungary	5
Sweden	12	Norway	5
Austria	12	Russia	3
Germany	11	Japan	3
Great Britain	9	Finland	3
U.S.A.	9	Italy	2
Canada	7	Yugoslavia	1
France	6	Denmark	1
Czechoslovakia	5		

The total number of sites adds up to more than the total number of championship years because in the early years there were sometimes separate sites for the singles events.

APPENDIX 3

Leading Host Cities for World Championships

Stockholm, Sweden	11	Paris, France	5
Davos, Switzerland	10	Oslo, Norway	5
Vienna, Austria	10	Colorado Springs, U.S.A.	5
Berlin, Germany	7	Ottawa, Canada	2
Budapest, Hungary	5		

APPENDIX 4

Olympic Gold Medals by Country

MEN		WOMEN		PAIRS		DANCE†	
U.S.A.	6	U.S.A.	5	Russia*	9	Russia*	5
Sweden	4	Norway	3	Germany	3	Great Britain	1
Austria	3	Germany	3	Austria	2		
Great Britain	2	Great Britain	2	France	2		
Germany	1	Austria	2	Canada	1		
Czechoslovakia	1	Canada	1	Finland	1		
Ukraine	1	Sweden	1	Belgium	1		
Russia	1	Holland	1				
		Ukraine	1				

*Includes winners who skated for Soviet Union and Unified Team.
†Dance introduced into Winter Games in 1976.

APPENDIX 5

World Championship Gold Medals by Country

MEN		WOMEN		PAIRS		DANCE	
Austria	22	U.S.A.	20	Russia*	27	Russia*	21
U.S.A.	22	Norway	10	Germany	11	Great Britain	17
Sweden	15	Germany	10	Canada	9	Czechoslovakia	4
Canada	9	Hungary	7	Austria	7	Hungary	1
Russia*	4	Austria	7	Hungary	5	France	1
Germany	4	Great Britain	6	France	4		
Czechoslovakia	3	Canada	4	Great Britain	3		
Great Britain	2	Holland	4	Finland	3		
France	2	Czechoslovakia	2	Belgium	2		
Switzerland	1	Japan	2	U.S.A.	2		
Ukraine	1	France	1	Czechoslovakia	1		
		Switzerland	1				
		Ukraine	1				
		China	1				

*Includes the former Soviet Union.

APPENDIX 6

Youngest Olympic Champions*

MEN		WOMEN	
Dick Button, U.S.A., 1948	18	Sonja Henie, Norway, 1928	15
Alexei Urmanov, Russia, 1994	20	Oksana Baiul, Ukraine, 1994	16
Manfred Schnelldorfer, Germany, 1964	21	Katarina Witt, East Germany, 1984	18
Robin Cousins, Great Britain, 1980	22	Anett Poetzsch, East Germany, 1980	19
Button, 1952	22	Peggy Fleming, U.S.A., 1968	19
Victor Petrenko, Ukraine, 1992	22	Dorothy Hamill, U.S.A., 1976	19
Hayes Jenkins, U.S.A., 1956	22	Henie, 1932	19
Karl Schafer, Austria, 1932	22	Barbara Ann Scott, Canada, 1948	19
David Jenkins, U.S.A., 1960	23	Carol Heiss, U.S.A., 1960	19
Brian Boitano, U.S.A., 1988	24	Tenley Albright, U.S.A., 1956	20
Scott Hamilton, U.S.A., 1984	25	Kristi Yamaguchi, U.S.A., 1992	20

*Source: USFSA Official Media Guide

APPENDIX 7

Leading Medal Winners at World Championships

MEN

Ulrich Salchow, Sweden	13 (10 gold, 3 silver)
Karl Schafer, Austria	11 (7 gold, 3 silver, 1 bronze)
Willy Boeckl, Austria	9 (4 gold, 3 silver, 2 bronze)

POST-WORLD WAR II

Jan Hoffmann, Germany	7 (2 gold, 2 silver, 3 bronze)
Dick Button, U.S.A.	6 (5 gold, 1 silver)
Hayes Jenkins, U.S.A.	6 (4 gold, 2 bronze)
Brian Orser, Canada	6 (1 gold, 4 silver, 1 bronze)
David Jenkins, U.S.A.	5 (3 gold, 2 bronze)
Alain Calmat, France	5 (1 gold, 2 silver, 2 bronze)
Ondrej Nepela, Czechoslovakia	5 (3 gold, 2 silver)
Kurt Browning, Canada	5 (4 gold, 1 silver)
Scott Hamilton, U.S.A.	4 (4 gold)
Brian Boitano, U.S.A.	4 (2 gold, 1 silver, 1 bronze)
Elvis Stojko, Canada	4 (2 gold, 1 silver, 1 bronze)

WOMEN

Sonja Henie, Norway	11 (10 gold, 1 silver)
Lily Kronberger, Hungary	6 (5 gold, 1 silver)
Herma Plank-Szabo, Austria	6 (5 gold, 1 silver)

POST-WORLD WAR II

Carol Heiss, U.S.A.	6 (5 gold, 1 silver)
Katarina Witt, Germany	6 (4 gold, 2 silver)
Sjoukje Dijkstra, Holland	5 (3 gold, 1 silver, 1 bronze)
Gabriele Seyfert, Germany	5 (2 gold, 3 silver)

PAIRS

Irina Rodnina, Russia	10 (10 gold; 6 gold with Alexander Zaitsev, and 4 with Alexei Ulanov, who also had 2 other silvers)
Oleg Protopopov Ludmila Protopopov, Russia	8 (4 gold, 3 silver, 1 bronze)
Walter Jakobsson Ludowika Jakobsson, Finland	7 (3 gold, 4 silver)
Marika Kilius, Germany	6 (2 gold, 2 silver, 2 bronze; 4 with Hans Baumber, 2 with Franz Nigel)

PAIRS (CONTINUED)

Elena Valova Oleg Vasiliev, Russia	6 (3 gold, 3 silver)
Lloyd Eisler, Canada	6 (1 gold, 3 silver, 2 bronze; 5 with Isabelle Brasseur, 1 bronze with Katherina Matousek)

DANCE

Irina Moiseeva Andrei Minenkov, Russia	8 (2 gold, 3 silver, 3 bronze)
Natalia Bestemianova Andrei Bukin, Russia	8 (4 gold, 3 silver, 1 bronze)
Marina Klimova Sergei Ponomarenko, Russia	8 (3 gold, 5 silver)
Ludmila Pakhomova Alexander Gorshkov, Russia	6 (5 gold, 1 silver)
Courtney Jones, England	5 (4 gold, 1 silver; 2 gold with Doreen Denny, 3 medals with June Markham)
William McLachlan, Canada	5 (3 silver, 2 bronze; 3 with Geraldine Fenton, 2 with Virginia Thompson)
Natalia Linichuk Gennadi Karponosov, Russia	5 (2 gold, 1 silver, 2 bronze)
Maia Usova Alexander Zhulin, Russia	5 (1 gold, 2 silver, 2 bronze)
Oksana Gritschuk Evgeny Platov, Russia	5 (3 gold, 1 silver, 1 bronze)
Lawrence Demmy Jean Westwood, Great Britain	4 (4 gold)
Pavel Roman Eva Romanova, Czechoslovakia	4 (4 gold)
Diane Towler Bernard Ford, Great Britain	4 (4 gold)
Jayne Torvill Christopher Dean, Great Britain	4 (4 gold)

APPENDIX 8

Winning at Home

Skating at a major international competition in your native country brings with it the added pressure of expectations from the home crowd. The following is a list of the skaters in the post–World War II era who have won the gold medal when the World Championships were held in their own country. Prior to that war, there were fewer countries entered and hosting, so there were several "hometown" winners. The Olympic list includes all Games.

WORLD CHAMPIONSHIPS (SINCE WORLD WAR II)

MEN*

1957 David Jenkins, U.S.A., at Colorado Springs
1959 David Jenkins, U.S.A., at Colorado Springs
1964 Manfred Schnelldorfer, Germany, at Dortmund
1967 Emmerich Danzer, Austria, at Vienna
1969 Tim Wood, U.S.A., at Colorado Springs
1973 Ondrej Nepela, Czechoslovakia, at Bratislava
1981 Scott Hamilton, U.S.A., at Hartford
1990 Kurt Browning, Canada, at Halifax

*When Germany was divided into two countries, Jan Hoffmann of East Germany won in Munich (1974) and Dortmund (1980).

WOMEN*

1952 Jacqueline du Bief, France, at Paris
1957 Carol Heiss, U.S.A., at Colorado Springs
1959 Carol Heiss, U.S.A., at Colorado Springs
1992 Kristi Yamaguchi, U.S.A., at Oakland
1994 Yuka Sato, Japan, at Chiba

*In 1974, Christine Errath of East Germany won at Munich, West Germany; in 1980, Anett Poetzsch of East Germany won at Dortmund, West Germany.

PAIRS

1960 Barbara Wagner and Bob Paul, Canada, at Vancouver
1964 Hans Baumber and Marika Kilius, Germany, at Dortmund
1984 Barbara Underhill and Paul Martini, Canada, at Ottawa

DANCE

1962 Eva Romanova and Pavel Roman, Czechoslovakia, at Prague

OLYMPICS (ALL-TIME)

MEN

1960 David Jenkins, U.S.A., at Squaw Valley

WOMEN

1908 Madge Syers, Great Britain, at London (Summer Games)
1960 Carol Heiss, U.S.A., at Squaw Valley

PAIRS

1936 Maxi Herber and Ernst Baier, Germany, at Garmisch

DANCE

None

ERNST BAIER

APPENDIX 9

Most National Titles

U.S.A.*

MEN

Dick Button	7
Roger Turner	7
Robin Lee	5
Brian Boitano	4
Scott Hamilton	4
Hayes Alan Jenkins	4
David Jenkins	4

WOMEN

Maribel Vinson	9
Theresa Weld Blanchard	6
Gretchen Merrill	6
Tenley Albright	5
Peggy Fleming	5
Janet Lynn	5
Carol Heiss	4
Linda Fratianne	4

PAIRS

Theresa Weld Blanchard/Nathaniel Niles	9
Tai Babilonia/Randy Gardner	5
Karol Kennedy/Peter Kennedy	5
Caitlin Carruthers/Peter Carruthers	4
Cynthia Kauffman/Ronald Kauffman	4
Nancy Luddington (Rouillard)/Ron Luddington	4
Maribel Vinson/George Hill	4
JoJo Starbuck/Ken Shelley	3

DANCE

Judy Blumberg/Michael Seibert	5
Judy Schwomeyer/James Sladky	5

*Source: USFSA *Official Media Guide*

CANADA

MEN

Montgomery Wilson	9
Brian Orser	8
Toller Cranston	6

MEN (CONTINUED)

Charles Snelling	6
Melville Rogers	5
Kurt Browning	4
Ormond Haycock	4
Donald Jackson	4

WOMEN

Constance Wilson (Samuel)	9
Karen Magnussen	5
Wendy Griner	4
Lynn Nightingale	4
Barbara Ann Scott	4
Petra Burka	3
Josée Chouinard	3
Elizabeth Manley	3
Suzanne Morrow	3
Carole Jane Pachl	3
Mary Rose Thacker	3
Kay Thomson	3

PAIRS

Isabelle Brasseur/Lloyd Eisler	5
Sandra Bezic/Val Bezic	5
Barbara Underhill/Paul Martini	5
Barbara Wagner/Bob Paul	5
Constance Wilson Samuel/Montgomery Wilson	5
Frances Dafoe/Norris Bowden	4

(Note: Ralph McGreath won six titles with three different partners; Lloyd Eisler won a sixth title with another partner, as did Constance Wilson.)

DANCE

(From 1960 on; prior to 1960 the title was divided into different sections.)

Tracy Wilson/Robert McCall	7
Louise Soper/Barry Soper	4
Shae-Lynn Bourne/Victor Kraatz	4
Virginia Thompson/William McLachlan	3
Lorna Wighton/John Dowding	3

APPENDIX 10

World Champions

SINGLES

YEAR	MEN	WOMEN
1896 (St. Petersburg)	Gilbert Fuchs (Germany)	
1897 (Stockholm)	Gustav Hugel (Austria)	
1898 (London)	Henning Grenander (Sweden)	
1899 (Davos)	Gustav Hugel (Austria)	
1900 (Davos)	Gustav Hugel (Austria)	
1901 (Stockholm)	Ulrich Salchow (Sweden)	
1902 (London)	Ulrich Salchow (Sweden)	
1903 (St. Petersburg)	Ulrich Salchow (Sweden)	
1904 (Berlin)	Ulrich Salchow (Sweden)	
1905 (Stockholm)	Ulrich Salchow (Sweden)	

The women's event was introduced at the World Championships in 1906. Madge Syers of Great Britain competed in the men's competition, finishing second in 1902, but women were banned from men's internationals after that year.

1906 (Munich and Davos)	Gilbert Fuchs (Germany)	Madge Syers (Great Britain)
1907 (Vienna)	Ulrich Salchow (Sweden)	Madge Syers (Great Britain)
1908 (Troppau)	Ulrich Salchow (Sweden)	Lily Kronberger (Hungary)
1909 (Stockholm and Budapest)	Ulrich Salchow (Sweden)	Lily Kronberger (Hungary)
1910 (Davos and Berlin)	Ulrich Salchow (Sweden)	Lily Kronberger (Hungary)
1911 (Berlin and Vienna)	Ulrich Salchow (Sweden)	Lily Kronberger (Hungary)
1912 (Manchester and Davos)	Fritz Kachler (Austria)	Opika Von Horvath (Hungary)
1913 (Vienna and Stockholm)	Fritz Kachler (Austria)	Opika Von Horvath (Hungary)
1914 (Helsinki and St. Moritz)	Gosta Sandahl (Sweden)	Opika Von Horvath (Hungary)

1915–1921 No championships held (World War I).

1922 (Stockholm)	Gillis Grafström (Sweden)	Herma Plank-Szabo (Austria)
1923 (Vienna)	Fritz Kachler (Austria)	Herma Plank-Szabo (Austria)
1924 (Manchester and Oslo)	Gillis Grafström (Sweden)	Herma Plank-Szabo (Austria)
1925 (Vienna and Davos)	Willy Boeckl (Austria)	Herma Jaross-Szabo (Austria)
1926 (Berlin and Stockholm)	Willy Boeckl (Austria)	Herma Jaross-Szabo (Austria)
1927 (Davos and Oslo)	Willy Boeckl (Austria)	Sonja Henie (Norway)
1928 (Berlin and London)	Willy Boeckl (Austria)	Sonja Henie (Norway)
1929 (London and Budapest)	Gillis Grafström (Sweden)	Sonja Henie (Norway)
1930 (New York)	Karl Schafer (Austria)	Sonja Henie (Norway)
1931 (Berlin)	Karl Schafer (Austria)	Sonja Henie (Norway)
1932 (Montreal)	Karl Schafer (Austria)	Sonja Henie (Norway)
1933 (Zurich and Stockholm)	Karl Schafer (Austria)	Sonja Henie (Norway)
1934 (Stockholm and Oslo)	Karl Schafer (Austria)	Sonja Henie (Norway)
1935 (Budapest and Vienna)	Karl Schafer (Austria)	Sonja Henie (Norway)

World Champions

SINGLES

YEAR	MEN	WOMEN
1936 (Paris)	Karl Schafer (Austria)	Sonja Henie (Norway)
1937 (Vienna and London)	Felix Kaspar (Austria)	Cecilia Colledge (Great Britain)
1938 (Berlin and Stockholm)	Felix Kaspar (Austria)	Megan Taylor (Great Britain)
1939 (Budapest and Prague)	Graham Sharp (Great Britain)	Megan Taylor (Great Britain)

1940–1946 No championships held (World War II).

1947 (Stockholm)	Hans Gerschwiler (Switzerland)	Barbara Ann Scott (Canada)
1948 (Davos)	Richard Button (U.S.A.)	Barbara Ann Scott (Canada)
1949 (Paris)	Richard Button (U.S.A.)	Alena Vrzanova (Czechoslovakia)
1950 (London)	Richard Button (U.S.A.)	Alena Vrzanova (Czechoslovakia)
1951 (Milan)	Richard Button (U.S.A.)	Jeannette Altwegg (Great Britain)
1952 (Paris)	Richard Button (U.S.A.)	Jacqueline du Bief (France)
1953 (Davos)	Hayes Jenkins (U.S.A.)	Tenley Albright (U.S.A.)
1954 (Oslo)	Hayes Jenkins (U.S.A.)	Gundi Busch (Germany)
1955 (Vienna)	Hayes Jenkins (U.S.A.)	Tenley Albright (U.S.A.)
1956 (Garmisch)	Hayes Jenkins (U.S.A.)	Carol Heiss (U.S.A.)
1957 (Colorado Springs)	David Jenkins (U.S.A.)	Carol Heiss (U.S.A.)
1958 (Paris)	David Jenkins (U.S.A.)	Carol Heiss (U.S.A.)
1959 (Colorado Springs)	David Jenkins (U.S.A.)	Carol Heiss (U.S.A.)
1960 (Vancouver)	Alain Giletti (France)	Carol Heiss (U.S.A.)

1961 No championship held (American team killed in airplane crash over Brussels).

1962 (Prague)	Donald Jackson (Canada)	Sjoukje Dijkstra (Holland)
1963 (Cortina)	Donald McPherson (Canada)	Sjoukje Dijkstra (Holland)
1964 (Dortmund)	Manfred Schnelldorfer (West Germany)	Sjoukje Dijkstra (Holland)
1965 (Colorado Springs)	Alain Calmat (France)	Petra Burka (Canada)
1966 (Davos)	Emmerich Danzer (Austria)	Peggy Fleming (U.S.A.)
1967 (Vienna)	Emmerich Danzer (Austria)	Peggy Fleming (U.S.A.)
1968 (Geneva)	Emmerich Danzer (Austria)	Peggy Fleming (U.S.A.)
1969 (Colorado Springs)	Tim Wood (U.S.A.)	Gabriele Seyfert (East Germany)
1970 (Ljubljana)	Tim Wood (U.S.A.)	Gabriele Seyfert (East Germany)
1971 (Lyon)	Ondrej Nepela (Czechoslovakia)	Beatrix Schuba (Austria)
1972 (Calgary)	Ondrej Nepela (Czechoslovakia)	Beatrix Schuba (Austria)
1973 (Bratislava)	Ondrej Nepela (Czechoslovakia)	Karen Magnussen (Canada)
1974 (Munich)	Jan Hoffmann (East Germany)	Christine Errath (East Germany)
1975 (Colorado Springs)	Sergei Volkov (Soviet Union)	Dianne de Leeuw (Holland)
1976 (Gothenburg)	John Curry (Great Britain)	Dorothy Hamill (U.S.A.)
1977 (Tokyo)	Vladimir Kovalev (Soviet Union)	Linda Fratianne (U.S.A.)
1978 (Ottawa)	Charles Tickner (U.S.A.)	Anett Poetzsch (East Germany)

World Champions

SINGLES

YEAR	MEN	WOMEN
1979 (Vienna)	Vladimir Kovalev (Soviet Union)	Linda Fratianne (U.S.A.)
1980 (Dortmund)	Jan Hoffmann (East Germany)	Anett Poetzsch (East Germany)
1981 (Hartford)	Scott Hamilton (U.S.A.)	Denise Biellmann (Switzerland)
1982 (Copenhagen)	Scott Hamilton (U.S.A.)	Elaine Zayak (U.S.A.)
1983 (Helsinki)	Scott Hamilton (U.S.A.)	Rosalyn Sumners (U.S.A.)
1984 (Ottawa)	Scott Hamilton (U.S.A.)	Katarina Witt (East Germany)
1985 (Tokyo)	Alexander Fadeev (Soviet Union)	Katarina Witt (East Germany)
1986 (Geneva)	Brian Boitano (U.S.A.)	Debi Thomas (U.S.A.)
1987 (Cincinnati)	Brian Orser (Canada)	Katarina Witt (East Germany)
1988 (Budapest)	Brian Boitano (U.S.A.)	Katarina Witt (East Germany)
1989 (Paris)	Kurt Browning (Canada)	Midori Ito (Japan)
1990 (Halifax)	Kurt Browning (Canada)	Jill Trenary (U.S.A.)
1991 (Munich)	Kurt Browning (Canada)	Kristi Yamaguchi (U.S.A.)
1992 (Oakland)	Victor Petrenko (Commonwealth Independent States)	Kristi Yamaguchi (U.S.A.)
1993 (Prague)	Kurt Browning (Canada)	Oksana Baiul (Ukraine)
1994 (Chiba)	Elvis Stojko (Canada)	Yuka Sato (Japan)
1995 (Birmingham)	Elvis Stojko (Canada)	Lu Chen (China)
1996 (Edmonton)	Todd Eldredge (U.S.A.)	Michelle Kwan (U.S.A.)

PAIRS

Pairs were introduced to the World Championships in 1908.

YEAR	PAIR	YEAR	PAIR
1908	Anna Hubler/Heinrich Burger (Germany)	1928	Andrée Joly/Pierre Brunet (France)
1909	Phyllis Johnson/James Johnson (Great Britain)	1929	Lilly Scholz/Otto Kaiser (Austria)
1910	Anna Hubler/Heinrich Burger (Germany)	1930	Andrée Joly/Pierre Brunet (France)
1911	Ludowika Eilers/Walter Jakobsson (Finland)	1931	Emilie Rotter/Laszlo Szollas (Hungary)
1912	Phyllis Johnson/James Johnson (Great Britain)	1932	Andrée Joly/Pierre Brunet (France)
1913	Helene Engelmann/Karl Mejstrik (Austria)	1933	Emilie Rotter/Laszlo Szollas (Hungary)
1914	Ludowika Jakobsson/Walter Jakobsson (Finland)	1934	Emilie Rotter/Laszlo Szollas (Hungary)
		1935	Emilie Rotter/Laszlo Szollas (Hungary)
1915–1921 No championships held.		1936	Maxi Herber/Ernst Baier (Germany)
		1937	Maxi Herber/Ernst Baier (Germany)
1922	Helene Engelmann/Alfred Berger (Austria)	1938	Maxi Herber/Ernst Baier (Germany)
1923	Ludowika Jakobsson/Walter Jakobsson (Finland)	1939	Maxi Herber/Ernst Baier (Germany)
1924	Helene Engelmann/Alfred Berger (Austria)		
1925	Herma Jaross-Szabo/Ludwig Wrede (Austria)	1940–1946 No championships held.	
1926	Andrée Joly/Pierre Brunet (France)		
1927	Herma Jaross-Szabo/Ludwig Wrede (Austria)	1947	Micheline Lannoy/Pierre Baugniet (Belgium)

APPENDIX 10 (CONTINUED)

World Champions

YEAR	PAIR
1948	Micheline Lannoy/Pierre Baugniet (Belgium)
1949	Andrea Kekessy/Ede Kiraly (Hungary)
1950	Karol Kennedy/Peter Kennedy (U.S.A.)
1951	Ria Falk/Paul Falk (Germany)
1952	Ria Falk/Paul Falk (Germany)
1953	Jennifer Nicks/John Nicks (Great Britain)
1954	Frances Dafoe/Norris Bowden (Canada)
1955	Frances Dafoe/Norris Bowden (Canada)
1956	Elisabeth Schwarz/Kurt Oppelt (Austria)
1957	Barbara Wagner/Robert Paul (Canada)
1958	Barbara Wagner/Robert Paul (Canada)
1959	Barbara Wagner/Robert Paul (Canada)
1960	Barbara Wagner/Robert Paul (Canada)

1961 No championships held.

YEAR	PAIR
1962	Maria Jelinek/Otto Jelinek (Canada)
1963	Marika Kilius/Hans Baumber (Germany)
1964	Marika Kilius/Hans Baumber (Germany)
1965	Ludmila Belousova/Oleg Protopopov (Soviet Union)
1966	Ludmila Belousova/Oleg Protopopov (Soviet Union)
1967	Ludmila Belousova/Oleg Protopopov (Soviet Union)
1968	Ludmila Belousova/Oleg Protopopov (Soviet Union)
1969	Irina Rodnina/Alexei Ulanov (Soviet Union)
1970	Irina Rodnina/Alexei Ulanov (Soviet Union)
1971	Irina Rodnina/Alexei Ulanov (Soviet Union)
1972	Irina Rodnina/Alexei Ulanov (Soviet Union)
1973	Irina Rodnina/Alexander Zaitsev (Soviet Union)
1974	Irina Rodnina/Alexander Zaitsev (Soviet Union)
1975	Irina Rodnina/Alexander Zaitsev (Soviet Union)
1976	Irina Rodnina/Alexander Zaitsev (Soviet Union)
1977	Irina Rodnina/Alexander Zaitsev (Soviet Union)
1978	Irina Rodnina/Alexander Zaitsev (Soviet Union)
1979	Tai Babilonia/Randy Gardner (U.S.A.)
1980	Marina Cherkasova/Sergei Shakhrai (Soviet Union)
1981	Irina Vorobieva/Igor Lisovsky (Soviet Union)
1982	Sabine Baess/Tassilo Thierbach (East Germany)
1983	Elena Valova/Oleg Vasiliev (Soviet Union)
1984	Barbara Underhill/Paul Martini (Canada)
1985	Elena Valova/Oleg Vasiliev (Soviet Union)
1986	Ekaterina Gordeeva/Sergei Grinkov (Soviet Union)

YEAR	PAIR
1987	Ekaterina Gordeeva/Sergei Grinkov (Soviet Union)
1988	Elena Valova/Oleg Vasiliev (Soviet Union)
1989	Ekaterina Gordeeva/Sergei Grinkov (Soviet Union)
1990	Ekaterina Gordeeva/Sergei Grinkov (Soviet Union)
1991	Natalia Mishkutienok/Artur Dmitriev (Soviet Union)
1992	Natalia Mishkutienok/Artur Dmitriev (Commonwealth Independent States)
1993	Isabelle Brasseur/Lloyd Eisler (Canada)
1994	Evgenia Shiskova/Vadim Naumov (Russia)
1995	Radka Kovarikova/Rene Novotny (Czech Republic)
1996	Marina Eltsova/Andrei Bushkov (Russia)

ICE DANCING

Ice dancing was introduced to the World Championships in 1952.

YEAR	COUPLE
1952	Jean Westwood/Lawrence Demmy (Great Britain)
1953	Jean Westwood/Lawrence Demmy (Great Britain)
1954	Jean Westwood/Lawrence Demmy (Great Britain)
1955	Jean Westwood/Lawrence Demmy (Great Britain)
1956	Pamela Weight/Paul Thomas (Great Britain)
1957	June Markham/Courtney Jones (Great Britain)
1958	June Markham/Courtney Jones (Great Britain)
1959	Doreen Denny/Courtney Jones (Great Britain)
1960	Doreen Denny/Courtney Jones (Great Britain)

1961 No championships held.

YEAR	COUPLE
1962	Eva Romanova/Pavel Roman (Czechoslovakia)
1963	Eva Romanova/Pavel Roman (Czechoslovakia)
1964	Eva Romanova/Pavel Roman (Czechoslovakia)
1965	Eva Romanova/Pavel Roman (Czechoslovakia)
1966	Diane Towler/Bernard Ford (Great Britain)
1967	Diane Towler/Bernard Ford (Great Britain)
1968	Diane Towler/Bernard Ford (Great Britain)
1969	Diane Towler/Bernard Ford (Great Britain)
1970	Ludmila Pakhomova/Alexander Gorshkov (Soviet Union)
1971	Ludmila Pakhomova/Alexander Gorshkov (Soviet Union)

APPENDIX 10 (CONTINUED)

World Champions

YEAR	COUPLE
1972	Ludmila Pakhomova/Alexander Gorshkov (Soviet Union)
1973	Ludmila Pakhomova/Alexander Gorshkov (Soviet Union)
1974	Ludmila Pakhomova/Alexander Gorshkov (Soviet Union)
1975	Irina Moiseeva/Andrei Minenkov (Soviet Union)
1976	Ludmila Pakhomova/Alexander Gorshkov (Soviet Union)
1977	Irina Moiseeva/Andrei Minenkov (Soviet Union)
1978	Natalia Linichuk/Gennadi Karponosov (Soviet Union)
1979	Natalia Linichuk/Gennadi Karponosov (Soviet Union)
1980	Kristina Regoeczy/Andras Sallay (Hungary)
1981	Jayne Torvill/Christopher Dean (Great Britain)
1982	Jayne Torvill/Christopher Dean (Great Britain)

YEAR	COUPLE
1983	Jayne Torvill/Christopher Dean (Great Britain)
1984	Jayne Torvill/Christopher Dean (Great Britain)
1985	Natalia Bestemianova/Andrei Bukin (Soviet Union)
1986	Natalia Bestemianova/Andrei Bukin (Soviet Union)
1987	Natalia Bestemianova/Andrei Bukin (Soviet Union)
1988	Natalia Bestemianova/Andrei Bukin (Soviet Union)
1989	Marina Klimova/Sergei Ponomarenko (Soviet Union)
1990	Marina Klimova/Sergei Ponomarenko (Soviet Union)
1991	Isabelle Duchesnay/Paul Duchesnay (France)
1992	Marina Klimova/Sergei Ponomarenko (Commonwealth Independent States)
1993	Maia Usova/Alexander Zhulin (Russia)
1994	Oksana Gritschuk/Evgeny Platov (Russia)
1995	Oksana Gritschuk/Evgeny Platov (Russia)
1996	Oksana Gritschuk/Evgeny Platov (Russia)

AMERICAN BEATRIX LOUGHRAN WAS THE FIRST NORTH AMERICAN TO WIN A MAJOR SKATING MEDAL, TAKING SILVER AT THE 1924 OLYMPICS AND BRONZE AT THE WORLD CHAMPIONSHIPS IN THE SAME YEAR. SHE ALSO WON A BRONZE IN 1928, AND A SILVER IN PAIRS WITH SHERWIN BADGER AT THE 1932 GAMES.

Skating Chronology

156 A.D.:	"Skates" first mentioned in Icelandic literature.
800–1000:	Scandinavians fashion crude skates from animal bones.
1190:	Bone skates described in letters of William FitzStephen, clerk of Britain's Thomas Becket.
1396:	Lydwina, who becomes the patron saint of skating, has her famous skating accident at Schiedam, Holland, beginning thirty-eight years of terrible ailments.
1500s:	Skating becomes popular on the canals of Holland.
1662:	Bitter winter makes skating popular among British royal court.
1750:	British develop curved, grooved blade, extended past heel. The first "figure" skate.
1840:	Jackson Haines, generally credited as the pioneer of "figure" skating for liberating sporting from its stiff and humorless European style, is born in New York City.
1849:	The first skating club in North America, in Philadelphia, is formed.
1850:	E. W. Bushnell patents the first all-iron skate in North America, removing the encumbrance of heavy straps required to strap blades to boots.
1858:	The first covered rink in Canada is erected at Quebec City. A second rink is built in Montreal the next year.
1863:	Jackson Haines wins the Championships of America. He also wins the next year but receives a less-than-enthusiastic response for his free-form style and goes to Europe, where he is an overnight success. His expressive movements and jumps give birth to the international style of figure skating.
1870:	The Acme Skate Company of Halifax, Nova Scotia, invents the "gutter," a deep groove in the blade that permits the use of either the inside or outside edge of the skate.
1875:	Jackson Haines dies after catching pneumonia while traveling from St. Petersburg to Stockholm via sled.
1876:	The world's first artificial ice rink opens at Chelsea, England.
1879:	The National Skating Association of Great Britain, the world's first national skating body, is formed by uniting English and Scottish clubs.
1879:	Madison Square Garden, measuring 6,000 square feet, or 1,800 sq. m (six times the size of Chelsea), opens as the first artificial rink in North America.
1882:	The first known international skating meet is held in Austria.
1887:	Louis Rubenstein, a Montreal alderman and internationally renowned skater, forms the Amateur Skating Association of Canada. Rubenstein also spearheads the formation of the National Amateur Skating Association of the United States and the International Skating Union of America.
1891:	Germany and Austria are dual hosts of the first European Championships.
1893:	The International Eislauf Vereinigung (IEV) is founded in Scheveningen, Netherlands, and becomes the governing body for figure and speed skating. The IEV later becomes known as the International Skating Union (ISU).
1896:	The first official ISU is held in St. Petersburg, Russia, replacing the European Championship.
1902:	Great Britain's Madge Syers-Cave wins the silver medal at the World Championship, nearly beating legendary Ulrich Salchow of Sweden, who wins the second of his ten titles.
1903:	The ISU votes to forbid women from entering the men's competition.
1905:	The first Canadian Championships are held, Ormond B. Haycock winning the men's title, Anne L. Ewan the women's, and Ormond and Katherine Haycock taking the pairs title.

Skating Chronology (CONTINUED)

1906: The first ISU women's championship is held in Davos, Switzerland, while the men's championship is held in Munich, Germany.

1908: Pairs, sometimes called hand-to-hand skating, is added to the ISU championship roster.

1908: Irving Brokaw, of Cambridge, Massachusetts, becomes the first North American to participate internationally, placing sixth at London's Summer Olympics, in which figure skating was included.

1914: A separate organization, the Figure Skating Department of the Amateur Skating Association of Canada, is formed to handle figure skating. The two founding clubs are Ottawa Minto and Montreal Earl Grey.

1914: George H. Browne organizes the first International Figure Skating Championships, under the umbrella of the International Skating Union of America, the governing body for both speed skating and figure skating in the U.S.A.

1915: World Championships are canceled because of World War I.

1915: The first North American ice-skating film, *The Frozen Warning*, starring Broadway sensation Charlotte, is released.

1920: Oscar Richard wins U.S. Junior Men's Championship. He is sixty-five years old. The senior men's winner, Sherwin Badger, is nineteen.

1920: Summer Olympics at Antwerp, Belgium, include figure skating.

1921: In New York, the United States Figure Skating Association is born out of the ISU of A and the National Amateur Skating Association to oversee figure skating and spread the sport across the nation. The seven original clubs represent New York (two clubs), Boston, Chicago, Philadelphia, Lake Placid, and Minneapolis–St. Paul.

1922: World Championships resume.

1923: North American Championships, to be held every second year, are established, with the inaugural event at Ottawa.

1923: *Skating* magazine publishes its debut issue.

1924: The first Winter Olympics are held at Chamonix, France, with figure skating as a centerpiece sport.

1924: Beatrix Loughran of the U.S. wins North America's first World Championship medal (bronze). Women and pairs winners are called world champions for first time instead of ISU champions.

1927: IEV approves editions of its rules in English, and in that language the sport's governing body becomes known as the International Skating Union (ISU).

1928: Canada makes first appearance at World Championships: Montgomery Wilson (7th), Jack Eastwood (9th) in men's at Berlin; Constance Wilson (4th) in women's; and Maud Smith and Eastwood (6th) in pairs, both events in London.

1930: New York is the first North American city to play host to a World Championship. Sonja Henie wins her fourth straight title and triggers a boom in American skating. Roger Turner is first American man to win a World Championship medal (silver). Beatrix Loughran and Sherwin Badger are first Americans to win a pairs medal (bronze). Cecil Smith wins women's silver, the first Canadian to earn a world medal.

1931: Lake Placid establishes a summer skating center, believed to be the first in North America. "Patch" (dividing ice into many sections for figures practice) is invented.

1932: Montreal is the site of first World Championship held in Canada. Montgomery Wilson becomes the first Canadian man to win a World Championship medal (silver).

Skating Chronology (CONTINUED)

1936: Shipstad and Johnson's Ice Follies are born in Tulsa, Oklahoma.

1938: Thirteen professionals meet in Lake Placid to form the Association of Professional Figure Skaters, the predecessor to the Professional Skaters Guild of America (PSGA).

1938: The Broadmoor Ice Palace is formed out of an indoor riding center in Colorado Springs, Colorado.

1939: The Figure Skating Department is renamed the Canadian Figure Skating Association.

1939: Sun Valley experiments with outdoor artificial ice.

1940: Ice Capades starts.

1940: World Championships are canceled because of World War II.

1944: Holiday on Ice is founded.

1947: World Championships resume, in Stockholm, Sweden. Barbara Ann Scott gives Canada its first world title. All World Championship disciplines to be held at same site, for good.

1947: National office of the CFSA is established in Ottawa as a volunteer association under Secretary-Treasurer Charles H. Cumming, who became the first full-time employee in 1958.

1948: Dick Button becomes first American to win a world title. First of twelve straight men's World Championships for the U.S. (Button five, Hayes Jenkins four, David Jenkins three), the longest uninterrupted streak in men's event.

1949: A professional ice-dance competition is held in London, England, using proposed ISU rules.

1950: Peter and Karol Kennedy become first Americans to win World Pairs Championship.

1952: Ice dancing is introduced to World Championships.

1953: Frances Dafoe and Norris Bowden win Canada's first world pairs medal (silver).

1954: Frances Dafoe and Norris Bowden win Canada's first World Pairs Championship.

1961: World Championships scheduled for Prague are canceled when the entire U.S. team is killed in a plane crash near Brussels.

1962: Donald Jackson lands first triple Lutz in history, giving Canada its first men's World Championship.

1964: Short program is introduced into pairs championships. Only one program had existed.

1965: Ludmila Belousova and Oleg Protopopov become first Russians (Soviets) to win a World Championship. Soviet reign of fourteen straight world pairs titles begins.

1971: The final North American Championship is held in Peterborough, Ontario.

1973: Skate Canada is established, with the inaugural event in Calgary.

1973: Short program is introduced to singles skating, reducing value of compulsory figures from 50 percent to 30 percent.

1973: Dick Button promotes a professional championship in Tokyo but cannot convince the ISU to become involved.

1976: Ice dancing is included in the Winter Olympics for the first time.

1976: U.S. Figure Skating Hall of Fame is established at Colorado Springs.

1977: Minoru Sano wins men's World Championship bronze, Japan's first medal.

1977: The first precision competition in Canada is held at Ilderton, Ontario.

1978: Canada's Vern Taylor lands first triple Axel in history at Worlds in Ottawa.

1979: Norton Skate, expected to be a one-time international competition, is held at Lake Placid, New York.

1980: World Professional Championships debut in Landover, Maryland, their permanent home.

1981: Lake Placid plays host to the first Skate America, which evolved from Norton Skate.

Skating Chronology (CONTINUED)

1984: The first U.S. National Precision Championship is held in Bowling Green, Ohio.

1987: Brian Orser wins world title, ending a twenty-four-year drought for Canada in the men's event.

1988: Kurt Browning lands first quadruple jump in history at Worlds in Budapest.

1989: Japan's Midori Ito lands first triple Axel by a woman and becomes the first skater from an Asian country to win a world title.

1990: Compulsory figures are skated for last time at a World Championship, in Halifax.

1991: Tonya Harding becomes the second woman, and the first American woman, to land a triple Axel, completing the three-and-a-half-revolution jump at U.S. nationals in Minneapolis.

1991: Despite the absence from the team of the defending world champion (injured Jill Trenary) and the bronze medalist (Holly Cook, who didn't make the team), American women take all three places on the World Championship podium: Kristi Yamaguchi, gold; Tonya Harding, silver; Nancy Kerrigan, bronze.

1992: In June, the ISU passes a new rule that allows previously ineligible skaters (pros) to be reinstated and skate in international competitions, including the Olympics. A skater can be reinstated only once.

1992: In November, USFSA holds its first-ever pro–am in Hershey, Pennsylvania. Nancy Kerrigan wins women's title over Tonya Harding and pros Caryn Kadavy and Rosalyn Sumners.

1993: U.S. fails to win a medal at World Championship for the first time since 1964. Oksana Baiul becomes second youngest women's winner at fifteen (Sonja Henie was fourteen). Canada, with Kurt Browning (gold), Elvis Stojko (silver), and Isabelle Brasseur and Lloyd Eisler (gold), has its best Worlds since 1962.

1993: When deadline passes for reinstatement of pro skaters, thirty-three pros are approved, eighteen of them from the U.S.

1994: In January, Nancy Kerrigan is attacked by an unknown assailant during practices for the U.S. nationals in Detroit, forcing her to withdraw from championships. Tonya Harding's husband and two associates are later charged and convicted. Harding is banned from competition.

1994: In February, Kerrigan returns from injury to finish second to Oksana Baiul, who narrowly wins Olympic gold. Alexei Urmanov wins Russia's first men's Olympic gold. Pros return to the Olympics for the first time.

1994: In March, the Broadmoor World Arena in Colorado Springs is scrapped to make room for a hotel addition.

1994: In April, 28,000 fans, believed to be the largest skating crowd ever, flood into the Thunder Dome in St. Petersburg, Florida, to see the Tour of World Figure Skating Champions.

1994: The fifth pro–am sponsored by the USFSA becomes the first one open to international skaters.

1994: The ISU recognizes precision skating as a separate division of figure skating.

1994: In December, the first Canadian Professional Championships are held at Hamilton.

1995: Lu Chen gives China its first World Championship. U.S. rebounds with medals in three of four disciplines. Elvis Stojko wins second world title.

1995: The ISU announces it will form a Grand Prix circuit Champions Series of five former fall internationals and an overall Grand Prix championship event early in the new year. Prize money will also be paid at the World Championships.

1995: The ISU closes the door on reinstatement of ineligible skaters, with an April 1 last-chance deadline.

Glossary

SINGLES

AXEL: Considered the toughest of jumps to triple, because it has an extra half revolution. The skater takes off from the forward outside edge of the skating foot. The landing is on the back outside edge of the free foot. Named for Norway's Axel Paulsen, who never skated in an official World Figure Skating Championship because he had earned money in speed-skating races in the late nineteenth century.

CAMEL SPIN*: The skater revolves around the blade of the skating foot, with the chest and free leg parallel to the ice and the back arched.

CROSS-FOOT SPIN*: An upright spin in which the skater gradually places the free foot behind the spinning foot, and continues the spin on two feet with the toes together.

DEATH DROP*: Similar to the back sit spin; it involves a jump, as in the flying camel, but the skater drops immediately to a back sit position.

FLIP: The flip is the same as the Lutz, except the skater takes off from the back inside edge of the skating foot instead of the back outside edge. For some skaters, it is more difficult than the Lutz. It is sometimes called a toe Salchow.

FLYING BACK SIT SPIN CHANGING THE FOOT OF LANDING*: A spin involving a jump from a forward outside edge to a backward outside edge, landing in a full back sit position.

FLYING CAMEL SPIN*: A spin starting with a jump from a forward outside edge and landing rotating in a back camel position parallel to the ice.

JUMPS: Jumps are really spins in the air. Jumps are defined by several elements: how many times the skater rotates in the air (single, double, triple, quad); what edges of the skates are used in the takeoff and landing; whether or not the toe pick is used to assist the jump, the way a pole vaulter uses a pole; and what foot is used to initiate the jump. The foot that pushes off the ice is the "skating foot," and the other foot is called the "free foot." There are three "toe" (pick-assisted) jumps (toe loop, flip, and Lutz) and three "edge" jumps (Salchow, loop, and Axel). All jumps except the Axel are entered with the skater facing backward. Most skaters rotate counterclockwise, but many top ones go clockwise.

JUMP COMBINATIONS: A back-to-back set of jumps in which the landing edge of the first jump becomes the takeoff edge of the second one. Top competitive skaters do triple–triple combinations.

JUMP SERIES: Several jumps in succession, but with steps, turns, hops, or changes of feet between the landing of one jump and takeoff of the next. Often used as an artistic climax to a program, or an advertisement for a skater's energy.

LAYBACK SPIN*: An upright spin in which the head and shoulders are dropped backward and the back arched.

LAYOVER SPIN*: A flying-camel spin involving a shift in body weight so that the spin rotates on an outside edge and the skater turns on his or her side instead of being parallel to the ice.

LOOP: The skater takes off from the back outside edge of the skating foot. The landing is on the back outside edge of the takeoff foot. The skates form a loop in the air. In Europe, the loop is sometimes called a Rittberger, named for Germany's Werner Rittberger, three-time world silver medalist, who did the first single loop in 1910.

LUTZ: A difficult jump that requires a long, gliding buildup. The skater is exerting force against the natural body movement; the jump is approached clockwise but is performed counterclockwise. The skater takes off from the back outside edge of the skating foot with assistance of the toe pick on the free foot. The landing is on the back outside edge of the free foot. Named for Austrian Alois Lutz, who never skated in the World Championship but invented the jump in 1913.

Glossary (CONTINUED)

SALCHOW: The skater takes off from the back inside edge of the skating foot. The landing is on the back outside edge of the free foot. The jump is named for Ulrich Salchow of Sweden, who won the first Olympic Championship and ten World Championships.

SIT SPIN*: A spin done in a sitting position. The body is low to the ice, with the skating knee bent and the free leg extended.

SPINS: Continuous turns pivoting on a blade that does not leave the ice.

TOE LOOP: Usually the first jump to be mastered, in one of its forms. The skater takes off from the back outside edge of the skating foot, with the help of the toe pick on the free foot. The landing is on the back outside edge of the skating foot. This jump is also called a cherry or, with a small turn (three-turn) just before the jump, a toe walley.

*From Skating … An Inside Look, a CFSA publication.

PAIRS

DEATH SPIRAL: In this dramatic move, the pairs couple act like a geometry compass. The woman, with her body horizontal and as close to the ice as possible, describes a circle around the man, who is the pivot and center of the circle. Holding his partner at arm's length by one hand as she revolves around him on one foot, the man, too, is doing a spin, with one foot the pivot and the other spinning on an edge. The spiral is defined by the direction (forward/backward) the female's body is moving and the skate edge (inside/outside) she uses.

HAND-TO-HAND LOOP LIFT†: A lift in which the man raises his partner, in front of him and facing the same direction, above his head. She remains facing the same direction, in the sitting position with her hands behind her, while her partner supports her by the hands.

HYDRANT LIFT†: A lift in which the man throws his partner over his head while skating backward, rotates a half turn, and catches his partner facing him.

LATERAL TWIST†: A move in which the man throws his partner overhead. She rotates, while in a position lateral to the ice, and he catches her.

LIFTS†: Lifts are just as they sound: pairs elements in which the man hoists his partner above his head with one or both arms fully extended. The lift consists of ascending, rotating, and descending movements that define the lift.

PLATTER LIFT†: A lift in which the man raises his partner overhead, with his hands resting on her hips. She is horizontal to the ice, facing the back of the man, in a platter position.

STAR LIFT†: A lift in which the man raises his partner by her hip, from his side into the air. She is in the scissors position, either with one hand touching his shoulder or with both hands free.

TOE OVERHEAD LIFT†: A lift in which the man swings his partner from one side of his body, behind his head, and into a raised position. She is facing the same direction as the man, in a splits position.

THROW JUMP†: A move in which the man assists his partner into the air and she performs the necessary rotations and landing.

†From the Official Media Guide of the USFSA.

Photo Credits

All photographs are by Barbara McCutcheon unless otherwise indicated.

Page *vii*: courtesy of the Canadian Figure Skating Association (CFSA); 4: © Stephan Potopnyk; 14: collection of Barbara McCutcheon; 16: Dick Button © Dick Button/Candid Productions Inc.; Sonja Henie, collection of Barbara McCutcheon; Barbara Ann Scott, courtesy of CFSA; Ulrich Salchow, courtesy of CFSA; Zeljka Cizmesija, courtesy of CFSA; Jackson Haines, courtesy of CFSA; 19: collection of Ron Demers; 20: collection of Barbara McCutcheon; 21: collection of Barbara McCutcheon; 22: collection of Barbara McCutcheon; 23: collection of Ron Demers; 24: collection of Ron Demers; 25: © Carole Swan; 30: © Stephan Potopnyk; 46: © Carole Swan; 58: © Margaret Williamson; 65 (right): © Stephan Potopnyk; 72 (right): © Margaret Williamson; 79: © Margaret Williamson; 83: © Cam Silverson; 87 (right): © Cam Silverson; 97: collection of Barbara McCutcheon; 105: collection of Barbara McCutcheon; 107: courtesy of CFSA; 115:© Dick Button/Candid Productions; 117: © Canadian Sport Images/Ted Grant; 123: collection of Barbara McCutcheon; 137: collection of Barbara McCutcheon; 138: © Margaret Williamson; 142: © Toronto Star/B. Weil; 146: © Paul Harvath; 150: courtesy of the Canadian Broadcasting Corporation; 155: collection of Barbara McCutcheon; 157: collection of Barbara McCutcheon; 158: courtesy of MGM-Pathe Communications Co.; 159: collection of Barbara McCutcheon; 161: collection of Barbara McCutcheon; 164: © Cam Silverson; 168: © Cam Silverson; 169: © Cam Silverson; 174: © Margaret Williamson; 177: courtesy of CFSA; 178: courtesy of CFSA; 182: collection of Barbara McCutcheon; 188: courtesy of CFSA.

The figure skating medals that appear on pages 32, 63, 108, 141, and 170 are reproduced with the permission of Elvis Stojko.

Index

Page numbers in **boldface** refer to illustrations or captions.

Index (CONTINUED)

Index (CONTINUED)

J

Jaaskelainen, Oula, 49
Jackson, Donald, 23–6, 56, 106–8, **107**, 128, 167, 171; 1960 Olympic bronze, 107; 1962 World Championship gold, 55, 106
Jackson, H. Kermit, 4
Janoschak, Mark, 92
Japan, 106, 165
Jefferson Pilot, 165–6
Jelinek, Maria and Otto, 24, 110; World Championship gold, 108
Jenkins, David, 23
Jenkins, Hayes, 23, 104
Johnson, Lynn-Holly, 157–8
Johnston, Lyndon, 99
Joly, Andrée, 81
Jones and Markham, 123
Josephine (Napoleon's wife), 18
Julin-Mauroy, Magda, 122

K

Kachler, Fritz, 123
Kadavy, Caryn, **62**, 120–1, 139; 1987 World Championship, 62
Karatek, Stanislav, 71
Kawahara, Sarah, 70
Kazakova, Oksana, **101**
Kelly, Gene, 97, 153
Kelly, Moira, **158**
Kenna, Monica, 151
Kerrigan, Nancy, 6–7, 9–10, 21, 71, 73, 88, 112, 114–15, **114**, 127, 141, **152**, 159; 1991 World Championship bronze, 104, 123; 1994 Olympic silver, 114; Kerrigan-Harding incident, 7, 12, 27, 50, 115, 126–7, 151
Keszler, Uschi, 66, 70, 89–90, 168
Kim, Netty, 55, 172
Kirby, Michael, 158
Klimova, Marina, **80**, 81, 83–4. See also Klimova and Ponomarenko
Klimova and Ponomarenko, 1992 Olympic gold, 81, 83, 92, 117, **120**, 121–2, 123
Kokko, Petri. See Rahkamo and Kokko
Kovalev, Vladimir, 78, 119
Kovarikova, Radka, 10. See also Kovarikova and Novotny
Kovarikova and Novotny, **96**, 97, 100–1; 1992 World Championship silver, 100; 1995 World Championship gold, 96–7
Kraatz, Victor, 7, **29**, 37, 87, 91. See also Bourne and Kraatz
Krieg, Nathalie, 65, 68
Krylova, Anjelika, 95. See also Krylova and Ovsiannikov
Krylova and Ovsiannikov, **87**
Kubicka, Terry, 119
Kuchiki, Natasha, 83
Kulik, Ilya, 15, 27, **46**, 47, 171; 1995 European Championship gold, 46
Kwan, Michelle, 7, 15, 37, **48**, 49–50, 70, **72**, **162**, **163**
Kwiatkowski, Tonia, **56**

L

Ladret, Doug, 9, 153. See also Hough and Ladret
Lagencamp, Heather, 151
Lake Placid, New York, 78, 89
Landry, Cindy, 99
Lavanchy, Pascal. See Minotte and Lavanchy
Leaver, Linda, 70
LeBlanc, Raoul, 159
LeBlanc, Roméo, 45
de Leeuw, Dianne, 136
Leigh, Doug, 34, 39–40, 43, 48–9, 91, 109, 120, 168–9, 171
Leitch, Kerry, 84, 126, 128, 158
Leonovich, Stanislav, 116
Lewis, Dorothy, 155
Liashenko, Elena, 55
Lillehammer, Norway, 7–8, 13, 63, 89, 112
Linichuk, Natalia, 95
Lipinski, Tara, **56**
Little Women, 159
Liu, David, 25, 27, 68, **68**
Lockwood and Radford, 123
Loughran, Beatrix, **188**
Louis XVI, 18
Luddington, Ron, 24
Lussi, Gustave, 78
Saint Lydwina, 17–18
Lynn, Janet, 9, 27, **72**, 73, 105–6, 128, 141

M

McCall, Rob, 4, 10, 89, **117**, 164
McErlane, Bridget, 151
Mack and Mabel, 64
McPherson, Don, 23
Magnussen, Karen, 9, 26
Makarov, Oleg, 116
Maltin, Leonard, 157
Manley, Elizabeth, 9–10, 119, **140**, 164; 1988 Olympic silver, 119, 141
Maple Leaf Gardens, 134
Mariposa Skating School, 39, 171
Martini, Paul, **88**, 164, 167. See also Underhill and Martini
Matousek, Katherina, 99
Menjou, Adolphe, 154
Meno, Jenni, 35, **35**, 82–3. See also Meno and Sand
Meno and Sand, **83**; 1994 U.S. Nationals gold, 83; 1995 World Championship bronze, 83
Menzies, Michelle, 89, **133**, 158. See also Menzies and Bombardier
Menzies and Bombardier, **90**; 1995 Canadian Pairs Championship winners, **90**; 1996 Canadian Pairs Championship winners, **90**

Meritorious Service Medal (Canada), 45
MGM, 154, 158
Millot, Eric, 63, **169**
Minotte, Sophie. See Minotte and Lavanchy
Minotte and Lavanchy, 1995 World Championship bronze, 95
Mishin and Moskvina, 123
Mishkutienok, Natalia. See Mishkutienok and Dmitriev
Mishkutienok and Dmitriev, 82, **101**; 1992 Olympic gold, 101
Mitchell, Mark, 46
Moore, Scott, 8
Moser, Ed, 78
Mrazkova, Jana, 104
MTV, 4
Muller, Jutta, 171

N

Nancy Kerrigan and Friends, 9
Napoleon, 18
Nations Cup, 165
Naumov, Vadim, 100
Navka, Tatiana, 95
NBC, 8, 128; *Hallmark Hall of Fame* series, 116
Nebelhorn Trophy, 91
Nepela, Ondrej, 56
NHK, 165
Nicks, John, 35, 83, 157
Nielsen, Aren, 46
Nightingale, Lynn, 136
Niles, Nathaniel, 46
Norris, Chuck, 45
North American Championships, 41
Novotny, Rene, 10

O

Oakland, California, 31
Oelschlagel, Charlotte. See Charlotte
Olympic Gold Medals, 179
Olympic Report '76 (Cootes), 78
On Thin Ice, 156
One in a Million, 154
Onstad, Neils, 156
Oppegard, Peter, 1988 Olympic gold, 83
Oppelt, Kurt, 36
Orser, Brian, 8–11, 25–7, **36**, 39–40, 42–4, 70, 82, 104, 108, 110, 125, 130–1, 139–40, 153, 164, 167; 1987 World Championship gold, 36; 1988 World Championship silver, 106, 116; Battle of the Brians, 10, 56, 64, 111–12
Ottawa, Ontario, 97, 99, 109
Ovsiannikov, Oleg, 95. See also Krylova and Ovsiannikov
Owen, Laurence, 24
Owen, Maribel Vinson, 1932 Olympic bronze, 24

Index (CONTINUED)

Index (CONTINUED)

Skate: 100 Years of Figure Skating

Project Editor: Michael Mouland

Copy Editor: Beverley Sotolov

Design Concept: Jean Lightfoot Peters

Electronic Formatting and Assembly: Heidi Palfrey

Production Editor: Louise Ward

Colour Separations: Quebecor Printing

Printed and bound in Canada by: Metropole Litho Inc.